# Marriage and its Discontents

# Marriage and its Discontents

*Women, Islam and the Law in India*

SYLVIA VATUK

women
UNLIMITED
an associate of
kali for women

*Marriage and its Discontents*
was first published in India in 2017
by
**Women Unlimited**
**(an associate of Kali for Women)**
**7/10, FF, Sarvapriya Vihar**
**New Delhi-110 016**

www.womenunlimited.net



ISBN: 978-93-85606-09-0

*Cover design:* Neelima Rao

# Contents

# Publication History

"Where Will She Go? What Will She Do?" was first published in G. J. Larson (ed.), *Religion and Personal Law in Secular India: A Call to Judgment.* Bloomington: Indiana University Press, 2001. "Muslim Women and Personal Law" was first published in Zoya Hasan & Ritu Menon (eds.), *In a Minority: Essays on Muslim Women in India.* New Delhi: Oxford University Press, 2005. "The 'Cancer of Dowry' in Muslim Marriages" was first published in Mushirul Hasan (ed.), in *Living With Secularism: The Destiny of India's Muslims.* New Delhi: Manohar, 2007. "Divorce at the Wife's Initiative" was first published in Archana Parashar & Amita Dhanda (eds.), *Redefining Family Law in India: Essays in Honour of B. Sivaramayya.* London and New Delhi: Routledge, 2008. "Islamic Feminism in India" was first published in Filippo Osella and Caroline Osella (eds.), in *Islamic Reform in South Asia.* Cambridge: Cambridge University Press, 2013. "Change and Continuity in Marital Alliance Patterns" was first published in Ravinder Kaur & Rajni Palriwala (eds.), *Marrying in South Asia: Shifting Concepts, Changing Practices in a Globalising World.* New Delhi: Orient BlackSwan, 2014. "What can Divorce Stories Reveal about Muslim Marriage?" was first published in Srimati Basu & Lucinda Ramberg (eds.), *Conjugality Unbound: Sexual Economies, State Regulation and the Marital Form in India.* New Delhi: Women Unlimited, 2015. "Maintenance for Divorced Muslim Women after the Muslim Women (Protection of Rights on Divorce) Act, 1986" was first published in Huma Ahmed-Ghosh (ed.), *Asian Muslim Women: Globalization and Local Realities.* Albany: State University of New York Press, 2015.

# Introduction

Earlier versions of the papers in this volume were originally published over a period of fifteen years—between 2001 and 2015—and are presented here in order of their original publication. All eight chapters are concerned, in one way or other, with Muslim marriage in India. Five deal with the impact of Muslim Personal Law (MPL) upon the lives of women, specifically in relation to marriage and divorce. A central concern of all but two of the essays is the question of what happens if a marriage that was entered into hopefully ends in disarray, with the couple facing one another in a civil court, before a community council, the *jamaᶜat* or the *imam* of their neighbourhood mosque or in the office of a local *qazi*. Hence the title: *Marriage and its Discontents.*

I became interested in questions of Muslim Personal Law, specifically with regard to its consequences for the well-being of Indian Muslim women, after more than a decade, off and on, of conducting ethnographic and historical research and writing on issues of gender, family and kinship among south Indian Muslims. I was inspired to turn my attention to this topic due to an increasing unease with the prevailing tendency of the popular journalistic—and even much of the scholarly—literature, to account for most of the social disabilities under which Muslim women suffer by reference to the personal law regime by which they are governed. I often encountered the same rhetoric when discussing my research with Indian colleagues and others of my acquaintance, who almost invariably wanted to begin the conversation by deploring the fate of Muslim women suffering under laws, peculiar to their religion, that permit polygamy and unilateral divorce and leave them bereft of any means of support, should their marriage be dissolved. I naturally recognised—and by no means wished to minimise the significance of—the severe gender bias that is entailed in these particular provisions of Islamic law or the damage they inflict on many Muslim women. Yet, in several years of ethnographic and archival research among Muslims in Chennai and Hyderabad, I had not found that issues of this kind dominated the everyday concerns of the women I had come to know. I therefore felt a need to examine the empirical basis for these widespread stereotypes about Muslim women suffering under the oppressive burden of personal law and thereby, perhaps, find a way of undermining some of the strength of the prevailing rhetoric.

There was already a substantial body of historical, legal and sociological literature on women and the law in India, including some that highlighted the problems that these and other gender biased provisions of Muslim Personal Law create for women. But empirical studies of what they, in particular, experience when they find themselves in a judicial setting, were lacking. Nor had scholars investigated the question of how they fared when they brought marital or other family disputes to non-state, religiously based dispute-resolution venues, such as *dar-ul qazat*, community panchayats or mosque committees (*jamaᶜat*).

In the 1990s, legal anthropologists and other scholars of law and society were increasingly viewing the law not as a set of rules that mould human behaviour, but as a *resource* that individuals make use of in their pursuit of personal goals, whatever these may be. With respect to women, in particular, ethnographers working in courtroom settings in a variety of countries around the world, were arguing that legal proceedings often facilitate attempts to resist 'patriarchal' domination in the home and in society at large. With these ideas in mind, I began to design a study that would explore Indian Muslim women's use of both civil and religious judicial institutions, asking whether and how MPL, as administered in practice in India, impacts their efforts to accommodate and/or overcome the constraints and disabilities to which they are subjected in a heavily male-dominated legal and social milieu.

I decided to begin by investigating these questions in one of the state courts of India. Since Independence, personal law cases had been adjudicated in the regular civil courts where, due to overcrowded dockets and other reasons, they often languished for extended periods of time before being resolved. In 1984, in response to a long-standing demand of the women's movement and various welfare organisations, the Indian parliament enacted the Family Courts Act (FCA), which obliged every state in the union to set up specialised family courts in cities of over one million population, to try cases arising out of marital and family disputes. The Act was rather slow to be implemented: the first family court was established in Rajasthan in 1987, and in the following year a number of others, among them the Chennai Family Court, began operations. I therefore returned to that city in 1998 and spent seven months observing the ongoing activities in that court, interviewing judges, counsellors, court staff and advocates, and talking with litigants as they sat, often for hours, outside the courtroom, waiting for their cases to be called. My research assistant and I also spent many hours in the family court records room, reading and copying by hand the details of a large sample of Muslim cases that had been heard in that court in earlier years.

Court petitions and most of the supporting documents included in these case files were written in English and I was able to speak to judges, counsellors and advocates in that language as well. But my inability to speak Tamil proved to be a significant barrier to conducting anthropological 'participant observation' or even interview-based research. Tamil is, understandably, the language used almost exclusively for court proceedings and for the counselling that litigants are required to take part in under the terms of the Family Court Act. My previous research in Chennai had been carried out among Urdu-speaking Muslims but the mother tongue of most Chennai Muslims is Tamil, and when seeking to interview Muslim litigants I only occasionally encountered one with whom I could communicate directly. Consequently, I was obliged to use an interpreter for much of my work, something that I had never done in my previous research.

To serve in this role I was fortunate to find an extremely competent, anthropologically trained, Tamil-speaking young woman, Ms. R. Saraswathy, who worked with me for several months as research assistant cum interpreter. It was she who made it possible for me to accomplish my purposes, both in the family court itself and in a variety of related settings, including an all-woman police station and a women's counselling centre run by the Tamil Nadu Legal Aid Society. This period of research led to my first publication on Indian women and the law, which is included in this volume as Chapter 1. It was inspired by my observations of the tenor of counselling sessions with women and married couples (of all religions) in the family court and in other state or state-associated dispute-resolution premises, where the wife was so frequently urged to return to the marital home, despite having been abused, abandoned or thrown out by her husband or in-laws in the past. When I asked the counsellor, advocate or judge why he or she had offered such advice, the standard response was, 'But where will she go, what will she do, if she has to go off on her own?' With reference to the notion put forward by previous scholars that the law can provide women an arena within which to exert a degree of independent 'agency', enabling them to take control of their own lives, my findings were mixed. I observed modest numbers of Muslim women approaching the judicial institutions of the state, in hopes of ameliorating the conditions of their domestic lives. So, in that sense, they were not entirely passive victims of a patriarchal order. However, the realities of their domestic and overall social situation, combined with the way they are treated in the court, are such that most were able to achieve only limited success in what they had hoped to achieve by asking the state for succour.

Around the time that this article was published, Ritu Menon and Zoya Hasan were putting together a research group, based at the Nehru Memorial Museum and Library in New Delhi, on "The

Diversity of Muslim Women's Lives in India". They had heard about my work and kindly asked me to join them and the other participants in the project. I had by then extended my investigations to Hyderabad and was able to use data collected there to supplement my Chennai research findings for a conference paper, and then a more broadly focused article on Muslim women and MPL that was published in the edited volume that resulted from the group's work. An updated version of that piece appears as Chapter 2 in the present volume.

My fieldwork in Hyderabad in 2001 was conducted both in the family court and, as in Chennai, in other related official institutions, but also in the offices (*dar-ul qazat*) of four of the city's seven government-appointed *sadr qazis,* and the *qazi* connected with the Andhra Pradesh State Waqf Board, which appoints and provides overall supervision of their work. In addition I met several times with members of the *jama*$^c$*at* of two neighbourhood mosques in the city. My purpose was to broaden my investigations of how women fare under MPL by looking into the role of non-state religious bodies in the administration of Islamic law. I had learned in my Chennai research that the number of women who approach the courts, the police or other state authorities when faced with marital or other family problems, is relatively small. It emerged from our interviews with litigants and from the court petitions we read that, if unable to solve her problems within the family or kinship circle, a woman almost always next turns for help to a local community or mosque council or to a religious authority of some kind. It is a rare woman who goes directly to filing a civil suit or making a criminal complaint against her husband or in-laws, unless she is led to do so by members of a women's NGO or is taken there by a male relative who is familiar with the ways of the judicial system.

With respect to the issue of divorce, I had noted that in Chennai the rate of resort to the Dissolution of Muslim Marriages Act was very low and this finding was confirmed when I examined comparable data from Hyderabad. After speaking with the Hyderabad *qazis* and examining some of their divorce files, I realised that, in any given year, the number of wife-initiated extra-judicial divorces (by *khulᶜ*) were many times the number awarded by the courts. The fact that this was an option available to Muslim women had hardly been noted in the scholarly literature, outside the standard legal textbooks. That it was an option widely used in practice by Muslim women wishing to extricate themselves from unhappy or abusive marriages had not come to my attention until then. This discovery inspired me to investigate the matter in detail, and when I was invited to contribute to a volume of essays on Indian family law being put together to honour a distinguished senior Indian legal scholar, I chose that as my subject. Chapter 4 in this volume is a revised and updated version of that article.

Ever since the 1985 Supreme Court judgment in the Shah Bano case and the subsequent passage of the Muslim Women (Protection of Rights on Divorce) Act (MWA), the fact that a divorced Muslim woman could no longer apply for a court-ordered maintenance award against her former husband (under Section 125 of the Criminal Procedure Code) had become a focus of criticism by feminist activists and others concerned about the fate of poor divorcées with no other means of support. The new law required men to maintain their former wives only through the approximately three-month *ᶜiddat* period. After that, if unable to maintain herself, the woman could ask a magistrate to order members of her natal family or her adult children to do so. But few women, no matter how needy, proved willing to alienate their closest kin by filing a criminal suit against them. In time, however, high court judges in several states began requiring men who had divorced their wives to make 'reasonable and fair provision' for their future, in addition to maintaining them until they complete their *ᶜiddat.* This novel interpretation of the wording of the Act was confirmed in 2001 by the Supreme Court of India (in the Danial Latifi case). Curious about what impact the Act and the recent judgments upon it had had over the two decades since its passage, I returned to India in the winter of 2005-06 to investigate the matter. I began my research in Delhi, but found that there the MWA was being used only for the purpose of defeating a Muslim divorcée's suit for maintenance under Section 125 of the CrPC. In Hyderabad, however, certain Muslim advocates had been filing MWA cases on behalf of women clients under the rubric of 'reasonable and fair provision' ever since the law had been passed and, in a number of cases, had won them substantial lump-sum payments in lieu of the monthly stipend that was typically ordered in a Section 125 case. This strategy had proved most useful to those whose former husbands had high incomes or substantial property or other assets. It was not as beneficial to the destitute women for whom the benefits of Section 125—which they could no longer access—had been designed, because their husbands were rarely in a financial position to make a one-time lump-sum payment of any significant amount. In an article published in 2015 I reported these and other findings from that research and have included it as Chapter 8 in the present volume.

Even before I embarked upon the project just described, I had become aware of a growing movement among Muslim women activists to address, from within the community, issues of gender bias in MPL. Like the so-called 'Islamic feminists' who had for some time been advocating reforms in the practise of Islamic law in various Middle Eastern and North African countries, these women were using religious—rather than human rights—arguments for achieving greater gender equity in MPL. They were urging Muslim women to read the sacred text for themselves, telling them that the male Muslim leadership had for centuries been distorting the true meaning of the Qur'an in order to further their own patriarchal interests. The Qur'an, they insisted, is not responsible for the bias against women that prevails in Indian Muslim society. Rather, misinterpretations of the sacred text by the entrenched *ʿulama* are to blame for denying women many of the God-given rights that are laid down in the Qur'an. Furthermore, many of the woman-friendly provisions of the *shariʿat* are being ignored in practise. For example, the religious authorities regard as valid, instantaneous unilateral divorce by 'triple *talaq*', and claim to recognise but fail to enforce the requirements that, if a wife did not receive her *mahr* during her marriage it must be paid when she is divorced or widowed, and that a man who has more than one wife must treat them all equally.

Wishing to learn more about this incipient Indian 'Islamic feminist' movement, I met with several of the women involved in Delhi and in Hyderabad, and also made short trips to Bangalore and Mumbai to interview leaders of Muslim-led NGOs in those cities. I enquired about their ideas concerning Muslim law reform, the advocacy initiatives they were engaging in, and the challenges they faced, both from within the Muslim community and from representatives of the larger 'secular' feminist movement. After my return from India I presented a paper in London at a workshop on Islamic reform in India, whose proceedings were published in 2008 as a special issue of the journal, *Modern Asian Studies.* Later, I had the opportunity to pursue further enquiries among these and other activists during subsequent trips to India. I expanded and updated the original essay when that special issue was republished as an edited book in 2013, and made further revisions for the present volume, in which it appears as Chapter 5.

Since I first wrote about this movement it has grown significantly, and other scholars have pursued the topic in their own publications. A number of new groups have been formed, one of which, the Bharatiya Muslim Mahila Andolan (BMMA), has recruited thousands of individual members throughout the country. The movement is no longer limited mainly to middle-class, college educated women in large cities, but includes small-town and rural women from a variety of socio-economic backgrounds. The movement is also much more in the public eye than it was at the time of my research, and some groups are taking on not only the *ʿulama*, as before, but the Indian government as well. Most recently, a newly created coalition of Muslim women's activist groups and some secular feminist organisations has been spearheading a campaign on a national scale to outlaw triple *talaq.* With their encouragement and support, a number of petitions from women divorced in this manner, asking that it be declared unconstitutional, are currently being heard by the Supreme Court of India. The male-dominated Muslim religious establishment continues to be resistant to such demands, but it seems apparent that it will not be able to hold out indefinitely against the increasing numbers of supporters—of both sexes—who are adding their voices to those of India's Islamic feminists in calling for changes in their personal law.

In Chapter 7 I approach issues of divorce among Muslims from a different angle, by examining 'divorce narratives' culled from a variety of sources, including family court petitions, narratives of matrimonial disputes in the files of the Tamil Nadu State Legal Aid Authority and an all-woman police station in Chennai, and Hyderabad *qazis*' divorce records, as well as interviews with separated and divorced Muslim women, advocates, legal aid staff, judges, court personnel, and Islamic clerics. I use these stories of how and why a narrator's marriage failed, as a lens into what Muslim men and women expect when they wed, in terms of the spouses' respective duties and responsibilities and their manner of behaving towards one another. This chapter originally appeared in an edited volume in 2015.

Chapters 3 and 6 depart from the theme of marriages in trouble that dominate the rest of the book. Both essays address questions of what happens *before* a marriage is contracted, what considerations are involved and what strategies are employed when a young person and his or her parents become engaged in the process of finding a suitable spouse and negotiating an agreement to marry. Two of the key issues that must be dealt with are whether to make a match with a close relative or a stranger, and what kind of financial outlay will be required or what financial benefit will accrue, if a particular choice is made.

Thus Chapter 3 is concerned with the custom of dowry, which, although it has no sanction in Islam, has now become extremely prevalent among Indian Muslims, a development that appears to be at least partly related to the fact (discussed in Chapter 6) that many Muslims have moved away from the former practise of marrying endogamously, within a relatively small circle of close relatives. In this essay, a revision of an article published in 2007, I review the historical evidence concerning gift-giving in south Indian Muslim weddings, and present data on contemporary practises from my own ethnographic research and other published sources. I then go on to examine Muslim attitudes—as reflected in articles and letters to the editor in two south Indian Muslim-owned newspapers—towards the way that the custom of dowry has spread within their community in recent years and the continued escalation of the amounts being transferred from the family of the bride to that of the groom. For the most part, the writers' remarks about the deleterious social and personal effects of 'the cancer of dowry' mirror those put forward by the many non-Muslim critics of the custom. However, some critics are particularly concerned about the Hindu origins of the practice, arguing that it is mainly for this reason that anyone aspiring to be a good Muslims should avoid participating in it, either as a giver or a receiver.

Finally, Chapter 6 is based upon a still-ongoing family history project that I had been engaged in for several years before I began to work on personal law issues. In this essay—a revised version of a paper first published in 2014—I describe and attempt to account for patterns of change and continuity over time (from the beginning of the 19th century to the present) in the matchmaking practises and strategies of south Indian Muslims. Using detailed genealogical data from the records of one large extended family of Muslims that has long been based in Chennai, supplemented by material from the work of other scholars of kinship and marriage among Muslims in the region, I show that there has been a movement away from the traditional practise, by which elders arranged marriages between cousins or other close kin with little or no input from the young people involved. Nowadays, they are allowing their offspring to more directly engage in the choice of a spouse. Consequently, they are giving greater consideration to the educational accomplishments, occupation and earning potential, as well as the appearance and other personal qualities, of the candidate. This means that a suitable candidate may not be available within the kin group; they must therefore be open to the idea of having their daughter or son marry an unrelated person, even one who belongs to a different Muslim *qaum* or sub-group. This trend is consistent with the changing marital alliance patterns that have been observed to be occurring among those south Indian Hindu castes that formerly practiced preferential cross-cousin and/or uncle-niece marriages. It does not mean that the Muslim preference for marrying one's offspring to a close relative has entirely disappeared. I have found, for example, that in certain branches of the family I studied most closely, even among those living in the diaspora, there are those who perceive marriages within the kin group to have important advantages over marriages with 'outsiders'. They believe that a couple who has been socialised within the same extended family will share the same values, customs and ways of living, and is more likely to live harmoniously than two people could, who come from entirely different backgrounds, even though sharing the same religious faith. Such a union, supported by the respective natal families of the pair who are tied together by blood as well as by the marital alliance that binds them, is the best designed to ensure a harmonious relationship between man and wife and the long-term stability of the marriage.

I owe many thanks and much gratitude to the many people in India without whom I could not have accomplished any of the research on which the chapters in this book are based. I include here not only my research assistants but all the people who took the time to talk to me about their work, shared many of their personal experiences with me and allowed me to participate, in varying degrees, in their lives. I have acknowledged many of these individuals by name in the endnotes attached to the chapters for which they provided assistance or information. Others have had to remain anonymous for reasons of privacy. A number of funding institutions in the United States and host institutions in India provided both financial and other kinds of supportive assistance for my research endeavours, for which I am extremely indebted. I have cited them in the endnotes to the pertinent essays. However, one institution that I have not properly acknowledged in that connection is the University of Illinois at Chicago Institute for the Humanities, where I held a resident fellowship during the academic year 1999-2000, to begin analysing and writing up the fieldwork data I had gathered in Chennai in the course of my first research project on Muslim women and the law.

There are, in addition, a number of individuals not cited in the endnotes whom I would like to thank for various kinds of help and encouragement during the writing process, at different times and in different ways, both while I was working on the original articles and when I was revising and editing them for publication in this volume: Flavia Agnes, Imtiaz Ahmad, Helene Basu, Srimati Basu, Zoya Hasan, Rajinder Kaur, Mindie Lazarus-Black, Lynn Lees, Filippo Osella, Rajni Palriwala, Avril Powell, Lucinda Ramberg, Mary Beth Rose, Mrinalini Sinha, Gopika Solanki, and Narendra Subramanian. And, for his unceasing, enthusiastic encouragement and support of my scholarly endeavours, and of everything else that I have attempted to accomplish over the thirty-eight years of our marriage, I am eternally grateful to my husband, George Rosen.

Ritu Menon is, of course, the person who deserves the most gratitude, first for suggesting that I put together into a single volume a selection of my articles on Muslim women in India, and second for her extreme patience while I very slowly fulfilled my commitment to update, edit and revise them into a form suitable for publication by her press.

# 1.
# 'Where Will She Go? What Will She Do?'
## paternalism in the administration of Muslim Personal Law in contemporary India

### Introduction

I argue in this essay that in India a 'paternalistic' approach towards women and their needs permeates the legal process, in particular the manner in which personal laws are administered in practice in the lower courts. I draw for this insight upon seven months of anthropological fieldwork during 1998–99 in the city of Chennai, where I examined the impact of Muslim Personal Law (MPL) on women. For much of this time I was observing, conducting interviews, and examining case files in the Chennai family court. Of course, these paternalistic attitudes affect all women, regardless of their religion, who have occasion to become involved with the court system; but because Muslim women were the specific focus of my research, I will focus here on their experience, as a particular case of a more widespread phenomenon.

The broad theoretical context for my research lies in current discussions in the legal-anthropological literature about issues of power and resistance in the relationship of individuals to the law. Students of law and society increasingly view the law not as a set of rules that mould human behaviour, but as a resource, utilised by active agents to negotiate the conditions of their lives, pursue personal goals, and resist hegemonic definitions of selfhood.[1] By observing what actually goes on when women seek help from the state in resolving family disputes and examining it within a broader social and cultural context, these scholars have suggested that women are frequently able to use legal proceedings to 'resist' male domination and pursue personal ends that may be quite extraneous to the official purposes for which these judicial institutions were designed.[2] With these ideas as a point of departure, my own study was intended to explore Indian Muslim women's use of religious and civil courts, asking whether and how MPL, as administered in practice, impacts women's efforts to accommodate and/or overcome the constraints and disabilities to which they are subject in a heavily male-dominated social milieu.

Despite all the rhetoric about gender bias in MPL and the frequent calls for its reform, we have almost no hard data on how Muslim women are actually affected in practice by this code of law. A great deal of scholarly and activist effort has been devoted in recent years to describing the ways in which women suffer as a consequence of the freedom given to men to divorce at will and marry multiple wives, but the literature on this subject is largely anecdotal and highly polemical. In part this is because statistics that might shed some quantitative light on these matters are difficult or impossible to come by. India has no system of compulsory registration of marriage or divorce. Most Muslim marriages and a significant proportion of unilateral divorces (*talaq*) and divorces by mutual agreement (*khul*ᶜ and *mubarat*) are recorded by the clerics who conduct them. Estimates of the relative prevalence of unilateral and other forms of divorce could be made on the basis of these records but, since there is no requirement to register one's divorce, this would provide only a very partial picture of the overall situation. As for polygyny, the clerics who preside over marriages do not enquire into the groom's marital status and therefore it is not possible to estimate its prevalence from those marriage records.[3] In any case, since these records are not public documents, they are not easily accessible and therefore have not been extensively used by scholars.[4]

In this research, one of my purposes was to partially remedy, from a qualitative rather than a quantitative perspective, the present lack of empirical information about how the existing system of personal law affects the lives of Muslim women. A second purpose was to contribute, from a comparative perspective, to the theoretical debates I have outlined above concerning issues of state power, the law, and women's resistance. My preliminary findings point to an ongoing tension between what I have called the 'paternalism' that pervades the administration of family law generally in India, and women's attempts—still very rare and usually only partially successful—to exert some control over their own destiny by making use of what the law purports to offer them in this regard. What these efforts often amount to is resisting, whether actively or through refusal to cooperate, the judicial system's attempts to exert patriarchal control over their life choices.

I employ here the important distinction, familiar to students of law and society, between the law as written and the law as practiced, between what the law *says* and what it actually *does*, when real women with concrete problems seek relief from the courts. Even where the law itself is free of obvious gender bias or is explicitly designed to confer some special benefit on women, the latter may have difficulty successfully availing themselves of its provisions. In the Indian context there are many reasons for this, one of the more important ones being the attitudes of those who are responsible for dispensing justice. These men (and women) harbour assumptions about what women are like and what roles they ought to perform—or are even capable of performing—within their families and in society at large. Such assumptions predispose them to take a paternalistic approach towards the needs of the women who come before them, whether as plaintiffs or respondents, in matrimonial and other related kinds of legal suits.

By 'paternalism' I mean an attitude based on a view of women as inherently weak and vulnerable and consequently in need of lifelong material and symbolic support and protection from the men in their lives: fathers and brothers before marriage, husbands thereafter, and sons or other close male relatives in the latter's absence. Those responsible for administering the personal laws tend to believe, as do most Indians, especially those of the upper and middle classes, that the proper place for an adult woman is within a marital relationship. They are inclined to consider it preferable, whatever the quality of that relationship, for her to remain under the conjugal roof rather than return to her natal home or strike out on her own. Their position is premised in part on the notion that a woman is by definition economically dependent on the earnings of a man. If she leaves her husband, some other man will have to take over this responsibility. For her to earn her own living is almost inconceivable.[5] The presumed social and sexual vulnerability of a woman without a male protector also plays a role in the paternalistic approach taken by those who administer the family law. Here the issue is one of preserving her status as a 'respectable' woman. Even if an unattached woman succeeds in remaining chaste, it is assumed that those around her will never cease to suspect otherwise. Fears related to the stigma of divorce combine with fears of its material consequences to produce the rhetorical questions that I heard repeatedly during the course of my research: 'Where will she go, what will she do, if she and her husband cannot be reconciled?'

In order to 'save' women by 'saving' their marriages, lawyers, court-appointed social workers, and judges alike make ample use of delays, attempts at mediation, and pressures to reach a compromise. Of course, bureaucratic delays are not deliberately designed to thwart women's access to justice, but are built into the Indian judicial system.[6]

## Family courts

Family courts operate today in the major cities of most states of the Indian Union, pursuant to central legislation passed in September 1984 as the Family Courts Act (FCA).[7] These courts have civil jurisdiction over all matrimonial suits, regardless of the religion of the parties, and are also empowered to decide cases registered under Chapter IX, Section 125 of the Code of Criminal Procedure (CrPC), which covers orders of maintenance for destitute persons, mainly wives, divorcées and children.[8] The Chennai family court was established in 1988. Initially one judge handled its entire caseload, but this number was later increased to three.[9]

The original impetus for the establishment of family courts came from women's activist organisations that were critical of, among other things, the adversarial nature of matrimonial proceedings in the existing civil courts, procedural complexities, and long delays in resolving cases.[10] They saw all of these features of the existing system as particularly disadvantageous for women, who tend to be less well-informed about the law than men, and to have fewer financial resources with which to fight a legal case. As eventually enacted, the FCA cites as its main purpose, 'to promote conciliation in and secure speedy settlement of disputes relating to marriage and family affairs'. To the former end, provision is made for family counsellors to guide disputing parties towards amicable settlements. Clarification as to the kind of settlement envisioned is found in the section concerning the selection of family court judges, where it is laid down that they should be 'persons committed to the need to protect and preserve the institution of marriage'.

Under the FCA, advocates are not permitted to represent clients in court, except under special circumstances as *amicus curiae* with the express permission of the judge.[11] This clause was intended to enable greater access to the courts by the poor as well as to create a more informal atmosphere, where litigants would be free to state their own cases, not in legalistic language but in their own words. In practice, however, it is almost impossible to navigate the court system without an advocate and few are so foolhardy as to attempt it. Any litigant who does come to court alone is quickly propositioned by a tout or by one of the enterprising advocates who operate makeshift and continually moving offices within the space of the family court itself. Advocates draft all petitions (in English), advise their clients, and accompany them to court, but it is still necessary for the parties to a suit to appear in person for each hearing, usually scheduled at one-month intervals. For many, especially for poor women, this is a great hardship. In part because of this requirement, a high percentage of cases are eventually 'dismissed for default of plaintiff', that is, because the plaintiff has failed to appear for three consecutive hearings.

In this and many other ways, the family courts have not lived up to the hopes of those who originally fought for their establishment.[12] The persistence of the problem of long court delays, one of the original rationales for setting up specialised family courts, is one focus of criticism. I am aware of no published studies that provide comparative statistics on how long it takes for cases to be resolved under the new system, though there is impressionistic evidence that matrimonial cases are indeed being processed faster than before. However this does not mean that anyone filing suit in a family court can expect a swift decision. Between 1988 and 1997, cases filed in the Chennai family court took anywhere from two months to seven years to be resolved; the median time was approximately two years.

Legal scholars and feminist activists are especially critical of the Act's avowed emphasis on preserving the family, pointing out the incompatibility of this goal with that of ensuring women's well-being. In the words of a social worker attached to a private welfare organisation in Chennai,

> The bias [in the family courts] is in favour of holding the status quo of the marriage. In this, it is always the woman who is pressurised into adjusting or submitting, particularly as in most cases she is less educated, less articulate and less assertive.[13]

The same theme is echoed by O. Chinnappa Reddy, a former justice of the Supreme Court of India:

> The Act is supposed to remove the gender bias and to put disadvantaged women in a position of advantage ... [T]he historically disadvantaged position occupied by women has been sought to be removed ... not by restricting the dissolution or disruption of the marriage but by the enactment of laws, giving the right of divorce and the right to maintenance to women ... The commitment [of the Act] should be not

to protect and preserve the institution of marriage but to endeavour to secure to women a life with dignity and honour.[14]

## Counselling in the family court

Couples engaged in matrimonial litigation or maintenance suits are required to undergo counselling (routinely referred to in case files as 'reconciliation') before their case goes before the judge. In Chennai, most of those engaged as counsellors have no professional training for the task. They are not paid a salary, but receive only a nominal *per diem* stipend that barely covers their transportation costs. Those who volunteer to serve the usual three-month term are well-meaning, socially conscious, upper-middle-class, Hindu or Christian, western-educated men and women, often retirees, who see their work as a way of contributing to the welfare of those less fortunate than themselves. They sympathise with the women they encounter in court and are often quite insightful about the complexity of the situations in which the latter find themselves. However, imbued as they are with the kind of paternalistic attitudes I have referred to, and operating within a system whose goal is to preserve the institution of marriage, they cannot but commit themselves to getting couples back together. With this end in view, they insist that couples return again and again to the court for repeated 'reconciliation' sessions. Only when they realise that there is no hope at all of saving the marriage do they turn to brokering some kind of compromise settlement.

Where, as in India, power asymmetries between husband and wife are marked and where the burden of adjustment within most marriages falls primarily on the wife, 'compromise' is a gender-linked concept. It is the role of the wife to meet her husband's needs and demands, to comply with his wishes, and to bear stoically all manner of personal hardships. Thus, in the process of working out 'mutually agreeable' settlements in the family court context, husbands tend to be given considerably more leeway than strict gender equity would dictate. Wives are often pressured, even browbeaten, by counsellors into settling for outcomes that may be grossly unfair and contrary to their best interests. Thus, divorce settlements regularly have the wife giving up all financial claims on the husband, including the *mehr* amount to which she is entitled,[15] often in return for custody of a young child in whom the husband has never shown any interest and would not, in any case, have a claim on for many years in the future.[16] Where maintenance is the issue, once reconciliation attempts have been abandoned, counsellors, lawyers, and judges all concentrate on trying to persuade the husband to offer to pay some modicum of support for his wife and children even if it is not enough to meet their needs. They rationalise this approach by pointing out that there is little value in issuing an order that realistically cannot be enforced, unless the man is a government employee and therefore subject to salary attachment. If he can be prodded into making a commitment to pay a modest amount, it is more likely that the money will actually be forthcoming.

In the context of family court negotiations, women are regularly encouraged to drop criminal charges they may have filed against their husbands, to withdraw or reduce property, maintenance, or custody demands, and even to resume living with men who may have subjected them to long-standing abuse in the past. A legal discourse of 'rights' is thus transformed into a discourse of 'welfare', whose defining terms are set, not by the woman herself, but by her counsellor, her advocate, the judge, and, in the last analysis, by the realities imposed by the society within which she lives.

## Muslim Personal Law

As in many other formerly colonised states in Asia, Africa, and the Caribbean, the Indian legal system is 'pluralistic'. Furthermore, a state-sponsored system of codified law and civil and criminal courts coexists with a whole range of other less formal and unofficial community or religious dispute-settlement bodies. For Muslims, these include *qazis*' offices, *shari'at* courts, caste, *qaum*, or sect panchayats, and *jamaat* committees or councils of elders associated with local mosques.[17] Men and women who are experiencing family difficulties normally approach such bodies before, or instead of, turning to the civil courts. The family court is a place of last resort; only a minuscule percentage of those who experience marital difficulties ever use it. Most still prefer to resolve family disputes by more familiar, informal, local means.[18] Both aspects of legal pluralism are a legacy of British colonial rule, inspired in part by pre-colonial Muslim practice, whereby non-Muslim subjects were permitted to govern themselves in matters related to the family and caste.[19]

MPL today is still largely uncodified. The statutes most relevant to the work of the family court are the Dissolution of Muslim Marriages Act (DMMA)—under which a Muslim woman may file for divorce—and the 1986 Muslim Women (Protection of Rights on Divorce) Act (MWA) which, notwithstanding its misleading title, denies a destitute, divorced Muslim woman the right to sue her ex-husband for maintenance under the relevant criminal code

**Table 1**
**Muslim cases as a percentage of all cases filed in the Chennai family court in 1996**

| | OP* | | OS** | | MC*** | | Total |
|---|---|---|---|---|---|---|---|
| | Number | % | Number | % | Number | % | |
| All cases | 1367 | 74 | 47 | 2 | 441 | 24 | 1855 |
| Muslim cases | 10 | 19 | 18 | 34 | 25 | 47 | 53 |
| % Muslim | | 0.73 | | 38.3 | | 5.67 | 2.86 |

* 'Original Petitions' (divorce, judicial separation, restitution under Hindu Marriage Act (HMA)—including Hindu-Muslim marriages—and Muslims married under the Special Marriage Act (SMA), injunctions, child custody)

** 'Ordinary Suits' (divorce, etc.—including all matrimonial cases between Muslims married under MPL).

*** 'Maintenance Cases' (under Chapter IX , Section 125, CrPC—including petitions from married Muslim women and from or on behalf of minor children).

**Table 2**
**Muslim 'OS' cases in the Chennai family court, 1988 to 1997**

| Year | Muslim cases | DMMA | RCR | Other* |
|---|---|---|---|---|
| 1988 | 6 | 3 | 3 | 0 |
| 1989 | 18 | 4 | 6 | 8 |
| 1990 | 14 | 5 | 6 | 3 |
| 1991 | 18 | 2 | 4 | 12 |
| 1992 | 21 | 6 | 6 | 9 |
| 1993 | 18 | 5 | 8 | 5 |
| 1994 | 27 | 12 | 11 | 4 |
| 1995 | 17 | 6 | 9 | 2 |
| 1996 | 18 | 9 | 7 | 2 |
| 1997 | 10 | 5 | 3 | 2 |
| Total | 167 | 57 | 63 | 47 |

* 'Other' includes suits for declaration of the validity of a marriage or a divorce or of the marital status of one of the parties. Also suits for child custody, maintenance above Rs. 500/month, injunctive relief, return of property, and three cases of Muslim men filing for divorce under DMMA, under the mistaken impression that they can or are required to do so in order to dissolve their marriages.

(see below).[20] For matters not falling under the purview of either of these Acts, family court judges have available to them a number of 'authoritative' English-language texts on MPL.[21] Most of those currently in use are of fairly recent vintage. They are authored by English-educated Indian legal scholars drawing upon classical Arabic *shari'at* texts (often in translation) and Indo-Persian commentaries thereon, supplemented by the large body of case law that has been produced by the British-Indian and post-independence courts over the course of the last two centuries.

## Muslims in the Chennai family court

In their daily practice, however, judges rarely need concern themselves with the intricacies of MPL. Firstly, in Chennai at least, they seldom encounter a Muslim case. Muslim litigants are represented at a much lower rate in proportion to their population than are people of other religions. The city of Chennai had almost four million people in 1991, of whom 8.7 per cent were Muslim, but in no year during the period 1988–1997 did more than four per cent of the cases registered in family court involve Muslims. In 1996, for example, Muslim cases represented less than three per cent of the court's caseload (Table 1).[22] Secondly, a substantial portion of the suits filed by Muslims in these courts do not involve issues of MPL at all. In each of the years studied, Muslims filed approximately twice as many maintenance ('MC') as matrimonial ('OS') suits (primarily for divorce or restitution of conjugal rights—see Table 2). Almost every maintenance suit was filed by a woman, under Chapter IX, Section 125 of the Code of Criminal Procedure (CrPC), against a husband from whom she was living separately. Section 125 provides relief to persons of either sex and of any religion, who are destitute and have no other means of support.[23] As per a provision in the 1986 MWA, a *divorced* Muslim woman cannot file a maintenance suit against her former husband under this section, but she may sue him under it for child support.[24]

The second most common type of case to be filed by Muslims in the Chennai family court is for 'restitution of conjugal rights' (RCR). This legal remedy is available to persons of any religion. Its purpose is to compel a spouse who has left the matrimonial home to return to it and, in the formulaic phrase repeatedly encountered in court documents, 'restore to the petitioner the comforts and bliss of married life'. A person of either sex can file for restitution. In court records I found numerous instances of Hindu and Christian women doing so, but every petitioner in the 63 restitution suits filed by Muslims in the ten-year period of the Chennai court's existence, was male.[25]

Suits for RCR often seem motivated by a desire to harass or threaten a wife, or to retaliate against her for making a police report or for filing for divorce or maintenance. This is consistent with the fact that the proportion of RCR cases dismissed as 'withdrawn', 'not pressed', or 'for default of plaintiff' is higher than for any other kind of case: almost 85 per cent. Those cases that are pursued to judgment almost invariably succeed. However, there are no mechanisms to enforce restitution orders. In some cases the mere filing of such a suit may be enough to induce a wife to return to her marital home. If she is determined not to return, there is little that a judge—or a husband—can do to make her come back to him. However, an order for RCR has the serious consequence of making a wife ineligible to claim maintenance from her husband.

The number of divorce suits filed by women under the DMMA are, in Chennai at least, only slightly lower than the number of RCR suits filed by men—57 in the years 1988-1997. The DMMA allows a Muslim woman to obtain a divorce from an unwilling husband, or from one whose whereabouts are unknown, on grounds that include his cruelty, desertion, failure to maintain or to perform his marital obligations, impotence, insanity, leprosy or 'virulent venereal disease', or being imprisoned for a period of seven or more years. It was passed in 1939 in response to pressure from the Muslim religious establishment, which was then concerned about a growing trend whereby Muslim women, desperate to extricate themselves from abusive or otherwise intolerable marital unions, had resorted to renouncing Islam and converting to another religion, usually Christianity. Under MPL at that time, such an act of 'apostasy' automatically voided their marriages. Faced by the unpleasant prospect of women abandoning the faith in droves, a group of prominent clerics drafted and managed to get enacted legislation that would offer them another way out, while at the same time making it no longer possible for them to dissolve their marriages through apostasy.[26]

Half of the divorce suits registered in the Chennai family court during the period covered were dismissed, either because the woman withdrew the suit or because she simply neglected to pursue it. In some cases the record shows that the husband had pronounced *talaq* or the couple had come to an agreement for a divorce by *khul*ᶜ while the case was still in litigation, making the matter moot. Most of the women who continued to pursue their suits succeeded in obtaining a divorce decree. Rarely, if ever, was a divorce suit dismissed by the judge for lack of evidence or for failure to prove the grounds cited, but almost invariably—unless the husband failed to contest the suit or his whereabouts were unknown—a 'compromise', usually drafted in the form of a so-called 'joint endorsement', accompanied the judgment.

Muslim men do not come to court for a divorce, since under MPL they may divorce extrajudicially and unilaterally by merely pronouncing the word *talaq* three times, either on three successive occasions or all at once.[27] A man is legally required at this time to pay his wife her *mehr*, in whatever amount he promised at the time of their marriage, and to maintain her for a period of approximately three months thereafter (*ᶜiddat*). There exists no enforcement mechanism for these financial obligations, however, and there is considerable evidence that they are honoured more in the breach than in the observance.[28]

It is also possible for a Muslim woman to initiate an extrajudicial divorce; however, she cannot do so unilaterally. In order to obtain this kind of divorce (called *khul*ᶜ), her husband must consent to release her from the marriage. In exchange, she must pay him a financial consideration. Typically this means relinquishing her claims to any outstanding *mehr* and to maintenance during the *ᶜiddat* period. If she has already received her *mehr*, she must repay him for it. Occasionally a man will bargain for some additional payment as well. If a woman cannot get her husband to agree to *khul*ᶜ, some schools of Islamic law provide that, if she is suffering great hardship, an Islamic judge (*qazi*) may be approached for a divorce decree (*faskh*). Even today there are *qazi*s who will accommodate a woman in this way, but most, in line with their understanding of *shari'at*, seem to regard it as beyond the scope of their authority.[29]

## Marital conflict

For the purpose of the following discussion I have analysed in detail the files in a random sample of 20 Muslim cases from the year 1992. The documents consist, for the most part, of petitions and counter-petitions by the parties involved. Since there is no way to establish the truth of any of the narratives, I am using them principally for what they reveal about general patterns of marital conflict and relief-seeking patterns among Muslims in this part of India. The women involved in these cases married at ages ranging from 12 to 49—for some in the higher end of this range, the marriage may not have been their first. The husbands are typically five to ten years older than their wives. Even though the minimum age at marriage for girls is 18 years (as per the 1978 amendment to the 1929 Child Marriage Restraint Act[30]), almost a third of these women admit to having been younger than this when they married. Twenty per cent were under 16 years of age when they wed. Most of the marriages were arranged by the respective parents; few couples had the opportunity to become acquainted with one another before the ceremony. There were a small number of 'love marriages', mostly involving Muslim men married (under MPL) to Hindu or Christian women converted to Islam. One love marriage took place in a Hindu temple, another under the Special Marriage Act. The men involved, though Muslim by birth, are not entitled to divorce their wives by *talaq* but must file suit for divorce under the Hindu Marriage Act or the SMA, respectively.[31]

Despite a long-standing preference among south Indian Muslims for arranging marriages within a close circle of kin[32], very few court petitions give any indication that the spouses were related prior to the marriage. It is impossible to know whether silence on this matter indicates that no such relationship existed or that the information was not considered relevant to the narrative at hand. I am inclined, however, to accept the former interpretation. If I am right, the data suggest that couples who are close relatives are perhaps less likely than those who married as strangers to have the kinds of problems that bring couples into family court. Furthermore, if they do have marital difficulties, they are less likely to resort to the law as a way of solving them.

Almost without exception, the women in this sample were living apart from their husbands and often had been for many years. Most were married for only a short time before the separation occurred, but several years had usually elapsed after that, before a court case was filed. Almost every woman had at least one child and was living—usually with that child—in the household of her own parents or that of an adult sibling. If she was living with another man, this fact was, of course, unlikely to appear in any petition filed by her. Occasionally, such an allegation was made by a husband in a plea for RCR or in a counter to a divorce or maintenance petition filed by his wife.

Women's petitions often referred to 'dowry' gifts: cash, jewellery, and other material goods given by their parents to their husband and his parents at the time of the wedding.[33] After the wedding, the wife had almost always joined the household of her husband and his parents and siblings, thus beginning married life in an extended family household. Very few couples set up housekeeping on their own immediately after the wedding or moved in with the wife's parents.

The specific nature and source of the marital tensions that eventually led to the filing of a suit in court naturally vary from case to case, but certain patterns recur. Complaints about in-laws, especially mothers- and sisters-in-law, are common. The latter are reported to have insisted that the new bride take on the lion's share of the housework, prevented her from spending time alone with her husband, and forbade her to visit her natal family on holidays or in times of illness. They allegedly criticised her for the way she performed her household tasks, accused her of laziness or slovenliness, of showing insufficient respect and deference to them and to her husband, or of behaving in a seductive manner towards other men. They reportedly harassed her with recriminations about the quantity or quality of the dowry items they received and subjected her to demands that she extract additional money and goods from her parents. Verbal harassment was said to have escalated sooner or later to physical abuse, and eventually led to the woman either being forcibly ejected from the house or leaving on her own initiative, usually with the help of members of her natal family.

A common theme in these petitions is the husband's 'suspicion' of his wife, sometimes culminating in accusations of adultery. More than one woman reported having been regularly beaten and/or locked in the house every time her husband went out, ostensibly so that she would be unable to seek out male companionship in his absence.[34] One educated working woman told of visits by her husband to her place of employment, where he spied on her and subjected her to public rebukes. In his response to her petition he claimed that his actions were justified by her refusal to quit her job as he had demanded.

A high percentage of the women also complained that their husbands had been sexually unfaithful, usually with a neighbour, co-worker, or close relative. Others complained of his having contracted another marriage and then either bringing the second wife to live in the same house or setting her up in a separate household that drew assets needed by the first wife and her children. In one case a second wife petitioned the court with a complaint that when she married, her husband had failed to reveal that he was already married. He made her live in the same home with his first wife and do all the housework, while he neglected her needs for food and clothing. Other common allegations against the husband included alcoholism, drug abuse, and gambling. In two cases, a mother-in-law was accused of performing black magic, the first in order to cause her daughter-in-law to abort, the other to make her sexually repellent to her husband.

There is evidence in some of the petitions that men are not always eager to take advantage of their freedom to pronounce unilateral divorce, even when they have no desire to remain married. For example, in one petition the wife complained that her husband refused to pronounce *talaq*, demanding instead that she go to the religious authorities to ask for *khul*ᶜ. She refused to do this, not wanting to put herself on record as the party initiating the divorce. She knew that if she did so, she would 'get a bad name' in society. She was also unwilling to give up all financial claims on her husband, as she would have to do if they divorced by means of *khul*ᶜ. Her husband eventually did pronounce *talaq*, doing so in the courtroom of the first additional judge on the day he was summoned to answer his wife's suit for maintenance! Like many other Muslim men, he was aware of those provisions of the MWA that were being interpreted by most courts as enabling a man to avoid financial responsibility for a divorced wife after the three-month ᶜ*iddat* period.

Before approaching the civil authorities, most couples had made repeated attempts, often extending over a period of several years, to find a solution to their marital problems. They had sought the advice of family members, more distant kinsmen, neighbours, friends, and work associates. Later, many turned to the local mosque committee or to a local cleric for help. Typically these consultations ended in the drafting of a joint agreement, whereby both parties promised to improve their behaviour in the future, but such agreements seldom held for long. Eventually some of the women went so far as to file criminal charges against their husbands and/or parents-in-law for domestic abuse or dowry harassment. Those women who went to the police or ended up in court almost always received considerable financial, practical, and moral support from their natal families—parents and brothers in particular. Without such help, few women, regardless of their economic stratum or level of education, are able to take legal action against their husbands. Those parents who assist a married daughter in this way are atypical. It is fairly unusual for parents—whatever their religion and no matter how fond of their daughter they may be—to actively intervene when she is having marital problems. They tend to be reluctant to take such a daughter back into their home once they have given her in marriage, often at very great expense, and thus usually pressure or even compel her to remain with her husband. In this they are often motivated by a fear of incurring social disgrace and by an inability or unwillingness to assume the financial burden of supporting her for the rest of her life. Even if they can afford to do the latter and are not unduly fazed by the prospect of having to defend their action to outside critics, they may still have doubts about whether the best solution for their daughter is to live out her life as a divorcée, a veritable social outcast.

When I raised the issue of the stigma of divorce with Hindu legal practitioners, some expressed the view that a Muslim woman has an easier time in this situation than a Hindu, because Muslim parents are less likely to insist that their daughter remain with an abusive husband. They believed the stigma of divorce to be minimal among Muslims and pointed also to the possibility that a divorced Muslim woman could remarry, something that for a Hindu divorcée is still almost out of the question.[35] Muslim interviewees tended to begin by crediting their religion with being more realistic and humane than Hinduism, in allowing easy divorce for couples who find it impossible to live harmoniously together, and in permitting—even encouraging—remarriage for both partners. However when pressed, they also cited the stigma of divorce as a serious problem for Muslim women seeking a way out of unhappy marriages. They also acknowledged that, whatever the Qur'an may say, in practice it is difficult to find a man willing to marry a divorced woman, especially if she is no longer very young or is the mother of children.

## Conclusion

It is quite clear that, when one begins to examine the actual practice of MPL, one is faced with a far more complex situation than appears on the surface. At this point I am not far enough along in my analysis to make any definitive sweeping generalisations about the impact of this code on Muslim women. However, I can make some preliminary observations and point to certain issues that need further study.

First, it seems clear that in practice, the family courts play a very limited role in Muslim matrimonial disputes, very few of which ever reach the courts: they are nearly always dealt with informally at the family and community level, and with the help of various kinds of religious bodies, functionaries, and private religio-legal experts. Of course, the same is true for other religious communities, but Muslims make even less use of the family courts than others. One important reason for this is the ready availability for Muslim men—and to a lesser extent for women—of extrajudicial divorce. Another is that divorced Muslim women are ineligible to apply for maintenance under Section 125 of the CrPC. However, my study in Chennai suggests that even in situations where they have the same opportunity to obtain relief under the law, Muslims are less likely to do so than are Hindus or Christians.

Second, when Muslims do come into the family court, they are most likely to file under a law that is not part of MPL at all—for example, to ask for maintenance or child support under CrPC or to file for RCR. By comparison, very little use is made of the two chief MPL statutes, the DMMA and the MWA.

Third, neither the situations that bring Muslim, Hindu, and Christian women into court, nor the way their problems are dealt with by the judicial authorities and other court staff, nor the outcomes of their time in court, are very different, notwithstanding the differences in their personal law codes. Although my study was not designed to compare the family court experiences of Muslims with those of Hindus and Christians, I draw this conclusion from a count of all cases, by type, filed in the Chennai family court over a one-year period (1992) and from reading an unsystematically chosen sample of those cases. A careful comparative study of this question would be a valuable contribution to our understanding of the way the Indian personal law system works and to what extent one code has—in practice—any clear advantages over the others, in terms of their impact upon women's well-being.

Unilateral, extrajudicial divorce and polygyny are the provisions of MPL that have attracted the most negative attention and are the chief foci of criticism by proponents of a uniform civil code (UCC) of personal law. My research was not designed to determine the prevalence of these practices, but rather to put them into some kind of context. My evidence suggests that even though the possibility of being unilaterally divorced doubtless weighs heavily upon the wife in any troubled marital relationship and accentuates the need for her to be submissive and placating at any cost if she wishes to remain married, most *talaq*s are probably not pronounced 'on a whim', as the popular stereotype would lead one to believe. Interviews and court petitions reveal that a great deal of calculation—and frequently negotiation with the wife—usually goes into the decision to pronounce a divorce. Muslim men are sometimes reluctant to take advantage of that provision of MPL that allows extrajudicial divorce because of the social opprobrium it attracts. Among other things, a man who has pronounced *talaq* may have difficulty finding another wife. This is probably one of the main reasons why men often try to induce their wives to ask for *khul*ᶜ rather than simply divorcing them unilaterally. Financial considerations may also weigh more or less heavily in their calculations, depending upon the amount of *mehr* that had been promised and the likelihood that they can avoid paying it. If there is some clear advantage to divorcing the wife, rather than just living separately from her, then it is likely that a man will divorce her. Evading a maintenance suit (as per the MWA) provides just such a motivation, as my data clearly indicate, but otherwise, many men don't bother with this formality. In this they do not differ from their Hindu and Christian fellow countrymen, for whom the inclination to simply desert the wife (or kick her out of the marital home) rather than divorce her is even more compelling, since in most cases the latter can only be accomplished via a lengthy and expensive court procedure.[36]

If the allegations contained in women's court petitions are to be relied upon, extramarital liaisons are very common among Muslim men, as they are among Hindus and Christians. Polygynous marriages are also reported, though less frequently. Even though polygyny is an accepted practice in Islam and the simple fact that a man has taken a second wife is not generally regarded as a legitimate reason for the first wife to feel aggrieved, my data suggest that it frequently causes extreme marital discord. This is because the man almost inevitably shows favouritism towards one or the other wife or is at least perceived by one or the other to be doing so. And notwithstanding a Muslim man's right under MPL to marry up to four wives at a time, the courts tend, in practice, to be sympathetic to Muslim women who complain about their husbands' second marriage in a divorce or maintenance petition. Thus 'cruelty' under the DMMA is, not infrequently, interpreted to include a man's forcing his first wife to live under the same roof as the second.

Insofar as the actual administration of MPL by the family (and other civil) courts is concerned, I have identified in the approach typically taken by the judicial authorities to the women who come before them, a pervasive paternalism based upon unexamined assumptions about woman's 'nature' and her proper 'place' in society. Most important of these is the notion that the institution of marriage provides the only secure guarantee of a woman's well-being. Ideas like this are, of course, widely shared by people of all religions. They are not only consistent with but also help to perpetuate those economic and social structured realities of women's lives that force them into overall dependency on the men in their lives. The paternalistic attitudes towards women that this ideology generates ensure that even if a woman who is having marital difficulties can overcome the many barriers that hinder her access to the civil court system, her chances of actually obtaining there what the law theoretically has to offer her are relatively small.

The issue of women's 'resistance' in the context of legal proceedings in the family courts is difficult to sort out. I have ample evidence that the women with whom I spoke are impatient with the way counselling is carried out in the courts, that they resent the time and money spent coming to court month after month, sitting for hours, on the floor, without water or toilet facilities, while they wait, often only in order to hear that they should come back again next month. They may also distrust the intentions of the police, lawyers, judges, and other staff of the family court who hold such power over their lives. As they wait, they exchange with one another stories that help to reinforce their fears that nothing positive will come of their efforts to obtain justice; and they exchange advice about how to deal with what is happening to them. In the sense that these women are aware of what they are up against, but have decided to try to use the law to ameliorate their situation anyway, they cannot be regarded simply as passive victims of a patriarchal order that they are so often assumed to be. But, on the other hand, however much 'agency' they may exert in the process of dealing with the law, the realities of their situation are such that they can only hope for limited success.

### Endnotes

This paper was written while I was a Faculty Fellow of the Institute for the Humanities at the University of Illinois at Chicago. My research in India was supported by a Fulbright-Hays Senior Research Fellowship and a sabbatical leave from the University of Illinois at Chicago. In Chennai I was affiliated with the Madras Institute of Development Studies. For their cheerful assistance I am extremely grateful to my research assistant, Ms. R. Saraswathy, and to the employees of the record room at the Chennai family court, who patiently retrieved from their massive collection of materials the individual files that we required. I thank the then Chief Justice of the Chennai High Court for facilitating my research in the family court and the then Acting Principal Judge of that court for arranging for me to consult the relevant files under her jurisdiction.

[1] Mindie Lazarus-Black and Susan F. Hirsch, eds., *Contested States: Law, Hegemony and Resistance* (New York: Routledge, 1994).

[2] Susan F. Hirsch, *Pronouncing and Persevering: Gender and the Discourses of Disputing in an African Islamic Court* (Chicago: University of Chicago Press, 1998). The employment of such strategies is not, of course, restricted to female litigants. For India, see Bernard S. Cohn, 'Anthropological Notes on Disputes

and Law in India', *American Anthropologist* 67(6[2]) (1965): 82–122, and Robert S. Moog, *Whose Interests are Supreme? Organizational Politics in the Civil Courts in India* (Ann Arbor, MI: Association for Asian Studies, 1997).

3 The forms filled out by the cleric who performs the marriage has a space in which to enter the marital status of the bride and details about any previous marriages she may have had. But neither the marital status nor the marital history of the groom is enquired into.

4 In order to get an idea of what these records contain, I was kindly permitted by a *qazi* in another city to copy his divorce register for the year 1992. In a jurisdiction in which approximately 4,000 marriages are contracted each year, the register contained details on 450 divorces. Slightly more than half of these were of the *khulᶜ* type; in almost all these cases the woman was recorded as having given up her *mehr*. In cases of *talaq*, it was usually noted that the *mehr* due the wife had been deposited with the *qazi* and later paid out to her.

To put these figures into perspective, it must be stressed that there is no requirement that a divorce be pronounced in the presence of or registered with any religious or civil authority. The chief reason for a man to register a *talaq* is to obtain an 'official' paper documenting the dissolution of the marriage. Most men have no need for such a document. Since a woman cannot simply 'pronounce' *khulᶜ*, it is usual for her to go to a *qazi* or other cleric for help in negotiating with her husband and drawing up the necessary contract. For this reason, it is almost certain that a higher percentage of *khulᶜ* divorces than *talaq*s end up being registered.

5 The validity of the assumption that most married women in urban India depend on their husbands' earnings for support is borne out by statistics, although levels of labour force participation by women, especially among the poor, are certainly much higher than the proponents of this view realise. In my sample of Muslim women drawn from court files in Chennai, there were only a handful who had ever worked outside the home, though some engaged in home-based income-producing labour, such as making speciality food items, garments, hand-rolled cigarettes (*bidi*s), and the like.

6 Moog, *Whose Interests.*

7 See Devendra Kumar Tiwari and Mahmood Zaidi, *Commentaries on the Family Courts Act, 1984* (Allahabad: Alia Law Agency, 1997). By 1994 there were 50 such courts in operation. *Justice Delivery through Family Courts: Proceedings of the National Conference* (New Delhi: National Commission for Women, 1994), p. 19. Forty-one family courts had been set up by 2005 and five years later they reportedly numbered 194, spread out over 22 of India's then 28 states, plus the Union Territories of Delhi and Pondicherry (Flavia Agnes, *Family Law, Volume II: Marriage, Divorce, and Matrimonial Litigation* (New Delhi: Oxford University Press, 2011), pp. 273, 323–7.

8 In places where no family court exists, matrimonial cases and applications

for maintenance under the CrPC are handled, as in the past, by the regular civil and criminal courts, respectively.

[9] During most of my research year, however, there were only two judges on duty in the Chennai family court. Both were women: an Acting Principal Judge and an Additional Judge. A male Principal Judge was appointed towards the end of my stay. The FCA specifies that preference in the appointment of judges is to be given to women, presumably under the assumption that a female judge would deal more fairly and sympathetically with female litigants. The gender and marital status of the Chennai family court judges—neither of whom was married—was more than once spontaneously remarked upon by the lawyers and litigants to whom I spoke. There was no unanimity, however, in their answers to my questions about the relevance of these demographic characteristics to the manner in which the two dealt with matrimonial disputes.

[10] Committee on the Status of Women in India, *Towards Equality* (New Delhi: Government of India, Department of Social Welfare, 1974).

[11] In 1991 the Bombay High Court ruled that barring lawyers from representing clients in family court proceedings presents a severe handicap to litigants, particularly to those who are poor and uneducated. Since then a number of other high courts have issued similar judgments and in most family courts today lawyers are routinely allowed to appear on behalf of litigants, much as they do in any other civil court (Agnes, *Family Law, Volume II*, pp. 294–299).

[12] Flavia Agnes, 'A Toothless Tiger: A Critique of the Family Courts', *Manushi* 66 (1991): 9–16 and 'Family Courts and Minority Rights', *The Lawyers* 9(5) (1994), pp. 27–29; D. Nagasila, 'Family Courts: A Step Backward?' *The Hindu*, March 24, 1991; 'Family Courts: A Critique', *Economic & Political Weekly* 27 (1992): 1735–1737; and Geeta Ramaseshan, 'Family Courts, Wide Gaps', *Indian Express*, March 11, 1989.

[13] YMCA, Madras, unpublished letter, Mrs. Vanjana Clement to Organising Committee, Workshop on the Effectiveness of Family Courts (Office files, 1990).

[14] *Justice Delivery*, p. 9.

[15] The payment (or promise of payment) of *mehr*—a (usually) monetary gift from the groom to his bride—is one of the conditions for a legal Muslim marriage. If she does not receive the amount during their marriage, it becomes due when he divorces her.

[16] According to MPL, the mother is allowed custody of a minor boy until the age of seven or of a girl until puberty. Thereafter, she must turn him or her over to the father, if he so wishes. In case of disputes, however, the courts generally give priority to what they regard as the best interests of the child.

[17] See Moore's rich ethnographic account of one rural Muslim woman's

experience with such a body in the context of a long-running matrimonial dispute (Erin P. Moore, *Gender, Law and Resistance in India* [Tucson: University of Arizona Press 1998]).

[18] Moog (*Whose Interests,* pp. 60–63) maintains that in India the notion of the court as a place of last resort is by no means restricted to those who are having marital difficulties. This attitude is widespread among the populace, stereotypes about India as an excessively litigious society notwithstanding.

[19] Bernard S. Cohn, 'Law and the Colonial State in India', in J. Starr & J.F. Collier, eds., *History and Power in the Study of Law* (Ithaca: Cornell University Press, 1989); and Janaki Nair, *Women and the Law in Colonial India* (New Delhi: Kali for Women, 1996).

[20] The passage of this law followed a judgment by the Supreme Court of India that upheld a lower court's award of maintenance—under Section 125 of the CrPC—against the former husband of an elderly Muslim woman named Shah Bano. There is by now a huge body of literature on this case, on the debates that it unleashed, on the events that led up to the passage of the MWA, and its implications for divorced Muslim women's well-being. Engineer has collected many of the relevant documents as well as contemporary news items and public statements about the case (Ali Asghar Engineer, ed., *The Shah Bano Controversy* [Bombay: Sangam Books, 1987]). Some useful analyses include Madhu Kishwar 'Pro-Women or Anti-Muslim? The Shah Bano Controversy', *Manushi* 32 (1986): 4–13; Gregory C. Kozlowski, 'Shah Banu's Case, Britain's Legal Legacy and Muslim Politics in Modern India', in Y. Malik & D. Vajpay, eds., *Law, Politics and Society in India* (New Delhi: Chanakya, 1989), pp. 88–111; and Zakia Pathak & Rajeswari Sunder Rajan, 'Shahbano', *Signs* 14(3) (1989): 558–582.

[21] E.g., M. Hidayatullah & A. Hidayatullah, *Mulla's Principles of Mahomedan Law,* 19th edition (Mumbai: N.M. Tripathi, 1990).

[22] For example, in 1996 less than three per cent of the 1,855 suits filed in the Chennai family court involved Muslim litigants (see Table 1). Note that I am limiting my count here to cases filed under the three main headings of 'Ordinary Suits' (OS), 'Original Petitions' (OP), and 'Maintenance Cases' (MC). Other types of cases registered in that court include suits for orders of execution, interim orders, injunctions, etc. These, however, are always secondary to an earlier suit of the OS, OP, or MC type, and so have not been included in my calculations.

[23] See P.V. Muzumdar, *The Law of Maintenance of Wives, Children and Parents* (Allahabad: Malhotra, 1989); and B.R. Verma, *Muslim Marriage, Maintenance and Dissolution* (Allahabad: Alia Law Agency, 1988). Critical perspectives on the operation of the MWA through 1990 are offered by Flavia Agnes, *Give Us This Day Our Daily Bread: Procedures and Case Law on Maintenance.* Gender

Justice Series, Book II (Mumbai: Majlis, 1992) and 'Maintenance for Women: Rhetoric of Equality', *Economic & Political Weekly* 27 (1992): 2233–2235; Madhu Kishwar, 'Call for Action: Law Commission's Report on Maintenance; Humane Recommendations Ignored', *Manushi* 77 (1993): 27–31. See also Agnes, *Family Law, Volume II*, pp. 161–164; Narendra Subramanian, *Nation and Family: Personal Law, Cultural Pluralism, and Gendered Citizenship in India* (Stanford: Stanford University Press, 2014), pp. 236–247. For more recent developments in the relevant case law and on its administration in the lower courts, see my 'Maintenance for Divorced Muslim Women after the Muslim Women (Protection of Rights on Divorce) Act 1986: a View from the Lower Courts', in Huma Ahmed-Ghosh, ed., *Asian Muslim Women: Globalization and Local Realities* (Albany, NY: State University of New York Press, 2015), pp. 103–126, reprinted in this volume.

24 There has been some controversy over whether the jurisdiction of family courts as specified in the FCA is properly interpreted to include jurisdiction over maintenance suits filed under the MWA against a woman's natal relatives or, in their absence, the local Wakf Board. See Agnes, 'Family Courts'. In my perusal of the Chennai family court files for the years 1988–1997 I found two cases filed against the Andhra Pradesh state Wakf Board, neither of which resulted in a judgment. However, as the MWA specifically states that 'a magistrate' is to decide suits filed under it, I could presumably have found additional cases in the records of those courts, had I been in a position to examine them during my time in Chennai. In chapter 8 in this volume I discuss findings from a 2005–06 study of MWA cases in the magistrate's court in Hyderabad that deals mainly with cases of violence against women.

25 For a historical perspective on this legal remedy in Indian law, see Sudhir Chandra, *Enslaved Daughters: Colonialism, Law, and Women's Rights* (New Delhi: Oxford University Press, 1998). For more recent developments, see Flavia Agnes, *Family Law, Volume I: Family Laws and Constitutional Claims* (New Delhi: Oxford University Press, 2011), pp. 24–26 and *Family Law, Volume II*, pp. 22–27.

26 For further details and discussion of the events leading up to the passage of the DMMA, see Muhammad Khalid Masud, 'Apostasy and Judicial Separation in British India' in M.K. Masud, B. Messick, and D.S. Powers, eds., *Islamic Legal Interpretation: Muftis and Their Fatwas* (Cambridge, MA: Harvard University Press, 1996), pp. 193–203; Gail Minault, 'Women, Legal Reform, and Muslim Identity', *Comparative Studies of South Asia, Africa and the Middle East* 17(2) (1997): 1–10; Shahida Lateef, *Muslim Women in India: Political and Private Realities, 1890s–1980s* (New Delhi: Kali for Women, 1990); Rohit De, 'Mumtaz Bibi's Broken Heart: The Many Lives of the Dissolution of Muslim Marriages Act, 1939', *Indian Economic and Social History Review*, 46(1) (2009):

105–130; and 'The Two Husbands of Vera Tiscenko: Apostasy, Conversion and Divorce in Late Colonial India', *Law and History Review* 28(4) (2010): 1011–1041.

[27] Beginning in 1981 a series of High Court decisions have declared invalid divorces pronounced in this way, without any attempts at arbitration or adherence to other procedures that the Qur'an prescribes (see Agnes, *Family Law Volume I*, pp. 60–64; Subramanian, *Nation and Family*, pp. 247–251). But the lower courts are inconsistent in heeding these judicial precedents and, as far as the Muslim community at large is concerned, it is still the case that, once a 'triple *talaq*' has been pronounced, the couple is regarded as no longer married.

[28] For example, in a study of 100 divorced Muslim women in Mumbai, Merchant found that 60 per cent had not received their *mehr* after divorce. Munira Merchant, 'Indian Muslim Women: Post-Divorce Problems, Social Support and Psychological Well-Being', Ph.D. dissertation, School of Social Work, University of Illinois at Chicago (1992), p. 111. However, she does not distinguish those who were divorced by *talaq* from those who obtained *khul*ᶜ or a civil divorce under DMMA. Nor does she provide information concerning maintenance for the ᶜ*iddat* period for the women in her sample. In any event, *mehr* amounts reported in Chennai family court petitions tended to be minimal, almost regardless of the economic standing of the husband. The conventional figure of Rs. 568 was cited in the vast majority of cases and rarely did it exceed Rs 1,500.

[29] MPL also recognises other forms of divorce, including one by mutual agreement, *mubarat,* but these seem to be little known or resorted to, at least in the parts of India where I have investigated the matter.

[30] This law was superseded by the 2006 Prohibition of Child Marriage Act. However, no changes were made in the minimum marriage ages, which remain at eighteen for females and twenty-one for males.

[31] Technically, insofar as matrimonial cases are concerned, MPL applies to persons married under Muslim law, that is in a Muslim ceremony, the central features of which are the signing of a *nikah* contract and the payment (or promise of payment) of *mehr* by the groom to his bride. Thus someone married under the Special Marriage Act, even if he or she was born of Muslim parents, would be governed, in the event of a divorce suit, by the provisions of that Act. Conversely, a Hindu woman who contracts a *nikah* with a Muslim man must file for divorce under the DMMA, rather than under the Hindu Marriage Act.

[32] Mattison Mines, 'Urbanization, Family Structure and the Muslim Merchants of Tamilnadu', in I. Ahmad, ed., *Family, Kinship and Marriage among the Muslims in India* (New Delhi: Manohar Book Service, 1976), pp. 297–318;

C.G. Hussain Khan, *Marriage and Kinship among Muslims in South India* (Jaipur: Rawat Publications. 1994); F.S. Fanselow, 'Trade, Kinship and Islamisation: A Comparative Study of the Social and Economic Organisation of Muslim and Hindu Traders in Tirunelveli District, South India', Ph.D. dissertation, Social Anthropology, London School of Economics (1986); Sylvia Vatuk, 'The Cultural Construction of Shared Identity: A South Indian Muslim Family History', *Social Analysis* 28 (1990): 114–131.

[33] Although the practice of giving 'dowry' is not sanctioned by Islam, it has been spreading rapidly within the community in recent decades and is often cited by Muslims as a serious and growing social problem. See, e.g., Sylvia Vatuk, 'The "Cancer of Dowry" in Indian Muslim Marriages: Themes in the Popular Rhetoric from the South Indian Muslim Press', in M. Hasan, ed., *Living With Secularism: The Destiny of India's Muslims* (New Delhi: Manohar, 2007), pp. 155–176, reprinted in this volume.

[34] A study of women who had registered criminal cases for domestic abuse in the main All-Women Police Station in Chennai likewise cites the husband's 'suspicion' of his wife as a major precipitant of marital discord (Subadra Natarajan, 'A Study of Battered Women in Chennai', M.Phil dissertation. Chennai: Madras School of Social Work (1997) and Subadra [Natarajan], 'Violence against Women: Wife Battering in Chennai', *Economic & Political Weekly* 34 (1999): WS 28–33.

[35] These observations can be interpreted from one angle as a self-critique of excessive Hindu orthodoxy, but from another angle they are clearly part of a more general discourse about the relative 'immorality' of the Muslim woman in comparison to her Hindu sisters.

[36] The divorce procedure was, at the time of my research, especially onerous for Christians. A Christian man could get a divorce only on the ground of adultery. A Christian woman had to show that her husband had either converted to another religion and remarried or had committed adultery *as well as* desertion or cruelty (see Flavia Agnes, *Law and Gender Inequality: The Politics of Women's Rights in India* (New Delhi: Oxford University Press, 1999), pp. 141–163. However, in 2001, after years of pressure by Christian activist groups and non-sectarian women's organisations and in response to a number of High Court decisions and recommendations by the Indian Law Commission, the Indian Divorce Act 1869 was amended to allow Christians of either sex to file for divorce on any one of ten grounds or to divorce by mutual consent (Nandini Chatterjee, *Christian Personal Law in India: The Modern Origins of Yet Another Tradition.* [Cambridge: Centre of South Asian Studies, University of Cambridge, 2004]; and Subramanian, *Nation and Family*, pp. 252–259).

# 2.
# Muslim Women and Personal Law

## Introduction

The ongoing debates in India over the proposed enactment of a Uniform Civil Code (UCC) of personal law that would apply to all citizens, regardless of religious affiliation, have provided the main impetus for the research discussed in this chapter, which was conducted in 1998–99 and in autumn 2001 in the cities of Chennai and Hyderabad.[1] While the general principle that the State should assure equal protection under the law to all citizens provides the overarching rationale for legal reform in the family law area, proponents of a UCC focus, in particular, on the issue of gender bias in the existing Muslim Personal Law. Their critique is mainly directed at those provisions of the MPL that permit a Muslim man to have up to four wives at one time, to divorce his wife extrajudicially, and to be free of responsibility for her maintenance once an approximately three-month post-divorce period (*ᶜiddat*) has ended.

It is, of course, indisputable that these provisions of the MPL, both as codified and as developed through case law, favour the interests of the male partner in a failing marriage. However, notwithstanding all the rhetoric that has been expended on this subject, we have almost no hard data on how Muslim women are actually affected in their daily lives by these laws, how many are so affected, and for what reasons. These questions are important, whether or not one is in favour of the enactment of a UCC; believes that some other kind of reform in the existing MPL is desirable; or would prefer leaving the law as it stands. They are particularly so in the light of the current political realities, which make legislative reform in this area any time in the foreseeable future an increasingly remote possibility. Since it is almost certain that the status quo with respect to the MPL will, in fact, remain unchanged for many years to come, it is vital to try to achieve a more nuanced understanding of the MPL *as it is actually practised*, on a day-to-day basis, especially in the lower courts and in the *qazis*' offices or other religious venues where men and women most often encounter it. A great deal of scholarly and activist effort has been devoted in recent years to calling attention to the ways in which the freedom given to Muslim men to divorce at will, marry multiple wives, and leave those they have discarded without any means of support is detrimental to Muslim women's interests. However, much of the literature on this subject is highly polemical and the evidence presented is often merely anecdotal. The absence of any solid data on the frequency of divorce (unilateral or otherwise), on the actual prevalence of polygamy, or on the extent to which Muslim divorcées fall into destitution (and the social and economic contexts in which this occurs) makes it especially difficult to make valid generalisations about the relative deprivation of Muslim versus Hindu or Christian women in terms of actual legal practice, today.

My research was not intended to directly address the pros and cons of a proposed UCC but rather to gather empirical information on how the MPL actually operates and how the lives of Muslim women are impacted by it. Arguments on both sides of current debates about the alleged negative consequences of MPL for Muslim women are based largely upon interpretations of the codes themselves—as they are written—and upon case law, the accumulated judicial decisions of the various High Courts and Supreme Court of India over a period of more than two centuries. Little is known, however, about what happens when Muslim women today have reason to personally encounter and deal with those provisions of the MPL that are most strongly criticised by politicians, social and legal activists, and scholars. One place to begin looking at this is in the lower civil courts—which in large cities means the family courts—where Muslim women can bring suits for divorce (under the Dissolution of Muslim Marriages Act, 1939) or file for maintenance[2] and/or for child support (under Section 125 of the Criminal Procedure Code) and where they may be summoned to answer suits for restitution of conjugal rights brought by their husbands.[3] Another place to look for some answers to these questions is the women's cells of police stations (or the all-women police stations found in many large cities). Here complaints against husbands and in-laws for dowry harassment and cruelty (under Section 498A of the Indian Penal Code [IPC]) are registered. The criminal courts where such cases are tried are another important site for investigation. Finally, since MPL allows for extrajudicial divorce (when initiated by the husband or as a result of a negotiated agreement between the spouses), one can examine the operation of Muslim religious dispute-resolution bodies (sometimes referred to as *Shari'at* courts), of mosque committees that fulfil a similar function, and of the offices (*dar-ul-quzat*) where *qazi*s register marriages and divorces and provide occasional guidance on the fine points of Islamic inheritance and other laws.

In order to begin to fill this gap in our knowledge of the practise of MPL and to provide a firmer basis for future policy recommendations, I carried out a field investigation in a number of these sites, where Muslim women experiencing marital problems confront, directly or indirectly, the laws that govern personal relations in their community.[4]

Given the paucity of existing information on the subject, the study was exploratory in nature and no attempt was made to survey a systematic sample of informants for responses to a standard set of questions. Neither was any attempt made to gather data that would permit a comparison of the experience of Muslim women with that of women governed by Hindu or Christian personal laws. My aim was rather to get the broadest possible range of information on how, from the perspective of Muslim women living in India today, MPL actually works. Given the fact that any discussion of MPL in the context of a scholarly concern with its implications for gender equity is overdetermined by the public framing of the issue almost exclusively in terms of *talaq*, polygamy, and the Shah Bano case, I will limit the present discussion to these three facets of the law, although there are indeed other vital issues (such as that of women's inheritance rights) that are equally deserving of examination.[5]

One of my purposes is to complicate widely accepted understandings of the workings of MPL and, in particular, of its impact on women. I will endeavour to show, in relation to each of the legal issues raised, how popular understandings about what MPL means for women are undermined by some of my findings. The reality is not necessarily more favourable from the point of view of women's well-being than are some of the widely accepted misconceptions about Muslims in general and about the operation of Muslim personal law in particular. I will note these as I proceed. My second purpose is to call attention to some factors in the broader social structural milieu in which these women, not specifically as Muslims but as Indians, are living. I will argue, to paraphrase a statement by Srimati Basu, that the problem for these women lies not merely in the laws themselves, imperfect and often inappropriately implemented as they may be, but 'in the cultural configurations of gender and law and their relationship to the state', and (I would add) its representatives.[6]

## Social and cultural context of Muslim women's lives

This study was conducted in only two sites, both urban and in southern India, and inasmuch as the various samples of women from whom my data have been gathered is a very selective one—principally, women in unhappy marriages who had sought relief from the civil or religious authorities or had been compelled to answer to them because their husbands had taken legal action in connection with their marital problems. I can hardly claim that my findings describe the situation of all Muslim women in all parts of India. Only by comparing my findings with those of other researchers will it be possible to say how far it is valid to generalise from them.

Like most Indian Muslims, the women interviewed for this study and those whose cases were reported in the various records we examined were, with very few exceptions, Sunnis, followers of the Hanafi school of law. Otherwise, our samples were very diverse: economically, educationally, and in many other respects.

Reliable data on the women's economic status were difficult to obtain and the information we do have on occupation and income is sketchy and not supported by any kind of documentation. Many of those interviewed in Hyderabad appeared, from their own accounts, their dress and appearance, to be living at a bare minimum level of subsistence. On the other hand, a few divorce petitioners interviewed in the family court in Chennai came from middle-class families. In both cities, however, the majority of litigants belonged—as far as we could gauge—to the low to lower-middle income strata.[7] Their husbands were employed in a wide range of relatively low-paying occupations: manual labourers, autorickshaw drivers, office workers in small private firms, traders or owners of small businesses, or low-ranking government servants.[8] Women's petitions for maintenance in the Chennai family court usually provide estimates of the husband's monthly earnings. Typically, husbands dispute the amounts cited by their wives, claiming to earn much less or even to be unemployed.[9] But even allowing for this kind of discrepancy, the figures confirm what can be deduced from the occupational data about the economic standing of the women's families.

Very few of those interviewed had ever been employed outside the home, although some who had been separated from their husbands for a long time told of having intermittently earned small amounts doing home-based work: embroidery, sewing, preparing speciality food items, assembling cardboard boxes, giving religious instruction to children. A small number of college-educated women whom we interviewed had worked in government offices or as school teachers, but very few of the women submitting petitions to the Chennai family court indicated that they had ever been gainfully employed.[10] And only a handful of the brides married by Hyderabad Qazi A were described on their marriage certificates as anything other than 'housewife'. Some may have actually engaged in some kind of home-based handwork before their marriage, but such women's ways of earning small amounts of money are typically regarded (by men, in particular) as merely 'sideline' or 'leisure time' activities and are unlikely to be entered as a woman's 'occupation' (*pesha*) on an official (or quasi-official) form.

Not surprisingly, almost all of the women we interviewed, as well as most of those who provided this information in court petitions, described their marriages as having been arranged by their parents.[11] Most of them claimed to have taken little or no part in the discussions that had led up to their elders' acceptance of a marriage proposal for them. Few had met or even seen their husband-to-be before the wedding, although they had usually been 'seen' and perhaps 'interviewed' by some of his female relatives. Some indicated that they had not felt ready to marry when the initial proposal came—either because they had wanted to continue studying or for some other reason. However, for the most part they had not expressed their preferences outwardly—or at least not very emphatically—but had simply accepted passively whatever their elders decided.

Typically the prospective groom or his parents had taken the initiative in proposing the match.[12] Sometimes relatives, neighbours, or matchmakers—professional or otherwise—had made the initial approach. Often those presenting the proposal were very insistent, pressing the girls' parents for a quick decision and insisting that the ceremony be held very soon thereafter. When a proposal is received from a virtual stranger—which appears to have been the case in a high proportion of cases—a girl's elders naturally try to find out as much as they can about the young man. However, for families living in crowded urban centres it is difficult to thoroughly check a stranger's credentials, especially when the only mutual acquaintance is the go-between, who typically has a personal interest, financial or otherwise, in promoting the match. Furthermore, when parents receive what appears, at least on the surface, to be a 'good' proposal, they often find themselves on the horns of a dilemma. Would it be wise to turn it down and risk the chance that another equally or more suitable groom will not present himself in the future? There is considerable evidence that many families do not, or are unable to do, as thorough an investigation as prudence might dictate. This is especially likely if the girl's father is deceased or has left the family and her mother has no close male kinsman willing or able to take on this responsibility in his place.

In any event, the husbands of a substantial number of the women in our sample had allegedly provided false or misleading information about themselves, especially about their educational achievements, employment, or previous marital history. Even when there was no explicit attempt on the part of the man's family to misrepresent his qualifications or hide significant facts about his past, he sometimes had serious personality or character flaws about which the woman's family was unaware. Once the woman's parents have verified, through official channels, the educational and employment claims of their prospective son-in-law, there is little more that they can do without common (and well-disposed) friends, relatives, or neighbours willing to supply them with the inside information that he is also lazy, financially irresponsible, of a violent disposition, addicted to drugs, alcohol, or gambling, accustomed to frequenting prostitutes, keeping a mistress, or in love with his cousin.

Notwithstanding the expected preponderance of arranged marriages, a disproportionate number (22 per cent) of women in the Chennai litigants' sample had had a 'love match'. Such couples had met as neighbours, relatives, co-workers, fellow students, family friends, fellow-tenants in the same house, or in a landlord-tenant situation. In many of these cases one partner (usually the woman) was a non-Muslim. Typically, neither set of parents had given their consent to the match and the couple had eloped, going to a *qazi* or other Muslim religious functionary to have the non-Muslim partner converted to Islam and their *nikah* read.[13] The fact that so many of the couples who ended up in court were parties to love marriages is an indication not only of the exceptional stresses to which such unions are subject, but also of the fact that couples who have married without parental approval lack access to the usual family or community support systems when conflicts do arise between them.

## Age at marriage

Contrary to the common belief that early marriage is the usual practice among Indian Muslims, data from our sample of Chennai family court litigants show a mean age at first marriage of just under 21 years. Whereas 70 per cent of those who married before 1978 (when the revised Child Marriage Restraint Act was passed) claim to have been under 18 years of age at the time of their wedding, this was true of only 20 per cent of those who married after that date. Every one of the women married in 1990 or later met—at least according to their petitions—the minimum legal age requirement.[14] Interview data (not to mention periodic newspaper reports) make it clear that, despite the existence of this law, marriages of girls below the age of 18 years do continue to take place in Chennai (and elsewhere in India), even though both the parents of the underage bride and the person performing the marriage are liable for prosecution under the Act.[15]

In the past few years there have been a few well-publicised cases of *qazis* accused of knowingly falsifying the age of a bride on the marriage certificate. However, probably more common are situations in which parents, intent upon getting their daughter married, simply tell the *qazi* that she is 18 years old and he asks no further questions. Or without even asking how old the bride is, the *qazi* may simply write down '18' in the appropriate column on the form. Since few brides have an official birth certificate with which someone could prove differently and since there would rarely be anyone present at the *nikah* who was motivated to raise the issue, such an act does not carry a very great risk. As one illiterate young woman told us, 'I was only 16 at the time of my *shadi*, but they wrote 18 on the certificate, because otherwise the government won't recognise the marriage.'

## Reproductive histories

A surprising 57 per cent of the couples involved in the Chennai family court suits were childless—19 per cent of the women filing for maintenance and 69 per cent of those involved in other kinds of suits. Of those who had borne children, most had become pregnant very soon after the consummation of the marriage and, if the couple stayed together, had additional children in fairly rapid succession. However, most of the couples encountered in the files had separated relatively soon after their weddings.[16]

Court petitions not infrequently described a scenario in which the woman had become pregnant within a few months of the marriage, had gone back to her natal home for her confinement (as is customary in these communities) and had never returned to her husband's home, usually because of mistreatment she had earlier received from her husband and in-laws and/or because the latter had either neglected or refused to come to see the child or take the new mother and child back to their home after the obligatory 40-day period of post-partum impurity (*cilla*). Women filing for maintenance were understandably more likely to have children than were those who came to court for some other reason, but few of the litigants in either category had more than two offspring.

Almost invariably it was the mother who had physical custody of any small children at the time the suit was filed (by her or her husband) in family court. The only exceptions involved a few somewhat older children who had remained behind when their mother left or was ejected from the marital home. This finding contradicts the general belief that custody rules under MPL virtually ensure that women will lose their children upon divorce. In fact, if the evidence of family court cases can be trusted, it seems to be quite rare for men to seriously try to get custody of small children, although they frequently use the threat to do so as a bargaining chip in a divorce or maintenance suit.

### Proximate causes of marital conflict

The reasons that had brought these women to court naturally varied greatly in their details, but certain patterns can be identified. Generally the crisis that immediately precipitated the couple's separation had been provoked by the husband, who for one reason or another was dissatisfied with some aspect of his wife's behaviour, had berated her verbally, abused her physically, and finally thrown her out of the home. Sometimes the woman, unable or unwilling to put up with mistreatment sustained over an extended period of time, had left of her own accord, occasionally assisted by natal relatives. Reasons for a husband's displeasure were many; one of the most common was 'suspicion' of the wife's chastity. Women reported being unjustly accused of immodesty or sexual misconduct, failing to keep strict purdah, appearing before or talking to unrelated men, or even engaging in extramarital sexual relations.

Other commonly cited reasons for the husband's dissatisfaction with the wife were her alleged neglect of or poor skills in housekeeping, cooking or childcare, her arguing with or talking back to him, failing to show sufficient respect and obedience towards his parents, questioning him about his activities or plans, corresponding with or attempting to maintain friendships with relatives, friends, or neighbours of whom he did not approve, and leaving the house in his absence without obtaining his permission. Since most of the couples moved in with the husband's family upon marriage, conflict with the husband's mother and other (mainly female) in-laws often led to marital problems, even when the couple's relationship had started off on a solid footing. Frequently, it was said to be the mother-in-law who provoked her son to berate or beat his wife, by complaining to him about the way she behaved in his absence. The failure of her family to have provided sufficient 'dowry' at the time of marriage or their refusal (or inability) to meet further monetary demands very frequently were cited by women as precipitating mistreatment at the hands of the husband and parents-in-law.

A conflictual relationship between a man and his parents-in-law—whether arising out of dissatisfaction with the dowry they have given or for other reasons—is also typical of the cases that come to the family court.[17] It appears that from the very inception of the marriage a virtual tug of war often ensues between the two families that are joined by the marriage of their children, a war that is waged over the body of the wife. Thus, men complain that their wives visit their natal homes 'too often' or 'without informing' them or 'without securing permission'. Women complain that their husbands try to force them to cut off all ties with their parents or refuse to allow regular visits, even for the legitimate purposes of attending religious ceremonies or life cycle celebrations or helping to nurse an ill parent.

Whatever the specific problems a particular couple may have, the overarching issue seems to be that of a man's need—and his right—to establish and maintain control over his wife and bend her to his will in every aspect of life. This notion is consistent with data we collected on approximately 350 divorces recorded in the *dar-ul-quzat* of Qazi B in Hyderabad. Although Islamic law does not require that a man provide a reason when he pronounces *talaq* (or when he 'registers' a *talaq* after the fact), more than half the men who registered a *talaq* with this *qazi* provided at least a brief explanation for their action. To be sure, for most of these divorces the records contain only a conventional formula, to the effect that 'for various reasons it has become impossible for us to continue the marriage'. However, about one-quarter of those providing reasons for the divorce were more specific: the most common complaint was that the wife was 'disobedient' and/or 'stubborn'.[18]

As I have already indicated, both psychological and physical abuse of wives by husbands and sometimes by in-laws as well was very frequently reported, both by the women we interviewed and in the family court petitions. Among those filing suit for maintenance in the Chennai family court, 70 per cent reported experiencing domestic abuse, often, though not always, associated with 'dowry harassment'.[19] Demands that the wife get her family to provide cash for such purposes as setting up a business, buying a vehicle or household appliances, acquiring land, building a house, providing a dowry for her husband's sister's marriage, or financing her husband's efforts to secure work in the Middle East or one of the Gulf states were often reported.

The specific forms of abuse ranged from verbal insults to physical attacks. These took many different forms, from refusing to allow the wife adequate food, beating her with fists or kicking her, striking her with heavy objects, pushing her into a cooking fire or into a body of water, dousing her with kerosene and threatening to set her alight, to locking her in or out of the house. Other forms of harassment reported included stalking her whenever she left the house, even on 'legitimate' and 'authorised' outings, following her to her place of employment and making a public scene there, forcing her to resign from her job (even when, in a few cases, her earnings were the family's main source of income), misappropriating her jewellery or other possessions (in one case, the deed to her landed property) in order to fulfil ritual obligations or realise cash for some other purpose (including gambling or supporting another wife), or forcing her to engage in sexual relations with a male relative or friend.[20]

### Previous attempts to seek relief

When marital problems first arose, one or both partners typically sought the help of intermediaries—relatives or friends of one or both families—or consulted a community panchayat or the *jamaat* committee of the local mosque for mediation of their dispute.

Doubtless, most cases referred to these bodies never progressed to the point of either partner taking legal action. We were able to examine the case records of one such body, which calls itself a '*Shari'at* Court' and maintains files in a very similar manner to that used in the Chennai family court, employing a legal vocabulary and an identical system of numbering cases. Most of the 56 matrimonial cases[21] this body dealt with between 1995 and 1999 were brought either by husbands or by fathers (sometimes along with other female relatives) on behalf of their married daughters, granddaughters, or nieces. The avowed goal of this court, as explained to us by three of its sitting members, is to 'reconcile' the couple. In pursuing this end, the members take a more proactive role than the local *qazi* is usually in a position to do, making home visits, using the wife of the court's presiding officer to meet with the women involved. One reason this body feels that it is necessary for a woman to be deputed for this purpose is that they do not permit women to attend their hearings. They are also quite strict about not having their male members speak directly to women clients outside the court setting—or vice versa. They credit their involvement of this woman in their mediation activities (a rather unique practice for religious bodies of this kind) with enabling them to achieve a high rate of success in helping couples arrive at amicable solutions to their marital problems. Their main spokesman maintained in an interview, that in 90 per cent of the cases 'we succeed in getting the couple back together again'. This was an off the cuff estimate, not backed by any statistics, but it is indicative of the group's self-perception. Actual examination of their case files showed that many of the cases that come before them are dropped before a resolution is reached; others end in a *Shari'at* court-mediated divorce. It was difficult to determine how many of the rest had resulted in reconciliation, even one of temporary duration, because most of the files closed only with the brief and rather equivocal statement that 'the case was settled'.

## Police intervention

In 17 per cent of all case files examined at the Chennai family court there was evidence that the wife had gone (usually with some member of her family) at least once to the police to complain against her husband and/or her in-laws for domestic abuse, dowry harassment (under Section 498A of the Indian Penal Code), or for recovery of property that she had left behind in her marital home when the couple separated.[22] The actual number of women who took this step may well be larger than this, since not all petitioners may have considered it relevant or necessary to include this information in their petition or counter. Only a very few of these incidents appear to have led to prosecution of the man or his family members. In most cases, the police had evidently not even filed an FIR (first information report), but had simply made the man sign a commitment to cease his objectionable behaviour and had then released him.[23] Where a woman's conflictual relationship with her in-laws seems to the police to be a major contributing factor in the spouses' inability to live together peaceably, the couple is often advised to separate from the husband's parents and set up an independent residence. Men tend to be reluctant to take such a step, arguing that they cannot support two households or do not wish to leave their parents alone. Where the issue was retrieval of the wife's dowry items or other personal property, the police had typically gone to the house and forced the husband or in-laws to hand over all or most of what she claimed was rightfully hers.

## Resort to the family court

Typically, for woman litigants, filing a suit in the family court was a last resort, undertaken only after other measures of the kind described above had proved unsuccessful. On average, by the time a couple found themselves in court they had been married for about seven years, but few had lived together for this long. One-quarter had lived with their husband for less than one year, half for less than three years, and three-quarters for less than six. While there were occasional instances of women filing for maintenance or divorce after living together with their husbands for 30 years or more, the overwhelming majority of break-ups occurred within a few years of the wedding. Sometimes those couples who seek community mediation are still living together; by the time one or the other partner gets to the point of going to the *qazi* to get a divorce or to filing a civil or criminal suit, they are invariably living apart and often have been so for a considerable length of time.[24]

## Divorce

The most controversial provision of MPL is that which permits a man to dissolve his marriage extrajudicially, unilaterally, and automatically by pronouncing the word *talaq*, either directly to, or with clear reference to, his wife. He need not establish or even state any grounds for divorcing her and she need not be present when he pronounces the words. Indeed, for the divorce to be valid she need not even be informed that she has been divorced! If he *does* wish to inform her, he may do so through a third party or in writing.

There is a popular perception that the divorce rate among Muslims is very high. Whether the implied measure is against some ideal standard or as compared with the rate prevailing within the majority community is usually not specified. There are several different ways of calculating divorce rates, but most of these require that one know how many marriages were dissolved within a given period of time.[25] For no Indian population is it possible to obtain such a figure, in the absence of any comprehensive system of marriage and divorce registration. *Qazi*s' records, however, do shed some light on the question, although they do not permit calculating the 'divorce rate' according to any of the conventional methods.

Most Muslim marriages are recorded by the same *qazi* (or other religious functionary) who reads the *nikah*.[26] In both Chennai and Hyderabad, for example, standardised printed forms are filled in at the time the marriage is contracted. A copy is kept permanently in the *qazi*'s office and other copies are given to the groom and to the bride (or to her father or marriage guardian [*wali*]). In Hyderabad one copy is also deposited with the Wakf Board (which, among other functions, oversees the appointment and the work of *qazis* in the city and surrounding areas in Andhra Pradesh)[27] and another is supposed to be sent to the Andhra Pradesh State Archives.[28] From such records it is possible to obtain a good deal of information, not only about the number of marriages contracted but also about the demographic characteristics of the parties marrying within a particular period of time in the given *qazi*'s jurisdiction.[29]

Divorce records are maintained in a very similar manner. These are, however, much less complete than marriage records, largely because there is no obligation and much less motivation to involve a *qazi* in the divorce process than there is to invite him to preside over one's marriage ceremony. Whether or not a divorce has been registered has no bearing upon its validity but many men do go through this process, in some cases because they share the widespread, though erroneous, belief that a valid divorce must have the imprimatur of a recognised Muslim cleric. Otherwise, the only real reason to register a *talaq* is that, as Qazi B explained to me, 'nowadays people want to have a paper, something in writing to show as proof.' Marriage and divorce certificates are often produced in civil court cases. For example, a man may submit a *qazi*'s divorce certificate to counter his wife's suit for maintenance, as proof that he is no longer responsible for her support.[30]

When a previously married man wants to remarry, his prospective in-laws, unwilling to place their daughter in a polygynous marriage, may want evidence that his first wife is no longer in the picture. A man who needs to get a passport or a visa for travel overseas or is seeking a job in the Gulf has to show some documentation of his marital status. Government regulations bar their employees from having more than one wife and, although this rule conflicts with that provision of MPL that permits a Muslim man to have four wives at one time, attempts to enforce it upon Muslim government servants are not unusual. Here too, it may be necessary to be able to produce a divorce certificate in order to avoid losing one's job. It is obvious from the records of these two *qazi*s that not every *talaq* is registered at the time it is pronounced. There is often a gap of several years between the reported date of the divorce and the date of its registration. This is doubtless because at the time of the divorce the need for a certificate had not yet arisen.

The main services provided by *qazi*s in connection with divorce are to instruct the man in the proper way to formulate the divorce pronouncement and/or to 'register' one that has already been pronounced. When a client first comes into his office to consult him about a divorce, the *qazi* typically asks about the whereabouts of the man's wife, whether or not they have any children, what kind of job he has, and how much he earns. He may also ask the man to explain briefly why he wants to divorce his wife. If the reason strikes the *qazi* as too frivolous or ill-considered, he may suggest that the man go home and think about it and perhaps try to reconcile his differences with his wife before going through with his plan to end the marriage.[31] Or he may tell the man to bring his wife in for a joint consultation before discarding her irrevocably. However, most divorce cases seem to be handled with considerable dispatch and with relatively few questions asked. Having ascertained that the client is serious in his intention to dissolve his marriage, the *qazi* or his assistant commits the *talaq* to writing (a document called a *talaqnama*) and has the client and the requisite two witnesses sign it.[32] He then signs it himself and affixes his official seal. He enters the relevant information into a pre-printed divorce registration form which the man and his witnesses are also asked to sign. This document is kept in the *qazi*'s files for future reference.[33]

## Modes of divorce

Among Sunni Muslims of the Hanafi school of law, the religiously most 'approved' (*talaq-al sunna*) way for a man to divorce his wife is by pronouncing only one *talaq*, then abstaining from sexual intercourse with her until the end of the *ᶜiddat* period, that is when she has completed three successive menstrual courses. At any time before this he can revoke the divorce either verbally or by resuming cohabitation,[34] otherwise the *talaq* takes effect when the third menstrual period has finished. If the couple later wishes to reconcile, they must formally renew their marriage vows in a ceremony called *tajdid-i nikah*. The same rules apply if the man should on a later occasion pronounce *talaq* a second time. After a third *talaq* (called *talaq-ul bain*), however, the divorce takes immediate and final effect. This time it cannot be revoked and the couple cannot marry one another again unless the wife first contracts a *nikah* with another man, consummates that marriage, and is in turn divorced by him. This procedure is called *halala*.

It is also possible to pronounce three *talaq*s, one after another, without leaving the recommended month-long cooling-off periods between the first and second and the second and third *talaq*. When the word *talaq* is pronounced three times 'at one sitting', the divorce takes effect immediately and is irrevocable. The same result is accomplished if the man says simply, 'I divorce you by *talaq-ul bain* (irrevocable divorce)'. This so-called 'triple *talaq*' is generally agreed to be the least religiously approved method of divorcing one's wife. It is sometimes referred to as 'innovative' or 'new' (*talaq-ul bidᶜat*) divorce, because, it is said, it was not practised in the Prophet's time. Nevertheless, the vast majority of Indian Muslim men who divorce their wives do so in this way.

Those in positions of religious 'authority' (such as the *qazi*s to whom we spoke) often expressed regret that the 'triple *talaq*' is resorted to so often, in preference to the more approved methods of pronouncing divorce. Some claimed that, when they have the opportunity, they try to use their influence to inform and persuade the men who come to them of the wisdom of leaving open the possibility of a reconciliation. None of these clerics, however, thought it is desirable for the Indian State (or any other body) to try to halt the practise, and none had any concrete suggestions about how to lessen its prevalence, other than by trying to persuade men to be better Muslims.

## Timing

Although there is a popular perception that among Muslims the act of divorcing one's wife is often committed in the heat of anger, 'on a whim', my data suggest that most divorces are pronounced only after the couple is already living apart. This may be because the husband is working abroad or in another city, because he has ejected his wife from their home after a quarrel, or because she has gone back to her parental home of her own accord, typically either in order to give birth to a child or to escape mistreatment in the marital home. Rather than pronouncing divorce in the wife's presence, during or following a quarrel, it appears much more common to inform a wife that she has been divorced by sending her a letter, often by registered post and frequently through a *qazi* or advocate. In the upper strata of society, women sometimes report being informed through a newspaper advertisement, by fax, SMS, or by e-mail.

These latter methods are especially often employed by men who are working abroad, having left their spouse behind in India. Labour migration to the Middle East and the Gulf states means that spouses are often geographically separated in the early months of marriage, before they have become well-acquainted with one another or developed a strong bond of affection. This inevitably creates a situation in which misunderstandings can easily arise and fester. In one common scenario, the husband's parents complain about or pass on derogatory remarks to their son about their daughter-in-law's housekeeping abilities, mothering style, modesty, or morals. He eventually reacts by sending her a 'letter of divorce' by one or the other of the means described.

## *Mehr* and *ᶜiddat* payments

A man who gives his wife *talaq* is supposed to pay some amount to his wife to maintain her for a three-month waiting period, during which it is established whether or not the wife is pregnant. If she is, he is obliged to continue to maintain her until the child is delivered.[35] He is also required to pay her—if he has not already done so—the sum of money and/or other valuables, her *mehr*, that he promised his wife at the time of their wedding. Every Muslim marriage contract includes such a promise. The amount is not fixed, but is negotiated between the male elders of the two families before they seal their agreement to the match. It can range from as little as Rs. 51 or 101 to tens or hundreds of thousands of rupees, depending, among other things, upon the economic status and family customs of the bride and groom and whether or not the families are related—by blood or friendship—to one another.[36] *Mehr* may be 'prompt' (*muᶜajjal*: Urdu spelling, *mim ᶜain jim lam*), that is, handed over to the bride at the time of the wedding; much more commonly it is 'deferred' (*mu'wajjal*: spelled *mim wau jim lam*). In the latter case, the man makes a written commitment to pay his wife the agreed-upon sum at some unspecified future date. According to Islamic law, the *mehr* becomes due upon divorce (by *talaq*) or upon the man's death (in which case it becomes the first claim against his estate).

*Mehr* is often thought of as being a deterrent to divorce. A man, so the reasoning goes, will hesitate to pronounce divorce if he knows that he will be required to make good on his promise to pay her a substantial sum. From the perspective of a girl's parents, the higher the *mehr*, the more secure is their daughter's future. If she should be divorced, she will at least have a substantial nest-egg with which to begin life anew. However everyone also recognises that there is little point in negotiating a *mehr* so high that it will be beyond the son-in-law's ability to pay, if and when the time comes.

All of this assumes that there are mechanisms in place to ensure that in case of *talaq*, the *mehr* will in fact be paid. If a man does not voluntarily give his wife her *mehr* following the divorce, she has little recourse. Many women are not even aware of their right to claim their *mehr* at this time, others do not know what was promised to them when they married nor how to go about getting it. Although, theoretically, a woman can file a civil suit to get her *mehr* after divorce, in practice this option is expensive, has little certainty of success and is understandably only rarely resorted to. Furthermore, by the time they are divorced, many women have already waived their right to *mehr*, for young brides are often pressured by their husbands or in-laws very soon after the wedding to 'forgive' whatever was promised to them.

### Deferred *mehr*

The *mehr* of the overwhelming majority of the women for whom records are available was of the 'deferred' sort.[37] The amounts promised varied widely, not only within each city but also between the two cities and over time. The data for Chennai are relatively sparse, but what information there is indicates that *mehr* amounts in that city are very low by comparison with those customarily offered in Hyderabad. In Chennai family court petitions dated between 1988 and 1997, Rs. 585 is the figure most frequently cited,[38] although in a few cases the *mehr* was as much as Rs. 10,000 or more. In Hyderabad, on the other hand, in our sample of 260 marriages registered in 1990–91 by Qazi A, the amounts ranged from Rs. 500 to Rs. 51,000, with a mean of Rs. 8,200. Half the women sampled had been promised Rs. 5,000 or more; the most frequently cited figures were Rs. 5,000 (53 cases) and Rs. 11,000 (49 cases).

Ten years later, however, the average amount of *mehr* in Hyderabad had almost doubled. Ninety-one marriages contracted during the first three months of 2001 were randomly sampled from Qazi A's files. Now the *mehr* amount most frequently cited was Rs. 11,000. Amounts ranged from Rs. 5,000 to Rs. 1,25,000, the average being Rs. 16,000. In addition to cash, more than half the Hyderabadi grooms offered their brides between one and 11 dinars—gold coins used in Arabia at the time of the Prophet.[39] At the time of divorce, the *qazi* calculates the coins' cash value in terms of the current gold price. In 2001, for example, Qazi B was valuing the heavier *dinar-i surkh* at approximately Rs. 4,500 and the lighter *dinar-i shara'i* at Rs. 1,300.

All eight *qazis*[40] with whom I discussed this matter professed to be strongly committed to seeing that the divorced wife received her *mehr*. The *qazi* routinely enquires from the man how much *mehr* he promised when he married and, where possible, confirms this by referring to the original marriage certificate (*siyahnama*). He then calculates the total amount owed in both cash and gold, adds whatever figure he considers appropriate for the wife's maintenance during *ᶜiddat*, and instructs the man to hand this over to him, in cash or in the form of a bank draft.[41] If the husband has not brought enough money with him on this occasion, he is sent away and told that he must produce the amount before a 'certificate of divorce' can be issued. Once the money has been deposited, the *qazi* sends a registered letter to the wife, informing her that she has been divorced and instructing her to come, accompanied by two male witnesses, to take receipt of her *mehr*. When she arrives, all three are asked to sign or affix their thumbprints to his divorce register, acknowledging receipt of the money.[42]

According to Qazi B's records, 60 per cent of the women divorced by *talaq*, whose divorces were registered in his office during the Hijri year 1421 (2000–01), received payments averaging Rs. 21,000; in most cases, both *mehr* and *ᶜiddat* expenses were included. In a number of the remaining cases, the required amount had been deposited by the husband but had not yet been picked up by the wife at the time we examined the files in the fall of 2001. Most of the rest of the *talaq*s had been registered with the *qazi* well after the fact and the record simply noted that the husband had provided documentation of having paid the outstanding *mehr*. The nature of documentation or the amount paid were usually not specified.[43]

The data in Qazi A's 1993 divorce register are more or less

consistent with those we obtained from Qazi B. They show that 64 men (30 per cent of those who divorced by pronouncing *talaq*) deposited (either with him or with their advocate) the full amount of their wife's 'deferred' *mehr*, plus an amount designated for her support during the *ᶜiddat* period. Another 41 men (22.5 per cent) either paid their wife in the presence of the *qazi* or a member of his staff or provided satisfactory evidence (usually in the form of a signed receipt) that they had already paid her before coming to register the divorce. Thirty men (16.5 per cent) merely signed an undertaking in front of the *qazi* to pay what they owed sometime in the future. The following are some examples of the remarks entered in the register concerning such promises: '*Mehr* Rs. 1,100 *mu'ajjal* already paid in cash. Promised to pay Rs. 1,000 as *ᶜiddat* expenses of the lady and signed. Recorded with this statement.' 'Man has promised to pay through his advocate the *mehr* of Rs. 25,000 and Rs. 500 for the *ᶜiddat* expenses. Signed and recorded.' 'Man has agreed and promised to pay the lady her *mehr* (Rs. 12,000), the value of two gold coins (Rs. 2,580) and *ᶜiddat* expenses of Rs. 1,000. Total Rs. 15,580. Signed by both.' Whether any of these promises were ever fulfilled is not indicated in the record. It appears fairly certain that of the women divorced by unilateral *talaq* whose divorces were registered with either of these Hyderabad *qazi*s, almost 60 per cent received their *mehr* and the *ᶜiddat* expenses due to them, either at the time of the divorce itself or when it was registered. An indeterminate additional number may have received all or part of their *mehr* on a later occasion. Though these figures are not as high as one would hope, they are much higher than I had been led to expect from the existing literature.

How do these findings square with the persistent reports that men consistently evade paying *mehr* after pronouncing *talaq*? It is relevant to note that, according to the records we examined, somewhat more than half of all registered divorces take place not by *talaq*, but on the (ostensible) initiative of the wife, by an agreement for *khulᶜ*. In a divorce of this kind the woman has to forego her *mehr* as well as (usually) the expenses of her *ᶜiddat* period (see below). Most of those who have drawn attention to the problem of non-payment of *mehr* make no distinction between divorces by *talaq* and those effected by means of *khulᶜ*. If such a distinction is made, the more relevant statistic would be not the percentage of *all* divorced women, but the *percentage divorced by* talaq who had received their *mehr.* My findings suggest that, at least in the sample we surveyed, over half the women divorced by *talaq* did indeed obtain what is due to them under MPL.

However, one must also acknowledge that a sample drawn from *qazi*s' registers is almost certainly biased against men belonging to lower income groups. Poor men do not necessarily go to a *qazi*, either when contemplating giving *talaq* or after the fact. In part this is because they are much less likely than middle- or upper-class men to have any need for a divorce certificate. They are less likely to have a government job or one in the private formal sector, to be travelling abroad, or to be involved in civil litigation. These are the main activities for which proof of marital status is required. Even if a poor man decides to consult a cleric in connection with his divorce, he may be discouraged from registering it when he learns that the *qazi* will require him to come up with a sum of money that is well beyond his ability to pay. Even the small fee charged for the necessary paperwork will be out of reach for someone living hand to mouth.[44]

For example, once we were in the office of Qazi B when a very poorly-dressed young man came in with his elderly mother. The two were spoken to rather impatiently and with some disdain by the assistant on duty. Instead of being invited to come up and sit at his table along with the other clients who were present, the mother was directed with a wave of the hand to a chair in the corner of the small room, while the young man was obliged to remain standing. When asked what he had come for, he said that he had decided to divorce his wife because, in his mother's words, she had 'gone down a wrong path' ('*ghalat rasta*'—a euphemism for some unspecified 'immoral' act). A barrage of questions was then directed towards him about the whereabouts of his wife and children, what kind of work he did, and how much he earned. During all this, the mother kept interrupting in an effort to amplify and clarify her son's replies, but was repeatedly told to be quiet. Finally the question of the *mehr* was raised. The two consulted one another and agreed that it had been Rs. 1,000. After doing a brief calculation, the *qazi*'s deputy told the man to go to the *qazi* who had conducted his *nikah*, get from him a copy of his *siyahnama* and bring it back, together with Rs. 2,500 in cash for transmittal to his wife. At this, mother and son looked at each other, obviously quite distressed, and departed. I do not know whether or not they ever returned, but would not be surprised if they had decided to deal with the wayward wife in a more informal manner, either by divorcing her orally and not bothering about the registration or by simply throwing her out of the house without the benefit of divorce.

In any case, men often simply abandon their wives or expel them from the marital home when they wish to end the relationship, rather than give a formal divorce. This way of freeing oneself from an unsatisfactory marriage may, among many segments of the Muslim population, be as prevalent as the 'triple *talaq*', especially among the poor and less educated. In such cases, of course, there is no question of their paying *mehr*.

## Divorce by *khul$^c$*

Under MPL a woman cannot dissolve her marriage with the same ease as a man. As mentioned above, one of her options is to persuade him to release her from the marriage by negotiating a *khul$^c$* divorce. This procedure requires that the concerned spouses negotiate the release of the wife from her marriage vows in return for a 'consideration'. Typically the consideration offered is forfeiture of whatever *mehr* is still outstanding, along with the woman's right to maintenance during the *$^c$iddat* period.[45] Sometimes the husband will drive a harder bargain and ask for some additional financial compensation before agreeing to the divorce; or he may force her to waive her right to retain custody of their young children or to receive child support while they are under her care.[46] Once an agreement has been reached on the terms of the *khul*ᶜ, the husband pronounces *talaq-ul bain* (irrevocable divorce) and the marriage is dissolved.

Negotiations between the spouses over the granting of *khul*ᶜ may take place directly, but it is probably more usual for a wife who wishes to initiate the process to do so through an intermediary, a *qazi* or other religious leader, the local mosque committee, or an advocate. If she or her male relatives decide to consult a *qazi*—probably the most usual course of action—they can expect him to listen to her story and then send a registered letter to the husband, on his official letterhead, asking him to come to the office at a specified date and time to discuss the matter. If, after hearing the spouses' versions of their marital difficulties, the *qazi* feels that there is little or no chance of reconciliation, he may try to convince the husband to accede to his wife's request. If the husband is amenable, the *qazi* gives the parties an appointment to come in together, have an agreement drafted, and have the husband pronounce *talaq* in his presence. Sometimes, of course, the husband fails to respond to the *qazi*'s summons or steadfastly refuses the *qazi*'s advice to either pronounce *talaq* or assent to sign a *khul*ᶜ agreement. In such cases, the only option for a woman who is determined to end the marriage is to file for divorce under the 1939 Dissolution of Muslim Marriages Act. *Qazi*s regularly suggest this route if their attempts to put pressure on the husband are unsuccessful or if the man has deserted his wife and his whereabouts are unknown.

However, for reasons that I will elaborate below, most women whose attempts to free themselves from an unhappy marriage have reached this kind of impasse, simply reconcile themselves to living on in a state of limbo. For a Muslim man to leave his wife in this situation—still married but without the usual financial and sexual benefits of matrimony—is regarded as cruel and heartless. There is no religious mechanism to sanction him for this kind of behaviour and no religious authority can force him to free his wife if he is not inclined to do so.

More than half of all divorces registered in Hyderabad by the two *qazi*s whose records we examined were *khul*$^{c}$ divorces: 53 per cent of those registered by Qazi A and 56 per cent of those registered by Qazi B. The predominance of divorces ostensibly initiated by women is something that is not generally known, and was to me a somewhat surprising finding. However, there is reason to believe that there is more here than meets the eye: it would be premature to interpret these findings as proving that Muslim women are actually more likely than men to take the initiative in ending their marriages. Here again an important issue is that of the representativeness of the sample. I have already noted that many divorces are never registered, but there are several reasons to believe that divorces by *khul*$^{c}$ are more likely than divorces by *talaq* to be so. This is because, first of all, the average person is not as familiar with the procedure for obtaining a divorce by *khul*$^{c}$ as with the procedure for pronouncing *talaq*, and is therefore more likely to approach a *qazi* or someone with similar religio-legal knowledge for guidance in this situation. Furthermore, the procedure for *khul*$^{c}$ requires both parties to come to an amicable agreement, which is often difficult to do if the couple is either already separated or living together in an extremely conflictual relationship. In order to obtain the husband's consent to grant *khul*$^{c}$, work out the details, and write up the agreement in the proper form, the help of an expert intermediary such as a *qazi* is often essential.

Thus the fact that *khul*$^{c}$ divorces predominate in the *qazi*s' records is doubtless, at least partly, an artefact of differential rates of registration of the two kinds of extrajudicial divorces, but this does not entirely account for the difference in numbers between them. I first became aware, when examining case files in the family court of Chennai, that the issue of whether to end a marriage by *talaq* or by *khul*$^{c}$ was sometimes actively contested between husband and wife. In several maintenance or divorce petitions (filed by women) as well as in responses to petitions (filed by their husbands) for 'restitution of conjugal rights', women reported having been subject to threats and psychological and/or physical abuse because they had resisted their husbands' demands that they go to the *qazi* and ask for *khulᶜ*. These men were not desirous of continuing the marriage but they also did not want to give *talaq*, evidently for financial as well as social prestige reasons. Their wives, for their part, resisted going on record as wishing to dissolve their marriage. As one woman we interviewed explained her refusal to consent to her husband's demand that she request *khulᶜ*: 'I didn't want to be the one to get the bad name!'[47]

It is clear that for a man there are distinct advantages to granting *khulᶜ* rather than pronouncing *talaq*. The most obvious and most often cited advantage is financial, namely being relieved of the responsibility of paying *mehr* and *ᶜiddat* expenses, but there are also more subtle social advantages. While divorce is permitted in Muslim law, it is believed to be something that God greatly dislikes. A devout Muslim is enjoined to make every effort to adjust to his or her spouse before taking the drastic step of dissolving the marriage. In India generally there is considerable social stigma associated with divorce. Although their religion takes a relatively flexible approach to the matter, enjoining those who find it impossible to live harmoniously together to make a clean break, Muslims nevertheless tend to share their Hindu and Christian compatriots' negative attitudes towards divorce and divorced persons. Likewise, as among Indians of other religions, the stigma of divorce falls more heavily upon the Muslim woman than upon her male partner. Whatever the specific circumstances of the break-up, the woman is regarded as having failed to live up to society's ideal of the good, faithful, and forbearing wife. It is that much worse if she is the one who initiated the divorce; so the woman who takes *khulᶜ* risks being stigmatised, while the man who grants her request can present himself as the innocent and misused party who magnanimously agreed to set her free.

Contrary to the widespread belief that divorce does not carry the same stigma among Muslims that it does in the Hindu and Christian communities, for a young Muslim woman who is having marital problems, a major concern is the 'shame' that will attach to her and to other members of the family if she separates from her husband or is divorced. For this reason, the parents of a young woman locked in an unhappy or abusive marriage will often make every effort to persuade their daughter to bear whatever pain is being inflicted on her, rather than risk her future financial security and her reputation by leaving her marital home. Once she is separated or divorced, the task of preserving her modesty in her natal home is regarded as a very daunting one, as serious, if not more so, than the task of providing for her sustenance.

This said, it should also be stressed that most of the separated and divorced women we encountered had received very strong support from their parents and siblings, once the latter became aware that they were experiencing marital problems.[48] Several women told us that they had long delayed telling their families about their troubles, not wanting to hurt or distress them, burden them with the economic responsibility of supporting them if they returned to their natal home, or endanger the marriage chances of their younger sisters. However having found out what was happening, their parents, older brothers, or uncles had rarely hesitated to intervene. Often they had gone to the young woman's marital home to confront her husband and in-laws, had brought her and her children back to their home, and had proceeded in some cases to try to get help from a community panchayat, mosque committee, or *qazi*, or had accompanied her to the police station to file a criminal complaint. Some had eventually consulted a legal practitioner about filing a suit for divorce.

Women's groups activists in Hyderabad described as 'very prevalent in the Old City' a practice whereby a man gets a blank piece of stamp paper, brings it home, writes up a *khul*[c] agreement and threatens the wife with a beating if she doesn't sign it. Then he takes the signed form to a *qazi* and submits it for registration. Both the Hyderabad *qazis* to whom I spoke about this scenario denied that it could be enacted in their offices, insisting that the proper forms had to be filled out by them (or an assistant) and signed by both parties in their presence. Qazi B did not rule out the possibility that some unscrupulous, unauthorised *qazi* might be found willing to engage in such an activity for a fee. However, in the light of his description of the process as requiring the presence of both partners, it is somewhat difficult to understand why, out of the 213 *khul*$^{c}$ divorces registered by his office for the year 2000–01, only 8.5 per cent contained the wife's signature or thumbprint, albeit 81 per cent had been signed by at least two witnesses identified as representing her. All had been signed by the husband and one or more of his own witnesses. One explanation given by the *qazi*'s assistant (the question having been put to him before I had analysed the statistics and could confront him with them) was that some *khul*$^{c}$ divorces (like some *talaqs*) are not registered until some time after they have been contracted, and that in these cases the husband had to provide satisfactory documentation that the original *khul*$^{c}$ was properly processed. It does not seem beyond the realm of possibility that, as alleged by the activist cited above, the *qazis*' routine safeguards might sometimes be insufficient to prevent deceptive practices.

Both *qazis* did acknowledge that women are sometimes forced by their husbands to come to their office to take *khul*$^{c}$. They said that if they strongly suspect that this is the case, they will try to persuade the man to give *talaq* instead, so that the wife will at least be able to claim her *mehr*. They may also try to intervene if they suspect that the husband is making unreasonable demands on his wife in return for agreeing to a divorce that she has chosen to initiate. We happened to be present one day when a man and his wife came into the office of Qazi A, each accompanied by several relatives and friends, both male and female. When it was their turn to be interviewed, the woman told the *qazi* that she wanted *khul*$^{c}$ and intended to forego her *mehr* and allow their children to remain with their father. The *qazi* took some pains to question her about whether she understood the difference between *talaq* and *khul*ᶜ and whether she realised that it would be more advantageous to her if her husband pronounced *talaq*. When she insisted that she was taking this step of her own free will, he turned to the man and said, 'Why don't you simply divorce her?' After some further discussion, he stopped pursuing this line of questioning, wrote up the *khul*ᶜ contract, and had both parties and their witnesses sign it. Later, when they had left the office, he admitted to us that he had his suspicions about this case. The fact that the wife had agreed to give up her children had given him particular pause. His theory was that the wife probably wanted the divorce but the husband, instead of agreeing to give *khul*ᶜ in exchange for simply being released from the obligation of paying her *mehr* and *ᶜiddat* expenses, had compelled her to give up custody of their children as well.[49] However, he said, in as much as all 'legal' requirements for *khul*ᶜ had been met, there was nothing more that he could do.[50]

Without knowing the individual histories of the couples whose names appear in the *qazi*s' divorces registers, it is, of course, impossible to say how many women had been truly acting on their own initiative in seeking a divorce, and how many were persuaded or compelled by their husbands or others to assume that role. It is clear from our interviews that Muslim women are generally aware that negotiating for *khul*ᶜ is an option for one wishing to escape from an unhappy marriage, and many women do willingly, even eagerly, avail themselves of this provision of MPL.[51] However when trying to interpret the documentary record on the relative prevalence of *khul*ᶜ and *talaq*, it is important to be aware of the existence of the gender dynamics I have described and of their implications.

## The Dissolution of Muslim Marriages Act

The other option for a woman who wishes to end her marriage is to file a suit under the Dissolution of Muslim Marriages Act of 1939.[52] Under this Act, a woman can obtain a divorce from an unwilling or absent husband on nine different grounds, which include desertion, his suffering from insanity, obstructing her right to practise her religion, disposing of her property without her consent, charging her falsely with adultery, or subjecting her to mental or physical cruelty. The list of permissible grounds partly overlaps with, but is more extensive than, that provided under the Hindu Marriage Act. The DMMA is, however, little used as a legal resort by Muslim women. In the city of Chennai, over the ten-year period between January 1988 and December 1997 only 66 petitions were filed under the Act, for an average of 6.6 cases per year. In Hyderabad, the DMMA is resorted to somewhat more frequently than in Chennai, an average of 26 cases having been filed each year in the former city between 1995 and 2001. However, in comparing these statistics it is necessary to take account of the fact that the Muslim population of Hyderabad is several times larger than that of Chennai.

In Chennai, only 42 per cent (a total of 28) of the cases filed under the DMMA in the decade for which I have data were pursued to judgment. The rest were dismissed, usually because the petitioner had stopped making the required court appearances, whether because she had reconciled with her husband, had convinced him to give her *khul*ᶜ, had been divorced by him, could no longer afford to pay her advocate's fees, or for some other reason. All of the women who stayed the course did eventually succeed in obtaining a court-ordered divorce. However, most cases required months, if not years, of successive court appearances before they were resolved.[53] Furthermore, in almost every case the judgment was accompanied by a settlement agreement in which the wife waived her right to *mehr* and *ᶜiddat* expenses, sometimes in return for being allowed to retain custody of their children.[54]

Probably one reason that Muslim women do not file suits under DMMA in greater numbers has to do with the considerable social stigma that is attached to involving oneself in court proceedings, especially those that require exposing private family affairs to the scrutiny of strangers. Moreover, the precincts of the court are seen as a predominantly male space, where disreputable people are perceived to congregate and where unsavoury matters are publicly aired. These perceptions also serve as strong deterrents for any woman who might contemplate filing a suit under DMMA. For most women and their families, filing for a court divorce represents a last resort. Even if a woman is prepared to risk the stigma of repeated court appearances, she is rarely in a position to do so without the consent, active cooperation, and financial support of her natal family. Unless it is imperative for some reason that the marriage be legally dissolved (perhaps because they or she is considering her remarriage) most families would prefer that their daughter or sister, even though separated from her husband and not receiving any financial support from him, remain married unless and until he decides to divorce her.

However, a more compelling explanation for the relatively little use made of the DMMA is that a Muslim woman—unlike one of another religion—can get an extrajudicial divorce (*khulᶜ*) much more expeditiously and cheaply than she can obtain a 'court divorce', assuming that her husband can be persuaded to agree. Even legal practitioners and activist women's organisations routinely advise those who come to them, wanting a divorce, to first seek the help of a *qazi* in trying to get their husband to agree to grant *khulᶜ*.

## Remarriage

Another stereotype that is very prevalent is that Muslim women readily remarry after divorce. Theoretically, indeed, there is no bar to the remarriage of a Muslim divorcée. The Qur'an, in fact, encourages men to marry such women who are seen to be in particular need of both financial support and moral protection and, if they are still of childbearing age, of the opportunity to engage in legitimate sexual activity and fulfil their motherly instincts. Whereas, in some Muslim countries, the rate of remarriage of divorcées is quite high, the prevailing cultural mores in India are such that, even if a divorced woman and/or her parents are prepared to consider this option, it is usually difficult to find a man willing to accept her in marriage. Only a young and childless divorcée has a realistic chance of finding another husband.

Even if a man can be found who is prepared to take a previously married woman as his bride, he will rarely consent to take the child of another man into his home. This presents a divorced young mother with a difficult choice. In practice, women who remarry almost always leave their children behind, usually with their own parents or with a sibling.[55] Samira, living in her natal home with her six-year-old daughter, told us that her parents had entertained several proposals for her hand in recent years. She was willing to remarry, but did not want to leave her daughter behind. Only one of her suitors had expressed a willingness to allow her to bring the child with her, but Samira's mother would not agree to that arrangement. She insisted that if her daughter married, she herself would raise her grandchild. She felt that her daughter would almost certainly have more children with the new husband and no man, once he had his own children, could be trusted to give his stepchild the same kind of love and care that he lavished on those of his own blood.

Few of the divorced, separated, or widowed women we interviewed had even considered remarrying, although a few were under some pressure from family members to agree to do so. For the most part, those who had experienced serious problems in their first marriage seemed to feel that they stood a good chance of encountering very similar situations in a second marriage. Therefore they would prefer not to take such a risk.[56] Those women with children expressed strong misgivings about what their remarriage would mean for the latter's well-being.

The only available statistics indicate that the rate of remarriage for divorcées in this community is very low. In only three of the 226 case files examined from the Chennai family court was there any indication that the wife had been married before. Two of the women were divorcées and one a widow. Similarly, in only four per cent (that is, 141) of the 3,515 marriages recorded by Qazi A in 1990–91 and 2001 had the bride been married previously.[57] Information on the woman's marital status at the time of remarriage is available for only 120 of these women: 21 per cent had been divorced by *talaq* and 15 per cent by *khul<sup>c</sup>*. The rest were described in the records as widowed.[58] Not surprisingly, the mean age at remarriage for these women was about five years higher than that at first marriage, namely 26.5 years. Again, as one would expect, more than 80 per cent of the remarried brides were 30 years of age or younger. This is consistent with the pattern I have noted above: the chances of finding a husband for a divorcée or widow decline markedly as her age increases. However, it is worth noting that eight of the remarrying women were over 40 years of age.

The men these women married were also older, as one would expect, than those who married virgin brides. Eighty per cent were 40 years of age or less, but six were over 60. It is safe to assume that most of these men had also been married before. Not only were they in an age range at which there are relatively few single males in the population, our interviews make it clear that in this society a divorced or widowed woman would not be a preferred mate for a never-married man. Therefore, in the pool of potential husbands for a divorced woman, divorced men and widowers predominate.

## Polygamy

Another issue that has aroused considerable public discussion in recent years concerns that provision of MPL that allows a Muslim man to have up to four wives at one time. There is a widespread stereotype about Muslim men that many of them do have multiple wives; however, there are no solid statistics available to support this belief, nor have there been any serious attempts to investigate the actual prevalence of polygamy in the Muslim community. My data are insufficient to allow any very meaningful generalisations for India as a whole, or even for the two cities wherein my research was carried out. However, it is suggestive that of the 226 men in our sample of litigants in the Chennai family court, only 31 currently had two wives (including the wife with whom he was litigating) and two had three wives. Thus 14.6 per cent of the men were in a polygynous union, not a very large proportion, when one considers that this is a very selective sample made up entirely of couples with serious marital problems. Polygynous marriages are clearly likely to be over-represented in such a sample, given the kinds of tensions and conflicts that are almost inevitable when two wives and their respective children are competing for the affection and financial assets of one man. Rarely did the two wives live in the same house, which meant that the man was usually maintaining two separate household establishments. Problems in polygynous marriages resulted, in most cases, from the fact that the husband had to support two wives and numerous children—and often his own parents as well—on a limited income. He very often solved the resulting dilemma by neglecting one of his dependent families. The consequence, in some cases, was that the couple ended up in the family court.

On the other hand, where the husband had brought a second wife into his marital home and insisted that the two live together, conflict between the women and between the first wife and her husband was almost inevitable. The man's inability—or unwillingness—to treat both wives and their separate sets of children fairly and equitably is the principal grievance found in those court petitions submitted by women married to polygynous men. Since MPL permits a Muslim man to take more than one wife, it does not, of course, recognise as valid a complaint by the first wife that her husband has married again. Nor is his refusal to divorce the first wife when he marries another a ground for complaint on the part of the second. However, if he does not treat the two wives equally (which, as everyone recognises, is difficult or impossible to do), the wife who is neglected has a legitimate right to demand redress and, if he persists in his behaviour, has grounds for divorce under DMMA.[59] In the cases we examined from the Chennai family court this was not a common plea. Even women whose husbands had another wife and whose marital problems arose directly from the difficulty of living in a polygynous family, were more likely to charge physical cruelty, desertion, or expropriation of property. This is doubtless because these are easier to demonstrate in court than is the more amorphous 'unequal treatment'.

**Extramarital relationships**

In about five per cent of family court cases the woman complained that the husband had been engaged in one or more long-standing extramarital relationships. Some of our interviewees likewise alleged that their husbands were carrying on adulterous affairs that had lasted for an extended period of time (without marriage) and had, in a few cases, resulted in the birth of children. The existence of such adulterous relationships creates marital problems that are not very different from those that occur when the man has more than one legally married wife. Not infrequently, the man's paramour is a non-Muslim. For a married Muslim man who is sexually involved with a Hindu woman, marriage is not an option unless the latter is willing to convert to Islam. For this and other reasons, such a man may prefer to continue the adulterous relationship rather than go to the trouble of legitimating it under MPL. I might note here that charges of adultery are also very frequently made against their husbands by Hindu and Christian women who are filing for divorce or maintenance in the Chennai family court. One important difference, however, is that these women have legitimate grounds for divorce if their husband is carrying on an extended adulterous relationship.[60] This is not the case under MPL; only if the Muslim wife can show that the adultery takes the form of 'associating with women of evil repute', can she obtain a divorce on this ground under DMMA. This phrase is generally interpreted to imply repeated incidents of sexual misconduct, involving a series of women, rather than a long-standing extramarital but quasi-domestic relationship with one woman.

### Maintenance

A great deal of public concern has been expressed in recent years about the consequences of the passage of the Muslim Women (Protection of Rights on Divorce) Act, 1986. This Act made divorced Muslim women ineligible to file suit for maintenance against their former husbands under Section 125 of the CrPC. If a woman has no other means of subsistence, she may instead file under the MWA to obtain financial support from parents, siblings, other natal relatives, adult children, grandchildren, or—if these are lacking or without sufficient means—the Wakf Board of the state in which they reside. One of the questions that I would like to have been able to address in my research, is whether and to what extent the passage of MWA has created new hardships for divorced Muslim women. Clearly, fewer destitute, divorced Muslim women resort to Section 125 of the CrPC today than they did in the past. Those who would formerly have been eligible to do so must now seek support elsewhere, one option being to file suit under the MWA, but we lack any comparative data on the use of Section 125 of the CrPC by divorced Muslim women before 1986 that would provide a baseline from which to assess change over time.[61] Furthermore, I did not realise at the time I began my research in the Chennai family court that one could not determine from that court's records whether the MWA has become a viable alternative to those divorced women in need of financial support. The issue of whether family courts have jurisdiction over cases filed under MWA is still under dispute. In some states these courts do not accept such suits at all; however, one case was filed in the Chennai family court in 1992 and another in 1993. The first was dismissed within five months for default of the petitioner and the other (in which the Tamil Nadu State Wakf Board was the defendant) had not yet been decided when I examined the court's records in 1999. It is quite possible that other suits under the MWA may have been heard in the family court between 1988 and 1992,[62] and other courts were hearing them in the 1980s and 1990s but, as I was fully occupied with my research in the family court, I was not in a position to confirm this. The question of how much use divorced Muslim women actually make of MWA and what the outcomes of their suits are, should be given high priority by scholars of the sociology of law who are concerned with gender issues in the Muslim community.

My research nevertheless has made it possible to contribute something to what is already known about the larger question of how Muslim women fare financially after separation and/or divorce, and how they manage to support themselves once they can no longer depend upon their husbands to maintain them and their children. My findings show that, with few exceptions, divorced women are entirely dependent upon their natal families for shelter and subsistence. This was doubtless the case for the vast majority of women in their situation even before the passage of the MWA. A relatively small number do seek relief under the CrPC and a proportion of these—little more than half, according to my data—succeed in obtaining a maintenance award, either for themselves or for their minor children. However far fewer actually manage to collect, on a more or less regular basis, the monthly amount awarded to them.

None of the women we interviewed in Chennai and Hyderabad—except, of course, some of those whom we contacted at the court itself or through their advocates—had ever tried to make use of Section 125 of the CrPC, though most would have met the income and marital status criteria for obtaining a maintenance order, if not for themselves then for their minor children. The women we interviewed, like those whose family court petitions we read, were, without exception, living in the household of one or both parents and/or siblings. None was living on her own. Almost all were completely economically dependent on the earnings of others, usually their father or another male relative.

Very few of these women, even those who had some earnings of their own, could have survived without financial help from other family members. Some, for example, spoke of repeatedly taking loans that they had no hope of repaying or of receiving small gifts of money, clothing, or food on special occasions from better-off relatives. A few mothers reported receiving some child support given voluntarily by their husbands (or ex-husbands). Others were in receipt of court-ordered maintenance payments, to collect which they made monthly visits to the family court.

All in all, for women who are no longer living with their husbands, economic reliance upon one's family seems to be accepted as the natural state of affairs. There is no real expectation that a man would—nor even that he should—continue to support his former wife once they are divorced. Informants (women as well as men) often noted that in Islam, when a couple is divorced, it means that their relationship is completely severed and they should not even meet one another again if it can possibly be avoided. It seemed totally inappropriate to them for a woman to expect to receive regular support payments from an ex-husband, since this would inevitably mean maintaining an ongoing social relationship with her ex-husband. A generous lump sum financial settlement at the time of a divorce is not viewed in the same light, but very few of the men in these women's lives were in any position to offer enough, even if they had been willing, to maintain their former wife for more than a month or two at most.

Certainly none of the Muslim clerics with whom I spoke thought it inappropriate that a man's responsibility for his former wife should end after the three-month *ᶜiddat* period. They did acknowledge and professed to be distressed by the fact that divorce frequently put the wife at risk of destitution. Yet, although both the *qazi*s whose records we examined made a point of insisting that men who registered their divorces make some provision for their ex-wives' *ᶜiddat* expenses, the amount they actually levied for this purpose was quite minimal, even in those cases where the man involved apparently had substantial assets. Neither *qazi* seems to have regularly made any attempt to persuade those husbands who could afford it to either voluntarily continue to provide for their former wives after the three-month post-divorce period or give her a substantial lump sum settlement. Only occasionally do the *qazi*s' records show that a payment over and above the *mehr* and *ᶜiddat* amounts has been made to the wife. Evidence of such payments was found most often when the couple had negotiated a *khulᶜ* divorce rather than after a *talaq*. Although there is no way to be certain about this, I am inclined to interpret these payments as representing reimbursements of the wife's dowry or of the value of other personal property that she brought into the marriage, rather than settlements by way of maintenance.

Those men and women whom I interviewed rarely expressed the idea that a divorced or separated woman should, or even could, find a way to support herself once she could no longer rely on a husband's earnings. Many non-governmental organisations (NGOs) in Chennai and Hyderabad, focusing on the needs of poor women, concentrate their efforts on trying to develop self-confidence, a desire to be self-reliant, and the skills to engage in some form of income-generating work among the separated and divorced women who form a large segment of their clientele. However, prevailing notions about the fundamental complementarity of male and female roles and the appropriate division of labour are strong hindrances to their success in this direction. Especially within the Muslim community—though hardly limited to it—there are deeply felt concerns about female modesty that further discourage women whose marriages have broken down from seeking extra-domestic employment. There are also important structural factors that are at least as influential as ideology in keeping such women in an economically dependent role. Their lack of education, job skills, or work experience, the difficulty of managing household responsibilities and childcare while working outside the home, a scarcity of employment opportunities for unskilled female workers, and the very low wages they can command even if they find work are only some of the practical problems facing women who wish, or have no other choice than, to be economically independent of male family members.

In order to get some sense of the range of outcomes for those women who tried to address their economic insecurities by filing suits under Section 125 of the CrPC in recent years, we analysed the information contained in one MC (maintenance case) register of the Chennai family court. This register contains entries for the 2,551 maintenance suits that were filed in that court between March 1992 and March 1997. Of these 132 had been filed by Muslims.[63] We also reviewed a more limited set of 54 individual case files from all maintenance suits filed by Muslims in the years 1993 and 1996. These files contain much more detailed information than is provided on the same cases in the register. In 42 per cent of the 132 Muslim cases filed in the period covered by the register, the petitioner's suit was dismissed before any judgment was reached. Dismissal in most cases was 'for default', that is, because the petitioner had missed three consecutive court hearings without providing any explanation or asking to be excused. The specific reason for a petitioner's default never appears in the case file, but observation and interviews with litigants and court staff make it clear that in most cases women stop coming to court because they have found it too costly, in money and in time, to pursue their case. Other petitioners simply become discouraged about the way their suit is proceeding and give up the idea of continuing it. The husband's failure to appear causes others to default. Unless the man can be brought before the court to answer the charges made against him, the wife's suit cannot move ahead. Men who are neither regular salaried employees of the government nor work for a large private firm are often able to elude process servers by frequent changes of residence. Sometimes they bribe the carrier of the summons to report that they were unable to find the respondent at the address provided. Another reason why a woman may default is because her husband has divorced her (by *talaq*), rendering her ineligible to continue a suit for maintenance under the CrPC.[64]

A smaller number of the cases in our sample were dismissed 'as not pressed', a phrase used when the petitioner (or her advocate) informs the court that she has decided not to pursue her claim, usually because she and her husband have either reconciled or have reached a private financial agreement. The court encourages such outcomes, preferring not to hand down an *ex parte* judgment against a man, on the theory that if he can be persuaded to agree to pay some amount—even if it is much less than what the woman has asked for—he is more likely to actually come through with the cash each month. To this end, couples are required to undergo 'counselling' or 'reconciliation' by an appointee of the court, before the judge considers whether and how much maintenance to grant.[65]

Almost all of the remaining maintenance cases filed resulted in the petitioner obtaining a maintenance award, although this was rarely in the full amount she requested, even when the husband was in a position to pay. With very few exceptions, petitioners asked for the maximum allowable amount, namely Rs. 500 per month for each claimant—the petitioner herself (if eligible) and each of her minor children.[66] The amounts actually awarded, however, were sometimes as low as Rs. 100, with the average award just under Rs. 300 per month. In several cases where Rs. 500 per month was initially ordered, the man usually appealed successfully to get the amount reduced.

It took just over a year, on average, for the court to hand down a judgment in a maintenance case, but many other cases dragged on without being resolved for two or more years. During this time, hearings which the petitioner was required to attend were scheduled on a more or less monthly basis. Women would have to arrive early in the morning on the assigned day and wait for their case to be called. If their husband did not show up, the case would be continued for another month and they could return home.

Otherwise, they would have to wait some more, perhaps in order to meet with their advocate, undergo counselling or, eventually, to meet with the judge.[67] They might easily spend an entire day each month, sitting on the floor in the hallway, often with babies and young children in tow, and provided no access to water or toilet facilities as they wait for their turn to be seen. This, after perhaps a long and complicated bus ride from their home in a distant part of the city and, for those who are employed, the additional cost of taking an unpaid day off from work. It is easy to understand why these women occasionally miss hearings and many give up on the whole enterprise even before the judge has had the opportunity to render a decision.

Seventy per cent of the 54 women in our sample of maintenance cases in Chennai were filing either for maintenance for themselves and their minor children or for their children alone. The remaining 30 per cent either had no children or had only adult children and were filing on their own behalf. The vast majority of petitioners (47 women, 87 per cent of the total) were still married, though separated from their husbands, when they filed suit. This stands to reason, inasmuch as divorced Muslim women are ineligible to claim maintenance from their former husbands under the CrPC. The seven divorced women in this sample were filing not for themselves but on behalf of their minor children.

Thus, court records from Chennai (and from Hyderabad as well) show that many women do continue to turn to Section 125 of the CrPC when attempting to obtain financial support from their husbands or ex-husbands.[68] However, as is to be expected, they do not do so in numbers proportionate to their representation in the total population. Thus, in Chennai between March 1992 and March 1997, a total of 2,551 maintenance cases were filed under the CrPC in the family court. Notwithstanding the fact that 8.7 per cent of the population of Chennai is Muslim, only five per cent of the petitioners (132 women or their children) belonged to that community. Yet, if one considers that *divorced* Muslim women are precluded from seeking relief under this section, the figures suggest that those women who *are* eligible are probably just as likely as women of other religions to do so. This finding was somewhat unexpected and leads back to something that I have already mentioned in my discussion on the prevalence of divorce in the Muslim community, namely that the practice of simply abandoning the wife, without formalising the break-up by pronouncing *talaq*, seems to be quite common. One consequence of this is that it allows many women to continue to take advantage of the CrPC in order to get their husbands to provide for them. On the other hand, their doing so not infrequently provokes the husband to utter a divorce. Even if he was not already aware of this provision of the law, it is quite certain that as soon as he consults an advocate to defend himself against the maintenance suit, he will be immediately enlightened in this regard and encouraged to take the easy way out of the situation in which he finds himself.

## Conclusion

Muslim women confront MPL, whether in a religious venue or in a civil court in the context of a 'patriarchal' social system. The term 'patriarchy' of course, refers to the exercise of power by men over women, but there is more to this complex than naked power politics. A key aspect of 'patriarchy', one that enables those in control to justify—to their own satisfaction and that of the women they endeavour to keep in their place—is a 'paternalist' ideology that serves to legitimate the exercise of power and at the same time masks it even from their own consciousness. This ideology is premised upon a conception of women as inherently weak and vulnerable and consequently in need of lifelong material and symbolic support and protection from the men in their lives: fathers and brothers before marriage, husbands thereafter, and sons or other close male relatives when the husband dies or decamps.

It will not surprise any of my readers to learn that the Muslim clerics who discussed with me their roles in dispensing *shari'at* law (as they saw it) hold paternalistic views in relation to women, for even (or should I say, especially) a passing acquaintance with Islamic religious texts would provide ample support for their taking such a stance, just as would a perusal of the core Hindu legal texts or the Christian Bible. What might be somewhat unexpected to some readers is these men's perception of themselves as extremely sympathetic to and solicitous of the welfare of women. More than once I was told that when a woman comes to them with a marital problem they invariably take her side, because they know that only a woman whose situation is desperate would seek outside help. They sincerely believe, as do other devout Muslims, that their religion is exceptional and superior to other faiths in the degree to which it accords respect to and care for women. To the extent that they have the opportunity to do so, they try to spread this message to their co-religionists. They see around them countless instances of the mistreatment of wives, the misappropriation of their property, and similar 'un-Islamic' behaviour. The disjuncture between their ideals and the everyday reality is something to which they can, however, propose no solution, other than hoping that in time the two will be brought into line with one another, through their and others' efforts to spread more widely within the community a truer understanding and appreciation of God's own legal code.

An opposition is routinely drawn between the ideas of so-called 'obscurantist' Muslim clerics and modern, educated, secular citizens in terms of their contrasting attitudes towards women. Paternalistic attitudes, not too dissimilar from those I heard expressed by clerics, are widely shared beyond the community of religious experts, including by those middle and upper class men and women who are responsible for administering on the civil side the personal laws of all religions. For those in the legal professions, the law is perceived as offering the kind of solution to women's marital problems that (for obvious reasons) eludes the clerics, and if the current laws are not adequate to the task, then new laws can be designed to be so. However those who administer the law also believe that the proper place for an adult woman is within a marital relationship and that she should do everything in her power, no matter what the cost, to ensure that she remains there. They too are inclined to consider it preferable for her to remain under the conjugal roof, whatever the quality of that relationship, rather than return to her natal home or, even worse, strike out on her own. This view is premised on the notion that a woman is, by definition, a dependant creature. She is (and should be) not only economically dependent on the earnings of a man, but also under his 'protection' and 'guidance'. If she leaves her husband, some other man will have to take over these responsibilities: her father or her brother or a second husband. For a woman to 'stand on her own two feet', to earn her own independent living, is almost inconceivable, unless she is highly educated and trained for a profession.[69]

Even then, the presumed social and sexual vulnerability of a woman without a male protector generates a paternalistic approach towards her well-being among those who administer the family law, as it does in society at large. Here the issue is one of preserving her status as a 'respectable' woman. Even if she should succeed in remaining chaste, those around her will never cease to suspect otherwise. Fears related to the stigma of divorce combine with those concerning its material consequences to produce a generalised anxiety within all segments of society about allowing a marriage to end. The couple should 'compromise' and resume living together.

Where power-asymmetries between husband and wife are marked and the burden of adjustment within most marriages falls primarily on the wife, however, 'compromise' is a gender-linked concept. It means, as often as not, that the wife is to meet all of her husband's needs and demands, comply with his wishes, and bear stoically all manner of personal hardships. This can be seen in the process of working out 'mutually agreeable' settlements in the family court context: husbands tend to be given considerably more leeway than strict gender-equity would dictate. Wives are often pressured, even browbeaten, by counsellors and judges, into settling for outcomes that may be grossly unfair and contrary to their best interests, as these may be 'objectively', though perhaps not always subjectively, defined. Thus, divorce settlements regularly have the wife giving up all financial claims on the husband, including the *mehr* amount to which she is entitled, often in return for custody of a young child in whom the husband has never shown any interest and would not in any case have a claim on for many years in the future. Where maintenance is the issue, once reconciliation attempts have been abandoned, counsellors, lawyers, and judges all concentrate on trying to persuade the husband to voluntarily offer to pay some amount of support for his wife and children. They rationalise this approach by pointing out (correctly, no doubt, in many cases) that there is little value in issuing an order that realistically cannot be forced, unless the man is a government employee and therefore subject to salary attachment. If a man can be prodded into making a commitment to pay a modest amount, it is more likely that some money, at least, will actually be forthcoming.

Thus, in the context of family court negotiations, women are regularly encouraged to drop criminal charges they may have filed against their husbands, to withdraw or reduce property, maintenance, or custody demands, and even to resume living with men who may have subjected them to long-standing abuse in the past. A legal discourse of 'rights' is thus transformed into a discourse of 'welfare', whose defining terms are set, not by the woman herself, but by her counsellor, her advocate, the judge, and, in the last analysis, by the realities imposed by the society within which she lives. In this respect it is almost irrelevant whether the woman is governed by Muslim or by Hindu or Christian personal law.

However, there are some significant differences between Muslim women and those of other religions in terms of the kinds of options they have available to them when faced with marital breakdown. First, with regard to the question of divorce, although the threat of 'triple *talaq*' is a real one, it is probably not as prevalent as is generally believed. *Talaq* is usually not uttered suddenly, 'on a mere whim', in the course of an argument, but is more often pronounced after the couple has been separated for some time. It is often motivated by the man's desire to marry another woman whose parents, notwithstanding that Islam countenances polygamy, may well be reluctant to give their daughter to a man who is already married to someone else. In any event, it appears that domestic violence perpetrated while the couple continues to live together is far more common than unilateral divorce. So are desertion, abandonment, ejection of the wife from the marital home, or forcing her through mistreatment to leave on her own. There is, however, no evidence that these latter threats are any more prevalent in the Muslim community than they are among Hindus or Christians. One might even hypothesise that since divorce is more difficult in the latter communities, these alternative means of ridding oneself of an unwanted wife may be more common among them.

One unexpected finding of my research was the statistical predominance of women-initiated extrajudicial divorce (*khul*ᶜ) over *talaq* in the records of Hyderabad *qazi*s. This pattern was also reported, though not verified, by *qazi*s in Chennai and Vanyambadi town. The option of obtaining an extrajudicial divorce by negotiating *khul*ᶜ seems, on the face of it, to represent a benefit for Muslim women that is not available to those of other religions, but it apparently has a darker side. Thus we note abundant evidence of husbands, intent upon dissolving their marriage without suffering any of the attendant negative financial and social consequences, exerting psychological pressure and even physical force on their wives to seek, against their will and better judgement, a *khul*ᶜ divorce. The role of *qazi*s in enforcing—to some extent at least—the payment of *mehr* and *ᶜiddat* expenses by husbands who have pronounced *talaq* is an encouraging sign. However, the fact that *mehr* amounts are set so low (especially in Chennai) and *ᶜiddat* payments are also minimal and seemingly almost standardised, bearing little relation to the ability of the husband to pay, are less so.

Stereotypes regarding the prevalence of remarriage for divorced

Muslim women are also not supported by my evidence. Although the remarriage of very young, childless divorcées does take place, and is probably somewhat more common than for women of other religions, the idea that such an option is readily available to anyone discarded by her first husband is certainly false. The stigma of divorce, especially for the woman, is strong within the Muslim community, just as it is among Indians of other religious groups. Women with children, in particular, have a very difficult time finding another mate, even assuming that they wish to do so. Most do not. Rarely will a never-married man agree to marry a divorcée and should he do so, he will almost certainly refuse to allow her to bring her child along. The most likely scenario, for a woman whose parents are intent upon getting her married, is that they will find a man who has himself been married before, possibly one who has children of his own. The parents will then keep their daughter's children to raise in their home while their daughter joins her new husband in his, perhaps to raise his children by an earlier wife, now deceased or discarded.

Questions about the impact of the passage of the MWA are difficult to answer on the basis of my data. It is evident that the road to a maintenance award via Section 125 of the CrPC is not, contrary to popular belief, entirely closed to Muslim women. However, there is no denying that a large class of women who would previously have been eligible no longer have this option available to them when they find themselves without any means of support. To put this in some perspective, however, it might be pointed out that the number of eligible women of any religion who actually avail themselves of this law is relatively small, that a high proportion of those who do file for maintenance give up the process before the case reaches the judgment stage, and that those who do persist and succeed in obtaining a maintenance award face years of monthly court visits to collect the pittance that, all too often, is not regularly forthcoming from their estranged husbands. Whatever religious community they may belong to, the vast majority of women whose husbands have left or divorced them or died must still rely on their natal kin, and to a lesser extent on their own efforts, to feed and clothe themselves and their children.

The more of their stories I hear, the more convinced I am that the major problem for the Muslim women we encountered—whether in person or through the various records we consulted—is not the particular code of law under which they live their lives, but the structures that limit their options to move beyond a definition of self as dependent minors, subject to others' life strategies and desires rather than entitled to work towards realising their own. These are not, however, issues that are peculiar to these women as adherents of a particular religion. These issues are systemic ones that have a largely cultural, rather than a purely religious, basis. Although legal reform doubtless has something real to offer those women unfortunate enough to find themselves in unhappy or even intolerable marriages, it will not be enough, unless other social changes accompany it.

## Appendix 1

### *Data sources and research methods*

My findings draw heavily upon the individual experiences of Muslim women who had in the past, or were currently experiencing, marital difficulties and had sought help from civil or religious authorities or local NGOs. In each site a research assistant and I observed the ongoing activities, conducted loosely-structured interviews with staff personnel and with women clients, and examined recent case records. In addition, we conducted unstructured interviews in these cities and elsewhere in India with other people, knowledgeable through personal experience, about the administration of MPL today. These included advocates practicing family law, former judges, police officers, women's activists, scholars, Muslim clerics and community leaders, and others. We also interviewed Muslim women in both cities who had at some time in their life experienced marital difficulties of some kind, but had not been directly involved in any kind of legal or quasi-legal action in that connection.

One of the richest sources of such material are the narratives of the women whom we were able to interview personally. Some of them were currently involved in family court litigation and were approached on court premises or introduced to us outside the court by their advocates. Introduction to other women willing to talk to us about their marital difficulties and how they dealt with them were facilitated through NGOs or other local contacts. In Hyderabad, we conducted all interviews in Urdu; in Chennai, the mother tongue of most of those interviewed was Tamil. There I used a Tamil-speaking research assistant, except in the rare case that the interviewee was also fluent in English or Urdu.

Case files maintained by the Chennai and Hyderabad family courts, by two all-women police stations in Chennai, by the Tamil Nadu State Legal Aid Authority, by a Chennai mosque committee engaged in family dispute settlement and by two government-appointed *qazis* in Hyderabad provide a large amount of individual case material that is more superficial in many respects but allows the possibility of quantitative analysis. The contents of the case files maintained by these different kinds of agencies vary greatly in terms of both quantity and quality. In almost every instance, however, they include a more or less detailed complaint (usually from the wife)[70] and sometimes a response from the spouse as well. Family court case files and those maintained by the all-women police station also include other supporting documents along with a running record of how the case proceeded and its outcome. A serious defect of these narratives, however, is that none allow us to hear the parties' own, unmediated voices. They have invariably been written by someone else: an advocate, police officer, *qazi*'s assistant, etc. Thus they lack the 'authenticity' of orally-elicited personal narratives.[71] Nevertheless, they do provide useful insights into the social structural context of marital discord and its resolution in the Muslim communities to which their subjects belong. A third source of individual women's stories was our discussions with other Muslims, male and female, who have related not their own personal experiences but those of relatives, neighbours, close friends, and acquaintances, and have reflected on these in response to our enquiries.

**Endnotes**

[1] The first phase of my research, funded by a U.S. Department of Education Fulbright-Hays Senior Research Fellowship and a sabbatical leave from the University of Illinois at Chicago, was carried out from October 1998 to May 1999 in Chennai, where I was affiliated with the Madras Institute of Development Studies. I undertook a further three months' field research in Hyderabad in the fall and winter of 2001, with the support of an American Institute of Indian Studies Senior Fellowship and a semester-long research leave from the College of Liberal Arts and Sciences of the University of Illinois at Chicago. In Hyderabad, I was hosted by the Department of Fine Arts of Telugu University. I thank all of these institutions for generously facilitating my work. I also owe a large debt of gratitude to R. Saraswathy, Rafia Anjum, Rina Ambikeshwar, and H. Rayees Fathima for their competent and cheerful research assistance.

[2] If they are married but separated from their husbands.

[3] Family courts operate today in the major cities of most states, pursuant to central legislation passed in September 1984, as the Family Courts Act. They have civil jurisdiction over all matrimonial suits, regardless of the religion of the parties, and are also empowered to decide cases registered under Chapter IX, Section 125 of the Criminal Procedure Code, which covers orders of maintenance for destitute wives and children. The Chennai family court was set up in 1988. In Hyderabad, a special family court was not put into operation until 1995.

[4] See the Appendix for a note on data sources and research methods.

[5] Also see Nasreen Fazalbhoy, 'Muslim Women and Inheritance', in Zoya Hasan and Ritu Menon, eds., *In a Minority: Essays on Muslim Women in India* (New Delhi: Oxford University Press, 2005), pp. 69–107.

[6] This quotation appears in the context of a discussion of what Basu calls 'the cultural workings' of Hindu women's inheritance law. See Srimati Basu, 'Indian Women and Inheritance Law', in G.J. Larson, ed., *Religion and Personal Law in Secular India* (Bloomington, IN: Indiana University Press, 2001), p. 180.

[7] Few litigants come from the ranks of the truly impoverished, largely because it takes money to fight a court case, even if one is able to avail oneself of the free legal aid that is provided on a limited scale. For a summary history of the

latter, see Roma Mukherjee, *Women, Law and Free Legal Aid in India* (New Delhi: Deep & Deep Publications, 1998), pp. 30–44.

[8] For example, fully 25 per cent of the 351 grooms sampled from Hyderabad Qazi A's marriage certificates were listed as engaged in 'trade' (*tajarat*), while another seven per cent were 'government servants' (*sarkari mulazim*). On the other hand, as many as 26 per cent of the men being sued for maintenance in Chennai family court under Section 125 of the Criminal Procedure Code were employed by the government. This selectivity in the latter sample is not surprising, since it is difficult, if not impossible, to enforce a maintenance order against a man unless he is a public employee liable to salary attachment.

[9] Of the 47 men being sued for maintenance during the years 1993 and 1996 who provided monthly income figures, 17 per cent claimed to be earning Rs. 1,000 or less per month, 43 per cent stated their earnings as Rs. 2,500 or less, and 72 per cent as Rs. 5,000 or less.

[10] Approximately seven per cent described themselves as white collar and professional workers, while 3.5 per cent reported earnings from unskilled or semi-skilled labour or home industry.

[11] Given the fact that so-called 'love marriages' in this social stratum carry a somewhat negative connotation and the fact of having been involved in a 'love affair' reflects badly on the reputation of the woman, in particular, it is quite possible that some marriages were described as having been 'arranged' when actually there had been some element of personal choice on the part of one or both the parties. Since in most cases we had only one meeting with each woman whom we interviewed, there was no opportunity to learn more about the circumstances that brought the couple together.

[12] This pattern is customary among Muslims: propriety and notions of self-respect and honour require that the girl's family wait for a young man to ask for her hand, rather than directly approach the family of a suitable young man to offer her in marriage. They may, of course, and usually do, actively seek out information about eligible prospects, spread the word among their social circle about her availability, and let it be known to third parties that they are prepared to discuss with interested parties the possibility of marrying off their daughter.

[13] There were also several cases in the family court files of Muslim men or women who had married non-Muslims under the Special Marriage Act of 1954, or who had converted to Hinduism or Christianity in order to marry under the personal laws of their respective partners. Such individuals would not be subject to MPL and therefore were not included in my sample.

[14] Given the legal consequences of marrying a girl under the age of 18 years, there may be reason to question the reliability of these data. However, since wife's age at marriage was calculated from information on current age and on date

of marriage, rather than from direct reports of age at marriage, there is less likelihood of manipulation of the figures to conform to the legal requirement.

15 According to *qazi*s' records, the mean age at marriage of women is somewhat lower: 19.6 years in the case of those married by Hyderabad Qazi A in 1990–91 and 2001. The bride's age is entered as 18 years on as many as 50 per cent of this *qazi*'s marriage certificates and not a single bride is recorded as having been younger than this. There is, therefore, a strong probability that the true age of some of the younger brides was concealed, either by the *qazi* himself or by the girl's parents.

16 Of those filing for maintenance in the Chennai family court, 25 per cent had been married for one year or less before separating, as had 40 per cent of those who came to the family court for some other reasons. Only 25 per cent of the 226 litigant couples had lived together for six years or more. The average number of living children—for those women who had any children at all—was 1.8. Most of the children were three years of age or younger at the time the suit was filed by the parent and many were still in their infancy.

It is also interesting, and likely to be significant (despite the relatively small total numbers), that in this sample of Muslim Chennai family court litigants, the number of living daughters is almost precisely equal to the number of living sons. This suggests the absence among these Muslim families of the marked son preference (and resulting skewed sex ratio) that is typical of Indian society at large and, to a somewhat lesser extent, of the state of Tamil Nadu.

17 Husbands not infrequently accused the wife's parents, particularly her mother, of causing trouble in the marriage, usually by encouraging their daughters' 'misbehaviour' and/or insisting that their son-in-law live with them as *khanadamad*, so that they can benefit from his earning capacity.

18 This does not mean that each man actually used these precise words to characterise his wife's faults. It is not the divorcer but the *qazi* (or, more commonly, his assistant), who actually enters the requisite information on the divorce form. Generally what happens is that he asks the man for an account of his marital difficulties and then sums it up in one or two brief sentences of his own choosing for the record.

19 In interpreting these findings it should be noted that it is much easier to get the police and the criminal court system to take action under Section 498A of the IPC if the alleged abuse is related to dowry demands than if it is precipitated by some other dispute between the spouses.

20 There is nothing peculiar to Muslims in terms of the kinds of harassment of wives that I have been describing here. The noted advocate Indira Jaising, for example, at the conference at which this chapter was originally presented, reported orally on a study in which she was involved, of women court clients

in Delhi, most of whom were Hindu. Her findings were almost identical to mine in terms of the kinds and precipitating causes of marital conflict and the nature and frequency of psychological and physical violence sustained.

[21] The group also hears other disputes involving Muslim clients, most of them related to business matters.

[22] Chennai had, at the time of my research, three All-Women Police Stations, where complaints of this kind are usually taken. There was one similar police station in Hyderabad.

[23] Often, it is said, after beating him up and/or extracting a hefty bribe.

[24] The couples in the Chennai family court sample had all been separated for periods ranging from less than one month to 21 years: the mean length of time between the separation and the filing of a lawsuit was 2.8 years.

[25] One measure, for example, is the number of divorces per a given number of existing marriages; another is the number of divorces per number of married women (above a certain age) in the population. One can also approach the question by looking at the distribution of the population in terms of marital status: that is, by determining what proportion of the adult population is, at a particular point in time, divorced. For India, it is possible to calculate only the last measure, by using census data. Not surprisingly, the number of Indians reporting themselves to census-takers as 'divorced' is relatively small and, in terms of percentages, there is little difference among the religious communities. For example, in 2001, 0.32 per cent of both the Muslim and the Hindu population are listed as 'divorced'. In both communities there was a significant difference between men and women in this respect. Thus, whereas 0.5 per cent of Muslim women were divorced, this was true of only 0.13 per cent of Muslim men. The Hindu figures are quite similar: 0.45 per cent of women, versus 0.18 per cent of Hindu men, were divorced, (Census of India 2001, C - Series, Social and Cultural Tables, Table C-3 Marital Status by Religious Community and Sex).

[26] It is neither a legal nor a religious requirement that anyone other than the parties to the marriage, the wife's guardian, and their witnesses be present when a marriage is contracted. But in practice, most families choose to invite a religious expert of some kind to preside over the event.

[27] The principal responsibility of this office is to oversee the financial management of Muslim religious endowments (*waqf*, plural *auqaf*). [Note the use of the letter K for the Arabo-Persian Q in the word *waqf*. In Indian official English this is the conventional way of transliterating it into Roman script.]

[28] It is there that I and a research assistant were able to examine Qazi A's marriage certificates (*siyahnama*) for eight months of 1990–91 and the first three months of 2001. Unfortunately, *qazi*s tend not to be regular in

depositing their records in the archives, whose holdings are therefore very incomplete.

[29] According to Frank Fanselow, even more extensive marriage records are maintained by mosque boards in different communities of southern Tamil Nadu. See his *Trade, Kinship and Islamisation: A Comparative Study of the Social and Economic Organisation of Muslim and Hindu Traders in Tirunelveli District, South India*, Ph.D. dissertation, London School of Economics, 1986.

[30] Under the Muslim Women (Protection of Rights on Divorce) Act, 1986, a divorced Muslim woman is not entitled to file against her husband for maintenance under Section 125 of the Code of Criminal Procedure, although a married Muslim woman who is merely separated from her husband is still entitled to do so. According to the MWA, a man must provide for his divorced wife during her *ᶜiddat* period but thereafter, if she has no other income, she must rely on her children, grandchildren, or natal kin or, if they are unable to support her, the Wakf Board of the state in which she resides. There has been considerable controversy and some conflicting judicial decisions concerning the correct interpretation of the passage in the Act that reads 'a divorced woman shall be entitled to … a reasonable and fair provision and maintenance to be made and paid to her within the *ᶜiddat* period by her former husband'. Some maintain that this means that the husband is obliged to pay during the *ᶜiddat* period an amount sufficient to maintain her for an extended period thereafter or even for life. However, according to the more commonly accepted interpretation, his responsibility ends three months after the divorce takes effect. For some recent developments, see chapter 8 in this volume.

[31] The *qazi*s I spoke to averred unanimously to be of the view that marital problems are a very private matter between husband and wife that should not be enquired into in any detail. They said it was particularly inappropriate to commit either of the parties' complaints to writing, not only to protect the couple's privacy but to allow for the possibility of reconciliation without the complainant having to justify any recriminations made in the heat of anger. Furthermore, I was told, this policy allegedly avoids the potential for (unspecified kinds of) legal problems being created when, at a later date, a complainant might be put in the position of having to substantiate his or her accusations. It is perhaps partly for these reasons that, even though there is a space on the divorce forms where details about the circumstances surrounding the divorce are to be entered, they rarely contain much information of this kind, even if it was imparted to the *qazi* during his interview with the clients. On most forms one finds the same standard explanation, written in almost identical words: 'Due to unavoidable circumstances it has become impossible for us to continue married life.' Only occasionally does the *qazi* or his assistant

write something more specific, such as the very common complaint that the man's wife is 'stubborn and disobedient'. A woman's reasons for desiring *khulᶜ* are almost never provided. For more details about this, see chapter 4 in this volume.

[32] Advocates provide similar services and many men choose to issue a *talaq* through a legal practitioner instead of (or in addition to) registering it with a *qazi*. In either case, the format of the *talaqnama* is the same. The cost of dealing through an advocate is considerably more, however. Another means of making one's divorce 'official', which is used either instead of or in addition to those already described, is to take out an advertisement in the newspaper announcing to the public that one has dissolved one's marriage. Several such advertisements appear daily in those Hyderabad and Chennai newspapers that have a predominantly Muslim readership.

[33] In the course of this research, we were able to consult a complete corpus of divorce records for an entire year from the files of two different Hyderabad *qazi*s. Unfortunately, we could only examine the marriage records of one of these men, Qazi A, and they were not for the same year as the divorce records. The *qazi* solemnised a total of 3,515 marriages over a period of nine months in 1990–91 and three months in 2001. In the 12 month period from January to December 1993, on the other hand, he registered 391 divorces. If we assume that the number of marriages performed remained more or less stable or increased only slightly from year to year, we come up with an estimated eleven divorces issued for every 100 marriages performed. This is certainly an underestimate, given the fact that while practically all marriages are registered, an unknown number of divorces are not. Furthermore, it is not necessary that one register one's divorce with the same *qazi* who performed one's *nikah*. Yet, inadequate as these figures are, they do give some idea of the prevalence of divorce in this community.

[34] This is the *ahsan* form of *talaq-al sunna*, that *talaq* which is in conformity with the dictates of the Prophet. A less desirable, but still 'approved', procedure is termed *hasan*. It has the man make three successive pronouncements of *talaq* during three consecutive periods of 'purity' (i.e., when the wife is not menstruating), during which no sexual intercourse has taken place between the couple. This form of *talaq* also leaves open the possibility of reconciliation before the third pronouncement makes the divorce irrevocable. See A.A.A. Fyzee, *Outlines of Muhammadan Law*, 4th ed. (New Delhi: Oxford University Press, 1974), pp. 150–55. See also M. Hidayatullah and A. Hidayatullah, *Mulla's Principles of Mahomedan Law*, 19th ed. (Bombay: N.M. Tripathi Private Ltd, 1990), pp. 223–76, for a good overview of MPL as it pertains to marriage and divorce.

[35] If she is found to be carrying a child, the *ᶜiddat* period (and the husband's

responsibility for his wife's maintenance) is extended until the child is delivered.

36 Generally speaking, the closer the kinship relationship, the lower the *mehr* amount. Parents marrying their daughter to a complete stranger are likely to bargain for a substantial sum.

37 None of the women interviewed in Chennai or Hyderabad had received 'prompt' *mehr* at the time of marriage, and only 6.5 per cent of our sample of 351 women who had been married by Qazi A in Hyderabad in 1990–91 and 2001 and five per cent of those whose divorces were registered by him in 1993 had done so. Statistics compiled from the 2000–01 divorce records of Hyderabad Qazi B show a very similar pattern: only 6.2 per cent of the 341 women for whom the information is available received payments (in amounts ranging from Rs. 501 to 1 lakh) at the time of their wedding.

38 The local explanation is that when the Prophet's daughter, Fatima, was wed, this was the amount offered by her husband. To accept this amount is considered religiously virtuous.

39 Two *dinars* was the most typical offering.

40 In addition to the two *qazi*s in Hyderabad whose records I was able to examine, I interviewed four other Hyderabad *qazi*s, the head Sunni *qazi* in Chennai, and a *qazi* in the town of Vaniyambadi in Tamil Nadu about their work.

41 Despite obtaining earnings estimates from their clients, *qazi*s seem, in most cases, to levy a quite standardised amount for *ᶜiddat* expenses, rather than calculating it each time with reference to the individual man's income. Thus, in 1993, Qazi A instructed most of his clients to pay Rs. 1,000 for maintenance during *ᶜiddat*. By 2000–01, most men who had their *talaqnama* processed by Qazi B were being told to deposit Rs. 2,100 for this purpose. A few men paid as much as Rs. 3,000 and one gave his former wife Rs. 4,500. It may be that the larger amounts were offered spontaneously by the husbands concerned, rather than waiting for the *qazi* to propose an appropriate figure.

42 I am somewhat confident that this procedure is actually followed in most cases, having not only examined the relevant documents in the files of two of these *qazi*s, but having also personally observed it being enacted on different occasions in three different *dar-ul-quzat*, two in Hyderabad and one in Chennai.

43 This information as well as the documents themselves are kept in the individual client's case files. We were not given direct access to these, though a few were brought out and shown to us by Qazi B, by way of examples.

44 It may also be the case that in some other parts of the country the religious authorities are less insistent upon seeing that divorced women receive their due.

45 Actually, according to MPL, when a couple is divorced by *khulᶜ* her *ᶜiddat*

expenses are supposed to be paid by her husband (see Hidayatullah and Hidayatullah, *Mulla's Principles*). However this rule does not appear to be generally known and seems rarely to be followed by the *qazi*s whose records we examined.

[46] Under Hanafi law, followed by most Indian Muslims, the mother is entitled to custody of a son until the age of seven years and of a daughter until puberty. Thereafter, the father has the right to claim their custody (see Fyzee, *Outlines*, p. 198).

[47] In her case, as in some others, once their marital troubles landed them in court, her husband, no doubt motivated by the threat of having to begin paying maintenance to his estranged wife, eventually did pronounce *talaq*.

[48] Of course, our samples are biased toward those who *did* get help from their natal families. Those whose parents insisted that they remain in an unhappy marriage would not have ended up in a family court or have been otherwise available to be interviewed for this study.

[49] My research shows that the mother usually does retain custody of the couple's young children after divorce (or separation). This was true in all but a handful of cases among those in the Chennai family court litigants' sample, for example. Aside from the fact that this is a recognised right of a Muslim mother, rarely does a husband seriously want to take on the responsibility of raising an infant or toddler, particularly if he has plans to remarry. If the children are older, the couple may divide the children between themselves, with the father usually keeping one or more of the sons. However, not infrequently a man will sue for custody of an infant simply in order to harass his wife or will use a demand for custody as a bargaining chip in a divorce case filed by his wife. Almost all divorce cases tried under the Dissolution of Muslim Marriages Act of 1939 in the Chennai family court and pursued to disposal ended with an 'endorsement' by both parties. Where children were involved, the wife almost invariably agreed to give up any claim to a financial settlement or future child support, in exchange for retaining custody.

[50] When referring to 'the law' in such contexts, the *qazi* and his staff make, at least implicitly, a distinction between *sarkari qanun* (government law) and *shari'at* (Islamic law).

[51] They do not necessarily fully understand the procedure or its implications: some women even seem to be under the impression (by analogy with the husband's ability to pronounce *talaq*) that they need merely 'pronounce' *khul*ᶜ for the divorce to take effect.

[52] This law was enacted in response to pressure from the Muslim religious establishment, then concerned about a growing trend whereby Muslim women, desperate to extricate themselves from abusive or otherwise intolerable marital unions, had resorted to the stratagem of renouncing

Islam and converting to Christianity or Hinduism. Under MPL at that time, there was no way that a Muslim woman could obtain a divorce without her husband's consent—the act of 'apostasy' served to automatically void her marriage. Faced by the unpleasant prospect of Muslim women abandoning the faith in droves, a group of clerics proposed legislation that would offer another way out to such women and, at the same time, make it no longer possible for them to invalidate their marriages through apostasy. For further details and discussion of the events leading up to the passage of the DMMA, see Shahida Lateef, *Muslim Women in India: Political and Private Realities: 1890s–1980s* (New Delhi: Kali for Women, 1990); Muhammad Khalid Masud, 'Apostasy and Judicial Separation in British India' in M.K. Masud, B. Messick and D.S. Powers, eds., *Islamic Legal Interpretation: Muftis and their Fatwas* (Cambridge, MA: Harvard University Press, 1996), pp. 193–203; Gail Minault, 'Women, Legal Reform, and Muslim Identity', *Comparative Studies of South Asia, Africa and the Middle East* 17 (2) (1997): 1–10.

53 The average length of time from filing to disposal for those cases pursued to judgment was one year and four months. The quickest case took just under two months to be decided, while the slowest took three years and six months. One of the goals sought by the authors of the Family Courts Act 1984 (FCA) was to shorten the time which disputing couples would have to spend in court waiting for a judgment. Previously, personal law cases were handled in the regular civil courts, where the backlog of other kinds of cases often made the wait for a divorce or a decree interminable. There is anecdotal evidence that the Act has improved this situation somewhat, but in the absence of statistics it is not possible to say for certain whether or not the authors' hope for speedier justice has been fulfilled.

54 According to the law, when a marriage is dissolved under the DMMA, the wife's *mehr* is immediately payable, along with a sum for maintenance during the *ᶜiddat* period (Fyzee, 1974, *Outlines*, p. 186). But since (in Chennai, at least) judges seem reluctant to grant a contested divorce under this Act, there is a tendency to endeavour to gain the husband's consent, even if this means that the wife has to accept a disadvantageous financial settlement. Thus the implicit model for a 'court divorce' seems to be the Islamic *khulᶜ*. It is likely that most women (and possibly some advocates) are unaware that, following a divorce award under the DMMA, the law allows, and indeed prescribes, the payment of their *mehr* and *ᶜiddat* expenses.

55 Note that in most cases the Muslim divorcée retains physical custody of any young children born to the couple. When a woman remarries the husband can reclaim the children, but my research indicates that this does not happen very often, especially if the couple separated when the child was still an infant. One reason why the mother's family more often ends up raising the children

of their divorced and remarried daughter or sister is that, by the time she remarries, the former husband is already raising another family and has no interest in taking on the responsibility of caring for a small child with whom he may not even have developed any kind of relationship.

[56] On the other hand, it is really not possible to know from a brief interview what these women's real feelings about remarriage might be, particularly given the difficulty, in their situation, of finding another husband.

[57] In the case of women's remarriage we recorded information on *all* remarried brides for whom marriage certificates were available, rather than using only the ten per cent sample from which other statistics presented here were calculated.

[58] It appears from the marriage forms we examined that the *qazi* does not simply ask the bride's father whether she was married before and how the marriage ended, but requires him to provide further details and perhaps some documentation of her marital history. On some forms the name of the former husband and the date of his death or of the divorce were also entered.

[59] See Fyzee, *Outlines*, p. 175, under the heading of cruelty.

[60] At the time of my research, a Christian woman would have to prove adultery in combination with some other fault in order to obtain a divorce. However, this provision of Christian Personal Law has since been changed, so that adultery alone, whether committed by the husband or the wife, constitutes grounds for the dissolution of a Christian marriage.

[61] The only cases for which printed reports are available are those which for some reason went on appeal to one of the High Courts or to the Supreme Court. In any event, their numbers bear no necessary relation to the total number of cases filed in the lower courts.

[62] The appropriate registers for these years could not be located by the clerk in charge when I was working in the Chennai family court record room.

[63] The MC register for the earlier years of operation of the Chennai family court could unfortunately not be located when I was working in the record room in the spring of 1999.

[64] If the court is aware that *talaq* has been pronounced (for example, if, as happens from time to time, the husband pronounces a divorce during a hearing of the maintenance suit) the case will be immediately closed, on the grounds that, as a divorced Muslim woman, she has become ineligible to file for maintenance under the CrPC. However, if the wife should receive the *talaqnama* outside the court, she will very likely simply not attend the next hearing and after two more absences her case will be dismissed for default.

[65] The FCA specifically cites the preservation of marriage as a principal goal. It instructs that judges are to be selected from among those who are committed to this effort. It also provides for the employment by the court of 'counsellors',

whose task it is to try to reconcile disputing couples. In Chennai, counselling is mandatory for all litigants. The counsellors appointed for this purpose are generally not professionally qualified social workers but well-meaning middle-class men and women, often retirees, who wish to devote some of their time to helping those less fortunate than themselves. They are not paid but receive a small daily expense allowance. In Hyderabad, I was told, a similar system was tried when the family court first went into operation, but the man serving as chief judge at the time of my research had at some point taken over this responsibility himself.

66 This was the maximum award at the time of my research. The Code of Criminal Procedure (Amendment) Act, enacted in 2001, removed all limits and made the award amount subject to the court's discretion: much higher awards are now possible.

67 Under the FCA, litigants do not have the right to be represented by legal counsel, except with special permission of the judge. This provision of the law is intended to facilitate a more informal mode of interaction between the litigant and the judge, in which the parties can use ordinary language rather than specialised legal jargon to explain their situation. It is also intended to free the court from adhering to the rigid procedural codes employed in regular courtrooms. However, in practice, it is almost impossible for even a well-educated petitioner to navigate her (or his) way through the process of filing a suit in the family court and pursuing it to completion without the assistance of an experienced advocate.

68 In Chennai, at the time of my research, there was a single family court, trying all matrimonial cases as well as suits for maintenance under Section 125 of CrPC. In Hyderabad, however, all cases filed under the latter statute were dealt with by a separate court, set up in October 2000 in an attempt to deal with the overloaded docket at the main family court. We were unable to examine the records of this latter body due to time constraints.

69 The validity of the assumption that most married women in urban India depend on their husbands' earnings for support is probably borne out by statistics, although levels of labour force participation by women, especially among the poor, are certainly much higher than the proponents of this view realise. In my sample of Muslim women drawn from court files in Chennai only a handful had ever worked outside the home, though some engaged in home-based income-producing labour (such as preparing speciality food items, sewing or embroidering garments, making hand-rolled bidis, and the like).

70 Seventy per cent of the approximately 540 Muslim cases filed in the Chennai family court during the ten years between 1988 and 1997 were filed by women, more than two-thirds of whom sought either a divorce (57 cases)

or maintenance for themselves and/or for their children (approximately 232 cases). Muslim women also filed, though in smaller numbers, suits for declarations as to the validity of a marriage or a divorce, for getting legal custody of a child, or for retrieving personal property in the possession of the husband or parents-in-law. Cases filed by men were overwhelmingly for 'restitution of conjugal rights', a legal remedy whose purpose is to compel a spouse who has left the matrimonial home to return to it and, in the formulaic phrase repeatedly encountered in court documents, 'restore to the petitioner the comforts and bliss of married life'.

71 Court petitions are written in English, a language with which very few female litigants are familiar. In the Chennai family court the proceedings are conducted mainly in Tamil, with English spoken from time to time by the judge, advocates, and the occasional more highly educated litigant. Speakers of Hindi, Urdu, Telugu, or some other language may engage an interpreter if they are unable to speak or understand Tamil. In Hyderabad, the judge mainly used Telugu, sometimes interjecting remarks in English.

# 3.
# The 'Cancer of Dowry' in Muslim Marriages
## themes in the popular rhetoric from the south Indian Muslim press[1]

### Introduction

Today in India the 'evil of dowry' has moved to centre stage as an object of social critique by the general Muslim public as well as by social reform-minded religious authorities and institutions. This development reflects the recent spread of a relatively new kind of transactional regime in connection with Muslim marriages. Whereas the specific object of the critique is new, the nature of some of the rhetoric is not. To be sure, the major themes in the popular Muslim discourse about 'dowry' closely echo those issuing from the Indian public at large and from women's NGOs and other feminist social reformers and activists. A careful reading of the Muslim press, however, also reveals the presence of other themes that represent a more specifically Muslim critique of the system. These recall some of the rhetoric of much earlier Muslim reformers in the subcontinent, who wished to purge Muslim lives of a wide range of customary rituals and ceremonial observances (*rasum*) regarded as objectionable because they had no religious sanction in the scripture, and even involved activities contrary to the dictates of Islam. Furthermore, according to some, they were to be avoided because they represented cultural 'borrowings' or 'survivals' from pre-Islamic or Hindu modes of worship and life cycle ceremonial.[2]

I use the term 'dowry' in its current popular sense to mean cash and other valuables transferred at the time of a marriage by the bride's family to the groom and his family, often—though not necessarily—in response to explicit or implicit demands, rather than of their own free will.[3] Over the past 25 to 30 years in southern India there has been considerable change in the pattern of marriage transactions associated with Muslim marriages.[4] Whereas previously parents endowed their daughters with a 'trousseau' of clothing, jewellery and household goods that were intended (in theory at least) to remain her personal property, now they are expected, in addition, to transfer significant wealth to her prospective groom and in-laws. I will first discuss the historical background of this change and then explore the community's response as reflected in discussions about the 'dowry' phenomenon that appeared in two south Indian Muslim newspapers in the late 1990s. I will analyse the various terms in which the critique of 'dowry' is framed in the press and assess their significance for understanding some of the social and political dilemmas in which ordinary Muslims find themselves today, as they pursue their daily lives as members of a minority community in an environment increasingly hostile to the kind of 'difference' they are perceived to represent.

## Historical background

Already in the nineteenth century the British colonial state had become aware of the prevalence of the 'dowry' practice among certain segments of the Hindu population, especially in north-western India. Convinced that it led to widespread rural indebtedness and female infanticide, they made many attempts to suppress it, but to little avail.[5] After Independence those concerned with trying to rectify gender inequalities in the existing Hindu laws of marriage, property, and inheritance turned their attention to 'dowry'. Most acknowledged that the longstanding practice of endowing the daughter with valuables at the time of her marriage was a legitimate way of expressing parental affection and compensating her for the fact that, under Hindu law, she would normally inherit no share of her father's estate.[6] However reports of extortionate demands made during matchmaking negotiations by prospective grooms and their families were a cause for serious concern. In 1961, the Dowry Prohibition Act was enacted. It banned the transfer of 'any property or valuable security given ... *as consideration for the marriage* [italics mine]' and made both giver and taker subject to prosecution.[7] Only a handful of cases ever came to trial under this act, and in 1974 a government-appointed committee surveying all aspects of women's status in India had to report that 'dowry is on the increase, and has penetrated communities and regions which did not practice it earlier'.[8] Women's organisations all over India echoed the committee's call for strengthened legislation, and the original Act was twice amended, in 1984 and again in 1986.[9] The practice of giving 'dowries' continued to spread, however, and ever-rising amounts were reported.[10] Furthermore, 'dowry demands' were being made not only during the marriage negotiations but for years thereafter. Women who were unwilling or unable to comply with the demands often suffered psychological and physical abuse and, in extreme cases, death.[11]

There has been no perceptible decline in the prevalence of 'dowry' since the latest legislative enactments took effect; if anything, the custom has continued to spread. While one can find exceptions to this generalisation, it is fair to say that most Indians today, of whatever social stratum or religion, take it for granted that, if they are to find a suitable husband for their daughter, the financial outlay will be substantial.

## Marriage transactions among south Indian Muslims: the historical evidence

Two fairly detailed descriptions of Dakkhani Muslim marriage 'customs' are available. Both were written in Urdu by local Muslim men, one in the 1830s[12] and the other at the turn of the twentieth century.[13] Both works begin their discussion of marriage transactions by describing *mehr*, a gift of money or other valuables that Islamic law requires the groom to offer his new bride.[14] The amount is always recorded in the marriage contract. It need not necessarily be handed over at the time of the wedding but, if not, it remains an outstanding debt until either paid to or 'forgiven' by the wife.[15]

These early observers also prominently mention *jahez*, the bride's trousseau.[16] Assembled and presented to their daughter by her parents it included, according to Jaffur Shurreef, 'a quantity of the bride's clothes which have been worn, jewellery, cosmetics, bed and table linen, furniture (including a bed and a storage trunk), kitchen utensils, pots and pans, plates and cups, and one or two domestic slaves and some animals'.[17] The *jahez* goods, he says, remain in the bride's possession 'as long as she lives'. They then pass to her children or, if she is childless, to her closest [natal?] relatives.[18] On the night before the wedding ceremony (*nikah*), the entire *jahez* is taken in procession, often with musical accompaniment, to the groom's house and laid out there for his relatives and friends to inspect and admire. With it is delivered—in reciprocation for the wedding dress that the groom's party had earlier delivered to the bride's house—a set of clothes and an elaborate flower veil (*sehra*) for the groom to wear at the wedding ceremony.

Neither account mentions anything resembling the contemporary 'dowry'. Aziz Jang Wala, writing specifically about customs of the Nawwayat community (*qaum*), does mention a cash gift—called *pend* or *paind*—that is presented to the groom by his future in-laws at the conclusion of the engagement ceremony (*mangni*).[19] He indicates that poor families would offer sweets instead; he further explains that the word and the custom itself is of Telugu Hindu origin. Though it passed from the bride's parents to the groom, it does not appear to have been a gift on a par with the modern 'dowry', in terms either of size or function.

## Marriage transactions in the more recent past

Several anthropologists carried out research among various south Indian Muslim communities between 1960 and the early 1990s. None of these reports addresses marriage transactions in great detail, but a careful reading suggests that, while it has long been customary to give the daughter as substantial a gift as possible of personal and household items at the time of her marriage, the practice of making payments of cash or valuable goods to the groom and his family was not widely followed in this region before the late 1970s or early 1980s. All mention the requirement that the groom make a commitment to give *mehr* to his bride. Otherwise, the principal marriage transfer described is the bride's 'trousseau'. Thus, Mines says that among Muslim merchants in the town of Pallavaram, Tamil Nadu, in the late 1960s 'a woman is said to receive her share of [her natal family's] wealth in the form of dowry ... such wealth belongs personally to her'.[20] The Tamil word *citanam* used for this gift by both Hindus and Muslims in the area is derived from the Sanskrit *stri* + *dhan*, 'women's wealth'. Though Mines translates it as 'dowry', what he describes is not what is commonly meant by that term today but corresponds rather to Shurreef's description of the *jahez* or 'trousseau'.

Fanselow, in an unpublished paper based on research among Muslim Ravuttars and Tarkanars in Tirunelveli district, Tamil Nadu in the early 1980s, likewise translates the Tamil *citanam* as 'dowry' in the context of a discussion of women's inheritance rights.[21] It consists of moveable property, mainly gold jewellery and silk saris, for the daughter's personal use. No mention is made in this account of any payments to the groom. However, in a later paper he documents from several decades of mosque records that, by the 1980s, a major portion of the *citanam* consisted of cash intended for the daughter's husband and in-laws. Whereas in the past the respective families' wedding expenses had been more or less equal, there was now a 'unilateral transfer of wealth' to the family of the bridegroom. Deploring this development, but unable to stop it, some local mosque committees (*jamaat*) had begun levying a tax on any groom who accepted a 'dowry'. However, this experiment was later abandoned because worshippers objected to benefitting from an activity so clearly contrary to the dictates of Islam.[22]

A much more detailed account of Muslim marriage transactions is provided by C.G. Husain Khan, who conducted research in the early 1980s among Urdu-speaking Muslims in Karnataka.[23] There the principal marriage gift is the *jahez*, presented to the bride by her parents and consisting of 'many pairs of clothings [*sic*] and personal effects for the bride, normally including several pieces of gold and silver jewellery which will remain her personal property'. In addition, there are 'household furnishings like a bed with bedding ... brass and copper cooking vessels ... and other miscellaneous items'.[24] Khan also notes that well-to-do Muslims had recently begun giving substantial gifts of cash and gold to the families of their prospective sons-in-law.[25] He associates this new transaction called *hunda*—which he identifies with the Hindu concept of *kanyadan*—with a growing preference among the wealthy for marriages outside the kin group, and notes the similarity between the Muslim practice and that of Hindus in the region.[26] Jackie Assayag, who did research in the early 1990s among villagers of both religions in the same general vicinity in Karnataka, makes a similar observation. He translates *hunda* into French as *dot* (meaning 'dowry' in English), 'a payment to the future husband', while translating *jahez* as 'trousseau'.[27]

### Marriage transactions today

According to my own observations and interviews conducted between 1983 and 2001 in Hyderabad and Chennai, mainly among Urdu-speaking Muslims, the sequence of wedding rituals and gift exchanges followed are similar in most respects to those described in nineteenth-century and early twentieth-century sources.[28] Ritually, the relationship between bride-givers and bride-takers tends to lack the element of asymmetry that typically characterises this relationship among Hindus. Most material exchanges and feasting are reciprocal rather than one-sided, and the sequence of rites held at the groom's and bride's homes before and after the wedding are roughly mirror images of each other.[29] Likewise, the sharp role distinction between the 'groom's side' and the 'bride's side', so crucial in Hindu marriage, is much less marked in a Muslim marriage, particularly, of course, when the union is endogamous to the *khandan* or local descent group.[30]

The major difference with the past is the expectation that the bride's parents will give substantial amounts of cash, goods, and other valuables to the groom and his family. With changing practices have come new linguistic usages. One expression that is frequently heard is *len-den* (literally 'taking-giving'). Traditionally a neutral term applied to the practice of exchanging gifts on a variety of ceremonial and festive occasions, it has acquired a more specific and negative connotation. The word *jahez* is still used, but its meaning has broadened as its content has changed. No longer consisting only of goods for the bride herself, a significant proportion of the goods is intended for use of the groom and his family. Furthermore, rather than being selected and freely given by the bride's family, what goes into the *jahez* is increasingly being dictated by the groom's family. The line between the bride's property and that of her conjugal family is consequently becoming blurred, and her ability to retain or control the disposition of any part of her *jahez* is greatly reduced.[31]

While the word *jahez* is now often used in a broad sense for the entire set of transfers from the bride's family to their daughter *and* her new family, the cash portion of the gifts to the groom is often singled out from the material items as *jore ka paisa*, or *jore ki raqm*, 'money for the set (*jora*) [of clothes]'. As noted above, the groom's wedding outfit was formerly made to order by the bride's family and delivered to him shortly before the wedding. A tailor would be sent ahead of time to take his measurements and sew whatever the bride's family thought suitable. Over time, however, the parents of young men began to take responsibility themselves for ordering the wedding suit. The girl's parents would then be asked to reimburse them in cash. Eventually the amount demanded began to greatly exceed the actual cost of the clothes. Nowadays, under the guise of *jore ki raqm*, the girl's family may be asked to give anywhere from a few hundred to (in extreme cases) several lakhs of rupees. There is no longer even a pretence that it is directly related to the actual expense of clothing the groom for the wedding ceremony.

In the extended family (*khandan*) with whose practices I am most familiar,[32] when cash began to replace the gift of a readymade outfit, a conventional amount of Rs. 50 was paid.[33] By the 1980s some families were paying amounts ranging from Rs. 500 to Rs. 5,000. When the groom was a close kinsman, the amount paid was usually nominal but larger amounts were transferred if the groom was a non-relative. This particular family is rather unusual in its collective reluctance to participate in the current practice of taking a large amount as *jore ki raqm* when they marry a son, and paying out correspondingly when marrying off a daughter. One way that they are able to do this is by continuing to marry within their own *khandan*, insofar as this is possible, given changing criteria of 'suitability' or 'eligibility' of grooms in terms of educational qualifications and employment prospects.

If they aspire—or are forced by the lack of 'suitable' candidates within the *khandan*—to seek an 'outsider' for their daughter, parents are aware that they may be obliged to give a more substantial *jahez* and a larger amount as *jore ka paisa* than if the groom were a close relative. Even when a young man of the *khandan* marries an 'outsider' girl, many prefer to adhere to their traditions and their religious principles, and refuse to demand or even to accept 'free-will' offerings of cash or expensive goods from the girl's parents. Therefore, as one woman said to me, only partly in jest, young men of their *khandan*—particularly those who are educated in the professions or are working in the Middle East—are regarded as 'bargains' in the marriage market!

When urban residents of Hyderabad or Chennai talk about the way marriages are being celebrated today, the issue of 'dowry' is central. In the fall of 2001, I had such a conversation with a fairly well-to-do middle-aged Hyderabadi whose sons were just finishing high school. He explained that 'all middle class people' want their sons to become doctors, but admission to government medical schools is extremely competitive, so most must seek admission in one of the private medical colleges. These require, he said, a 'capitation fee' of up to Rs. 8 lakhs and annual fees of Rs. 80,000 to 86,000. Therefore, parents look for a bride whose family is in a position to reimburse them for their son's education. On top of this, they want a fridge, VCR, colour TV, and a motor scooter or even a car. They will say to each of the prospective brides' families, 'We have spent so much on our son's education. How much can you give?' Then they will send the proposal to the one that offers the most.

A young single woman bank employee in her early 20s, belonging to a lower middle class family and working as a computer operator, had a similar story to tell. The most desirable grooms, she said, are those working in the Gulf. They can command as *jore ki raqm* Rs. 3 or 4 lakhs. Those who have secure salaried jobs in India are worth closer to Rs. 2 lakhs. Even if the young man is unemployed, his parents may demand this much so as to set him up in business. Or the girl's family will be asked to make arrangements for a job overseas and a visa and also to fund his travel. As *jahez* they will also have to give their daughter a substantial amount of gold jewellery and numerous sets of clothes (11, 21, 51, or 101 and so on) and at least one roomful of furniture. 'But it [the furniture] won't go into their own room. The husband's family will use it themselves!' As for the *jore ki raqm* ('So much money for one suit of clothes!'), the boy's family may use some of it to pay for the *valima* feast (on the day after the marriage is consummated). They may buy a few sets of clothes and perhaps some pieces of jewellery for the bride. The rest they will save for when their own daughter gets married.

Neither of these informants was describing the details of any particular marriage, and it is quite conceivable that they were exaggerating somewhat for maximum effect or at least presenting worst-case scenarios. Somewhat more specific—though not necessarily more reliable—are the data I obtained from interviews and case files of women whose failing marriages had brought them into the family courts of Chennai and Hyderabad. One young woman, a B.A. from a middle class family, told me that in 1985 her parents had paid her husband-to-be Rs. 15,000 as *jore ki raqm*. Her *jahez* included five tolas of gold and assorted furniture. After the marriage, her husband sold the gold and used the proceeds to finance his sister's marriage. He gave the furniture in his sister's *jahez* as well. The parents of several other women I interviewed, who had married between 1979 and 1989, had paid between Rs. 5,000 and 10,000 as *jore ki raqm* in addition to the usual *jahez* items. Of course, to properly assess the significance of the cited amounts it would be necessary to have information about the income and assets of these women's families.

Detailed schedules of items presented in *jahez* are sometimes found in court files. For example, in connection with a marriage that took place in Chennai in 1986, 44 items of household use are listed, including furniture and kitchen utensils, with a total value of Rs. 36,000. The petitioner also claimed that her parents had given her eight *tola*s of gold and 25 *tola*s of silver and her husband Rs. 10,000 in cash. Another bride, married in 1987, listed 19 silk saris, 65 *tola*s of gold, and extensive household furnishings and equipment as *jahez*. Her husband received Rs. 30,000 in cash, but soon after the wedding he and his parents further demanded a VCR, stereo, washing machine, cooking range, and Rs. 15,000 to invest in a 'side business'. When she refused to ask her parents to comply with these new demands, she was allegedly physically abused and eventually ejected from her marital home and forced to return to her natal family.

### The 'dowry evil' in the Muslim press

That the custom of making payments to eligible grooms in connection with marriage is regarded within the community as a pressing social issue can be seen from the frequent discussions on the topic in Muslim newspapers and magazines and, increasingly, on Islamic Internet sites originating in the subcontinent. I have sampled two south Indian newspapers for relevant articles and letters to the editor on this topic. The first, the daily *Siasat*, published in Hyderabad and also in Bangalore, originally appeared only in Urdu but now has English and Hindi editions as well. It is distributed throughout south India and puts out a web version that is read around the world. It is not a religious organ but its readership is largely Muslim, as are those who write for it. It covers local, national, and international news, sometimes written with a distinctly Muslim slant. It regularly prints articles about Muslim personalities and events in other countries and has a popular religious advice column. There is a once-a-week 'women's page' where most of the comments on 'dowry' that I discuss here have appeared. Women are well-represented among the authors of articles on this page. This is true as well of most of those responding with letters to the editor and one can assume that the page's readership is also primarily female.

The other publication sampled is the *Islamic Voice*, published in Bangalore. It is India's most widely read English-language Muslim newspaper.[34] It appears to aim more explicitly than *Siasat* to speak for and to a self-consciously religious Muslim constituency. It devotes much space to religious as well as to social and political issues of particular relevance and concern to its largely middle class, western educated, upwardly mobile Muslim readership. Articles dealing with social issues like that of 'dowry' appear irregularly. They tend to be written by locally or nationally prominent male religious and/or scholarly authorities and are typically highly didactic in tone. The paper does not provide a regular forum for readers' responses, so, although it has female journalists on its staff, the voices of women are otherwise largely absent from its pages.

Both papers are very critical of the phenomenon that in the Urdu press is variously referred to as 'the dowry cancer' (*jahez ka nasur*) or 'the evil spirit of dowry' (*jahez ka bhut*). Writers address the topic from a variety of vantage points. Many write to document the current situation with respect to the practice of 'dowry', while others are more concerned about the social and personal consequences of excessive *len-den*. Some try to assign responsibility for the prevalence of the custom and its spread or to ask where and why the custom originally came from. Finally, there is the vexing issue of what to do about it. Most of the proposed solutions take the form of the usual exhortations to 'simply say no' when the time comes to arrange a marriage in one's own family, but these recommendations are frequently buttressed by appeals to Islamic ideals.

Letters to the editor of *Siasat* documenting current practice typically draw upon the writers' own experience or upon that of relatives and acquaintances. As one young woman explains,

> A very close friend of mine got married recently. Her parents had to pay six lakhs cash as *jore ki raqm*, in addition to all the other expenses of the wedding. Altogether the marriage cost them 11 lakhs. When I asked her about it, my friend explained that the marriage was so expensive because he is a doctor. Otherwise, why should he marry an ordinary high school graduate like her?

A man reports the dilemma in which an acquaintance, the father of a young woman, currently finds himself:

> Five years ago, he negotiated the marriage of his daughter with a close relative. At that time there was no talk of dowry. Now, just before the day of *nikah*, the groom's father has demanded five lakhs rupees cash, a car, washing machine, fridge, colour TV and all the other household items! What can he do?

With respect to the issue of 'dowry demands', writers may refer to the time-saving device of presenting a 'list' at the onset of negotiations, in order to weed out unsuitable candidates and serve as a basis for serious discussion with the rest. Others outline the current 'market prices' for different kinds of grooms:

> A chauffeur, bus conductor, policeman, or office boy demands two lakhs rupees in cash, a motor scooter, five *tolas* of gold and plastic veneer furniture. A bakery worker demands 25,000 rupees cash, a motor scooter, three *tola*s of gold and metal furniture. The demand for grooms is shooting up like the market price of any other commodity. For

> example, for a doctor, five lakhs plus a Mercedes car. For a veterinarian, four lakhs plus a Suzuki car. For a civil engineer, five and a half lakhs and a Maruti. For a lawyer, three lakhs, etc, etc. These are the prices for professionals. Non-professionals have their own going rates.

Writers universally deplore the fact that the need to pay dowry is making it difficult for parents of moderate means to get their daughters married. Young women are remaining unmarried well beyond the desirable age for marriage and sometimes are unable to marry at all, because their parents cannot afford the dowries that are expected by 'suitable' grooms. One result of this is that girls are now seen as—and feel they are—burdens on their parents. This perception strikes at the very heart of the ideal parent-daughter relationship.

The question of who can and should exert control over the *jahez* is also raised by many writers. For example, one woman asks readers of *Siasat* to respond to the question of whether the bride ought to be required to share 'her' *jahez* articles with other family members. Some reply that she should be generous in allowing others to use her belongings, but also note that family members should in turn acknowledge her rights and give the items back to her when they have finished with them. Other writers point out that, in practice, there isn't much a woman can do if her in-laws take her belongings. In the words of one woman, 'There is nothing, other than her *jahez* clothes and jewellery, that the girl can keep for her own exclusive use.' In answer to this, several writers cite instances in which even the woman's jewellery has been taken by the husband or in-laws and sold to finance their own projects or to give away in the marriage of the husband's sister.

Many writers ask who is to blame for this 'aberration'. For some it is greedy grooms and their parents, for others it is the families of prospective brides who, in order to attract the most 'desirable' grooms, put ads in the paper offering large amounts of cash and promising an elaborate wedding. Such practices encourage dowry escalation and unfairly tempt young men who otherwise would be perfectly satisfied with modest gifts. The young women themselves are blamed by others for pressuring their parents to spend as much as possible, so as to heighten their own prestige and desirability. But most letter writers reserve their strongest ire for those bride-takers who make unreasonable 'demands', instead of looking at the qualities of the girl and accepting gladly whatever her parents choose to offer.

Writers also debate whether it is the younger or the older generation that is chiefly responsible for propagating the custom of dowry, and whether men or women are more prone to insist on retaining it. So, for example, some claim that grooms are pressured by their mothers into going along with dowry demands, while others say that young people are at fault for indulging in the modern craze for fashionable clothes, expensive jewellery, and consumer goods of all kinds. Their parents typically have no particular interest as such in these kinds of material things but are willing to do what they can to please their children.

Most of the anti-dowry rhetoric that I have cited so far conceptualises the issue of *len-den* as a social problem adversely affecting the lives of individuals and their families. It is because of its deleterious social effects that the custom should be suppressed. Another approach to attacking dowry, repeatedly expressed in the *Islamic Voice* but rarely encountered on the 'women's page' of *Siasat*, makes use of the notion that dowry and other undesirable marriage customs should not be engaged in by religious Muslims because they were originally Hindu practices. While this discourse shares with others the assumption that the social consequences of participating in dowry transactions are deplorable, it differs in that its appeal for reform relies on an appeal to historical origins, rather than to overall societal well-being or gender justice.

For example, one person writing in *Islamic Voice* introduces his essay by saying, 'Several traditions and customs which have been existing in the Indian subcontinent have nothing to do with the true Islamic spirit. They should be nipped in the bud at the earliest.' Another, after outlining how the demand for dowry places unbearable financial pressure on the parents of Muslim girls, elaborates upon this theme: 'The rich have copied this vulgar and criminal system from their counterparts in Hindu society and this practice has percolated to the poorest families too.' He goes on to criticise in particular the way that, before the *jahez* is delivered to the groom's house, the girls' parents

> ... display the vulgar luxurious goods in a mini-exhibition... Where is the spirit of Islam here?... If Islam is in danger right now in any sphere of human activities ... it is here (dowry).

In another issue, the same author, in an article entitled 'Dowry Deaths and Mute Muslim Society', reiterates that 'Hindu influence' is at the root of the problem:

> Dowry is an alien feature and totally prohibited under Islamic principles. This is a social evil eating away the Hindu society ... Its influence on the Muslims disgraces the very Islamic notion of respect, affection and kindness expected to be showered on women. Muslims of India are victims of the social evil of the Hindus.

Finally, in both newspapers the all-important question of how to rid society of the 'dowry menace' is addressed. Suggestions include getting young people and their parents to refuse to participate in the practice of *len-den* themselves and to boycott weddings where they know that the dowry given is excessive. This is another area where appeals to Islam are often encountered. There are repeated calls for so-called 'simple' marriages, which are more pleasing to Allah than the lavish celebrations current today. For example, in an article published in 1998 in *Siasat* the writer points out that God has directed man 'to use all of his belongings in humility and moderation'. It is counter to His teachings to waste money and other material resources by spending excessively on unnecessary things just in order to impress others. It is especially so if one's means are limited. An essay in *Islamic Voice* entitled 'Simple Marriages are the Need of the Hour' echoes this theme: 'For those who are born with silver spoons in their mouths this waste is not felt at all, but for poor and middle class Muslims, celebrating marriages has become a nightmare.' A letter to the editor of *Siasat* advises readers: 'If all Muslims followed the Sunnah of the Prophet (PBUH) and followed a simple life, then inshallah this problem could definitely be solved.'

A male correspondent cites as an exemplary model his own son's recent wedding:

> My son is employed abroad and earns 6,400 rials per month. His marriage was very simple and according to Islamic law. There were no traditional rituals. *Nikah* was held in the mosque and the guests then came to the function hall [for a meal]... *Mehr* was paid to the bride immediately. There was no band or videography. Those items of daily use that are usually given—such as copper and brass utensils, scooter, TV set, fridge, cooler, etc.—were absent. The bride brought only a bed, bed linen, a few clothes, a metal wardrobe, and 55 grams of gold. We did not make any demands.

A woman reader writes in a similar vein about a cousin working in Saudi Arabia: 'He got many proposals offering *len-den*, but he chose a poor girl from a respectable family.'

Both letters reflect and doubtless reinforce the common perception that young men who live for a time in Saudi Arabia or the Gulf States tend to become more religious than they had been before leaving India. Upon their return they are believed to adhere to stricter standards of Islamic practice, based on what they have seen and heard preached there. Evidence of such a trend is purely anecdotal so far but may have some basis in fact.

## Conclusion

I have argued that the giving and taking of dowry is widespread among south Indian Muslims today. It is indulged in quite unselfconsciously, especially in urban areas, just as it is elsewhere in India and among people of other religious communities. While recognised as a relatively new and decidedly negative addition to the repertoire of practices associated with Muslim marriages, it is reluctantly accepted as something that is perhaps an unavoidable accompaniment to the modern dilemma of growing economic insecurity and a lack of employment opportunities at a time of rising aspirations, among the young in particular, for the acquisition of ever more consumer goods and 'modern' lifestyles. But as the practice continues to flourish, so too does an ever more strident social critique that is reflected in the use of such phrases as *jahez ka nasur* and *jahez ka bhut.*

Most of the critique that emerges from the Muslim rank and file is identical in tone and content to the familiar pan-Indian anti-dowry discourse, whose history reaches far back into the early colonial period, though Muslims were not, until very recently, implicated among its perpetrators. It focuses on the deleterious effects of the practice on families and on marriageable and young married women and tries to find ways to explain and suppress its excesses.

Another theme, of more minor importance in the newspapers I sampled, reflects a more specifically Muslim critique. It stresses the 'alien' origins—from the perspective of worldwide Islam—of the 'dowry' custom. Underlying this critique of dowry is an implied conceptual opposition between 'Indian culture' and 'the Muslim religion' that has been heard often over the centuries from Muslim religious reformers. In this discourse, dowry is linked with a myriad of other undesirable Hindu customs that Indian Muslims have 'adopted' or 'retained' when their ancestors converted to Islam. I suspect that had I chosen to examine for this purpose one of the publications put out by any of the major Muslim religious bodies in India, this theme would have been even more prominent than it is in the newspapers I sampled. There is also an evident gender bias with respect to the terms in which the criticism is voiced. Women greatly predominate among the readers of *Siasat* who wrote to express their views about the 'cancer' of dowry. Women were also represented among writers of longer essays on the topic in this newspaper, though most were male. On the other hand, all the authors of essays that I read in *Islamic Voice* were male. Many were clearly well-versed in the textual traditions of Islam, something that women are in general much less likely to be.[35]

For the vast majority of Muslims, engaging in the practice of giving and taking dowry at the time of marriage presents no threat to their identity as both Muslims and Indians. Although they may resent its ubiquity for the entirely pragmatic reason that it so hampers their ability to arrange a secure and comfortable future for their daughters, they realise that it is a fact of life, something they must be prepared to deal with when the time comes. Some manage by resorting to such strategies as seeking a son-in-law within their immediate circle of close kin or—if they have a son of appropriate age—obtaining the necessary assets by first arranging *his* marriage to a girl whose parents are in a position to provide him a generous 'dowry'. Others turn to a like-minded community of devout Muslims pledged to stricter adherence to Islamic codes of conduct as a way of extricating themselves from dowry's stranglehold. For some of the latter, the familiar reformist discourse about fundamentally Hindu customs provides an especially strong and appealing rationale for going against the tide of lavish *len-den* that threatens a family's economic survival. To cease taking or giving dowry, then, becomes a compelling choice, not simply because of the harm it inflicts on them and their daughters, but because doing so threatens in a very fundamental way their identity as devout and observant Muslims.

I have noted here the presence of this latter discourse in some recent discussions in the contemporary Muslim press of the phenomenon of Muslim dowry. I am not in a position at present to say how prevalent it is in the Muslim press generally. It is not by any means the dominant theme of discussion in the two south Indian newspapers I was able to survey. However, it was encountered from time to time in the pages of a newspaper that attracts readers who are English-speaking and therefore more highly western-educated and presumably better off than the average reader of the Urdu press. According to Sikand, who has analysed editorials in the *Islamic Voice* in considerable detail, it tries to deal seriously and constructively with issues facing the Muslim community today, promulgating a message that encourages readers to find a way to reconcile their dual identities as religious Muslims and Indian citizens by adapting themselves to the many challenges of the milieu in which they live. Among other things, the publication is said to be dedicated to a strategy of trying to establish more direct and more positive relations with fellow citizens of other faiths.[36]

In the light of this overall assessment of the paper's orientation, it is therefore somewhat surprising to find that, at least with respect to the particular issue being discussed here, one finds in its pages numerous examples of utterances that might be interpreted as reinforcing negative stereotypes of Hindus and attempting to deliberately set Muslims culturally apart. To take this kind of position with reference to a social problem that afflicts Indians of all religions has its risks for Muslims living in a political environment where many in the majority community are eagerly looking for evidence that they are not only 'different' but that, in insisting on maintaining their difference, they represent a potential threat to the integrity of the Indian state. For this very reason there are many in the larger Indian Muslim community who are explicitly cautious about resorting to this kind of rhetoric when addressing issues like dowry.[37] My examination of some of the discourses on this matter leaves many open questions, not only about the political implications of some of the rhetorical choices that are being made by various individuals and segments of the community, but also about the potential of any of them for bringing about positive social change. Clearly, further research is needed before any of these questions can be satisfactorily answered.

**Endnotes**

[1] An earlier version of this paper was presented at a workshop sponsored by the Konrad Adenauer Foundation on the topic of 'Lived Islam: Liminality, Accommodation and Adaptation' held in Goa in December 2002. I thank the participants in that workshop and, in particular, its organisers, Helmut

Reifeld, Imtiaz Ahmad, and Shail Mayaram, for giving me the opportunity to benefit from their knowledge of and ideas about the issues discussed here. I have also profited from conversations and e-mail exchanges with Frank Fanselow, Mary Hancock, Dennis McGilvray, Diane Mines, Mattison Mines, Filippo Osella, Martha Selby, Yogindra Sikand and Theodore Wright.

2 Barbara Metcalf outlines the major issues and reviews the central arguments of some of these reformers in 'Islam and Custom in Nineteenth-Century India: The Reformist Standard of Maulana Thawani's [*sic*] *Bahishti Zewar*', *Contributions to Asian Studies* 17 (1982): 62-78. See also Book 6 of Muhammad Ashraf 'Ali Thanvi, *Bahishti Zewar* (New Delhi: New Taj Office, 1962) and Barbara Metcalf's translation of and comments on this chapter in her *Perfecting Women: Maulana Ashraf 'Ali Thanvi's Bahishti Zewar* (Berkeley: University of California Press, 1991).

3 Some have suggested that the terms 'groom price' or 'groom fee' are more appropriate than 'dowry' for the system as it operates today. However, since the latter is so widely used in India—often even when people speak in their mother tongue—I will use it here. On this question of terminology, see Lionel Caplan, 'Bridegroom Price in Urban India: Class, Caste and "Dowry Evil" among Christians in Madras', *Man* (n.s.) 19 (1984): 216-33; and Nicholas J. Bradford, 'From Bridewealth to Groom-Fee: Transformed Marriage Customs and Socio-Economic Polarisation amongst Lingayats', *Contributions to Indian Sociology* (n.s.) 19 (1985): 269-302.

4 I limit my discussion to southern India, although the phenomena that I discuss are widespread among Muslims elsewhere in India as well as in Pakistan and Bangladesh. My remarks are based largely upon my own research among Urdu-speaking Muslims in Chennai and Hyderabad, conducted since 1984, during several visits for periods ranging from two to 10 months in length. I also refer to the ethnographic literature on Muslims elsewhere in the south, excluding Kerala.

5 Veena Oldenburg subjects British analyses of the connection between dowry and female infanticide to critical examination in *Dowry Murder: The Imperial Origins of a Cultural Crime* (New York: Oxford University Press, 2002).

6 On the question of the relationship between dowry and female property rights in India see Jack Goody and Stanley J. Tambiah, *Bridewealth and Dowry* (Cambridge: Cambridge University Press, 1973); Stanley J. Tambiah, 'Bridewealth and Dowry Revisited: The Position of Women in Sub-Saharan Africa and North India', *Current Anthropology* 30 (1989): 413–35; Bina Agarwal, *A Field of One's Own: Gender and Land Rights in South Asia* (Cambridge: Cambridge University Press, 1994), pp. 198–248; Srimati Basu, *She Comes to Take her Rights: Indian Women, Property, and Propriety* (Albany, NY: State University of New York Press, 1999).

[7] The law applied to people of any religion, although at that time the practice of giving 'dowries' had not yet become widespread among Christians or Muslims.

[8] Committee on the Status of Women in India, *Towards Equality* (New Delhi: Government of India, Ministry of Education and Social Welfare, Department of Social Welfare, 1974), pp. 73–4.

[9] For more details see Werner Menski, 'Legal Strategies for Curbing the Dowry Problem', in W. Menski, ed., *South Asians and the Dowry Problem* (London: Trentham Books, 1998), pp. 97-149.

[10] It is not entirely clear to what extent this increase simply reflects an overall inflationary trend over the period.

[11] M.N. Srinivas analyses these and other post-Independence developments in his *Some Reflections on Dowry* (New Delhi: Oxford University Press, 1984).

[12] Jaffur Shurreef [Jafar Sharif], *Qanoon-e-Islam, or the Customs of the Moosulmans of India; Comprising a Full and Exact Account of Their Various Rites and Ceremonies from the Moment of Birth till the Hour of Death*, G.A. Herklots, trans, (London: Parbury, Allen, and Co., 1832), pp. 83-144. The author was a Dakkhani Muslim employed as a *munshi* by the East India Company. His original Urdu manuscript was never published and was apparently lost shortly after it was edited and translated into English by the British Army surgeon who had commissioned it. For further details about this book and its history see my 'Shurreef, Herklots, Crooke, and *Qanoon-e-Islam:* Constructing an Ethnography of "the Moosulmans of India"', *South Asia Research* 19 (1999): 5-28.

[13] Aziz Jang Wala, *Tarikh-un Nawwayat* (Hyderabad: Wala Akadami, 1976 [orig. 1904]), pp. 84-132. The Nawwayats are a relatively small community whose members are found widely dispersed throughout southern India. They trace their ancestry to Arab traders and preachers who came by sea to the western coast of India in the eighth century. Some of their descendants moved gradually to the east and south, serving in various religious and civil capacities in the administrations of successive Muslim rulers of the Deccan. See Victor S. D'Souza, *The Navayats of Kanara: A Study in Culture Contact* (Dharwar: Kannada Research Institute, 1955); Sylvia Vatuk, 'Identity and Difference or Equality and Inequality in South Asian Muslim Society', in C. Fuller, ed., *Caste Today* (New Delhi: Oxford University Press, 1996), pp. 227-62; and 'The Cultural Construction of Shared Identity: A South Indian Muslim Family History', in P. Werbner, ed., *Person, Myth and Society in South Asian Islam*, Special Issue, *Social Analysis* 28 (1990): 114-31.

[14] When Muslims speak or write in English they often use the word 'dowry' for *mehr.* This leads to considerable confusion, even in some of the scholarly literature. A more appropriate translation, long used by scholars writing about marriage transactions generally, is 'dower'.

[15] Sunni Hanafi law, followed by most Indian Muslims, recognises two categories of *mehr*, the 'prompt' and the 'deferred'. In some parts of the Islamic world the groom normally hands over all or a substantial portion of the *mehr* at the time of the wedding (see, for example, Annelies Moors, *Women, Property and Islam: Palestinian Experiences 1920-1990* [Cambridge: Cambridge University Press, 1995], pp. 77-150; Judith Tucker, *In the House of the Law: Gender and Islamic Law in Ottoman Syria and Palestine* [Berkeley: University of California Press, 1998], pp. 52-7). The rest comes due when her husband dies or divorces her by *talaq*. But in India the entire *mehr* is almost always 'deferred' and in practice few women ever receive it, even after divorce or widowhood.

[16] The Urdu word *jahez* comes from the Arabic *jahaz* or *jihaz*, the trousseau that is customarily given to the daughter in Arabia and other Middle Eastern countries. See, for example, Tucker, *In the House*, pp. 55-7.

[17] Shurreef, *Qanoon*, p. 117. The apparent reference to clothes that have been *previously worn* is somewhat puzzling. It may be a typographical error or an error in translation from the Urdu. It is certainly inconsistent with the contemporary practice of sending the bride to her new home with a generous set of *brand new* clothes, ideally enough to last her for several years.

[18] Shurreef, *Qanoon*, p. 121.

[19] *Pend* is also included in a list of 'harmful' wedding rites in a manifesto against 'wasteful' and non-Islamic ceremonials issued in 1863 by a group of reformist Nawwayat *ʿulama* in Madras (Muhammad Sibghatullah et al., *Zabitah-i Rasum-i-Nikah*, unpublished manuscript). See also the same author's *Gulzar-i-Hidayat* (Madras: Nizam-ul-Mutaba, 1873-4 [orig. 1847]).

[20] Mattison Mines, 'Urbanization, Family Structure and the Muslim Merchants of Tamilnadu', in I. Ahmad, ed., *Family, Kinship and Marriage Among Muslims in India* (New Delhi: South Asia Books, 1976), p. 303.

[21] Frank S. Fanselow, *Law and Custom Reconsidered: A Comparative Study of Hindu and Muslim Inheritance Laws and Practices in Southern Tamil Nadu*, unpublished paper, p. 28.

[22] Frank S. Fanselow, *Dan, Dakshina and Dowry: An Analysis of the Muslim Marriage Market in Tamil Nadu*, unpublished paper, pp. 11-14.

[23] C.G. Hussain Khan, *Marriage and Kinship among Muslims in South India* (Jaipur: Rawat Publications, 1994).

[24] Khan, *Marriage*, pp. 133-4.

[25] This term is doubtless the same as the Marathi *hunda*, 'money given at marriages by the father of the bride to the bridegroom and his party, instead of ornaments and clothes usually presented' (J. Molesworth, *Marathi-English Dictionary* [Pune: Shubhada Saraswat, 1986 [orig. 1857]), p. 905, cited in Véronique Bénéï, 'Changing House and Social Representations: The Case of Dowry in Pune District', in I. Glushkova and R. Vora, eds., *Home, Family*

*and Kinship in Maharashtra* (New Delhi: Oxford University Press, 1999), p. 130.

[26] Khan, *Marriage*, pp. 110-19. Poor Muslims, who were continuing to marry close kin, had not yet begun giving *hunda.*

[27] Jackie Assayag, *Au Confluent de Deux Rivières: Musulmans et Hindous dans le Sud de l'Inde* (Paris: Presses de l'École Française d'Extrême-Orient, 1995), p. 51.

[28] In 1998–99, in the course of research on women and Muslim family law in the Chennai family court, I also obtained some data on marriage transactions among Tamil-speaking Muslims in that city.

[29] This is consistent with a general Muslim tendency to endogamous and isogamous patterns of marriage alliance.

[30] In such cases the bride and groom and their other kinsmen are typically related to one another in multiple ways, making it difficult to definitively assign everyone to one or the other 'side' for ritual purposes.

[31] Of course, even in the past a husband or mother-in-law could (and sometimes did) forcefully or otherwise take possession of some or all of a woman's *jahez.* But the fact that it was well understood that this meant appropriating wealth that did not properly belong to them, doubtless served to constrain most people from taking such actions. Such constraints have now largely disappeared.

[32] This family, whose forebears were well-known Sunni *'ulama* in Chennai and Hyderabad, belongs to the Nawwayat community. See my 'Identity and Difference' and 'The Cultural Construction'.

[33] It is not clear when this change began to take place.

[34] See Yogindra Sikand's chapter on *Islamic Voice* in his *Muslims in India Since 1947* (London: Routledge Curzon, 2004).

[35] It is conceivable, although I have no evidence of it, that *Siasat* may have a policy of not publishing comments that could be seen as reinforcing religious stereotypes.

[36] Sikand, *Muslims in India.*

[37] I am indebted to a conversation with Filippo Osella for his insights into this question.

# 4.
# Divorce at the Wife's Initiative

## options and implications for women's welfare?[1]

### Introduction

The continuing public and scholarly debates over the desirability of enacting a Uniform Civil Code of personal law are heavily dominated by the issue of gender bias in Muslim Personal Law. Particularly controversial is the fact that a Muslim man can dissolve his marriage extrajudicially, unilaterally and with immediate effect, by simply pronouncing the word *talaq* three times. The alleged 'widespread abuse' by Muslim men of the 'privilege' of discarding their wives in this way is repeatedly cited by those who favour a thorough overhaul of the existing pluralistic system of personal laws.

Most non-Muslim Indians (and doubtless some Muslims as well) assume that the only way a Muslim marriage can be dissolved is at the initiative of the husband. According to this popular understanding, a Muslim woman is always the passive subject of divorce: she can only *be divorced*; she can neither prevent nor counter her husband's act, nor can she initiate the process. What is not widely known, outside the legal and social service professions, is that a Muslim woman who desires to extricate herself from an unhappy marriage has at least two well-established legal options. One is to file a civil suit for divorce under the Dissolution of Muslim Marriages Act, the other is to negotiate privately with her husband in order to *secure his agreement to release her* from the marriage, by *khul*ᶜ.

Considering that it is so rarely mentioned in popular or scholarly literature, I was surprised to discover in the course of my research that divorces by *khul*ᶜ are quite prevalent. Of course, *khul*ᶜ is routinely listed in every standard textbook or manual on MPL as one of several possible modes of dissolving a marriage. The procedure and case law pertaining to it are discussed as well in the texts.[2] Certain South Asian Muslim legal authorities, sensitive to allegations of gender bias in Muslim law, have also written about it, some of them actively seizing upon this provision of MPL to support their contention that Islam accords to women rights similar to those it gives to men. *Khul*$^{c}$, they claim, is simply the female equivalent of *talaq*.[3] But the only empirical studies of *khul*$^{c}$ that I have been able to find relate to its practice in the Middle East. Some historians of Muslim law, basing their conclusions on data from *shari'at* court records from Palestine, Egypt, and Ottoman Turkey, have suggested that the ability of women to initiate divorce—and the frequency with which, at least in the past, they actually did so—can be read as evidence of women's ability in those societies to exert 'independent agency' over the circumstances of their lives. This would undermine the prevailing view of Muslim women as invariably passive and submissive to the overbearing patriarchal control of their husbands.[4] My own ethnographic and archival investigations lead me to seriously question both these interpretations, at least insofar as their applicability to contemporary India is concerned. While there is no doubt that the ability to initiate an extrajudicial divorce is a positive right and has been, and continues to be, used successfully by many women to extricate themselves from unhappy marriages, *khul*$^{c}$ is hardly equivalent to *talaq*, in that it cannot be effected without the agreement of the husband.[5] Both sets of scholars greatly overestimate the extent to which one can validly use the availability of *khul*$^{c}$ in law and / or its prevalence in certain social settings as a measure of women's status. I will elaborate my reasons below, but first let me outline the main features of the law of *khul*$^{c}$ and present some observations about how it is implemented in those parts of India of which I have some personal knowledge. I will then briefly address the issue of woman-initiated *civil* divorce (under the DMMA), which represents an avenue of last resort for women who are unable to obtain *khul*ᶜ but are determined to have their marriages dissolved. Finally, I will revisit the larger question of how much of an advantage it is for the Muslim woman in marital distress to have available to her those options that MPL provides to wives who wish to initiate a divorce.

## Divorce by *khul*ᶜ

If a Hindu or Christian woman, or one married to a man of a different religion from her own, is determined to be legally free of her husband, she has no choice but to try to secure a 'court divorce' (by resort to the applicable Hindu Marriage Act 1955 [amended 1976], Indian Divorce Act 1869 [IDA—amended 2001] or the Special Marriage Act 1954 [amended 1970]).[6] A Muslim woman has another option. Assuming that she knows where to find her husband and has some hope of persuading him to release her from the marriage—either by making it financially worth his while or by offering some other inducement—it is much easier, quicker and cheaper, as well as more socially acceptable, to try for an extrajudicial *khul*ᶜ (or *mubarat*[7]) divorce. Even advocates and activist women's organisations routinely advise women who consult them for legal advice to try this route before resorting to the DMMA. As my data show, this form of divorce is a very real option for women in this situation and is frequently availed of in practice. Even where the marriage is ultimately not dissolved, or is dissolved by some other method, the fact that a Muslim woman can take the initiative in divorcing her husband plays an important role in the negotiations, power struggles, and manipulations that inevitably develop when one or both parties to an unhappy marriage considers the possibility of ending it.

## The *qazi's* role in facilitating *khul*ᶜ

As I have noted, under MPL, the wife cannot unilaterally declare herself divorced by *khul*ᶜ. The procedure requires negotiation between the spouses. The wife is supposed to take the first step, approaching her husband and offering him a 'consideration' for releasing her from the marriage. If he is willing, he accepts her offer and pronounces an irrevocable divorce, *talaq-ul bain*, just as if he were divorcing her at his own initiative. However, as I will detail below, the *consequences* of these two different forms of divorce are not identical, whether for the wife or for the husband.

A Muslim couple can effect *khul*ᶜ by the simple expedient of privately entering into an agreement between themselves. However it is more usual for the couple, or for the woman herself (typically accompanied by one or more male relatives), to consult either a Muslim cleric or an advocate knowledgeable about MPL to assist them in negotiating an appropriate agreement and drafting a written document. This is because they may not be sure of the correct procedure or because the wife and her family are unable or unwilling to contact the husband directly, or because they have already tried and been rebuffed. Or they may hesitate to make a private agreement because they are under the (false) impression that, in order to be valid, the divorce must have the written imprimatur of a recognised religious functionary.

In many parts of India, including the states of Tamil Nadu and Andhra Pradesh where I did my research, it is to a government-appointed *qazi* that Muslims most often turn for this purpose. A *qazi*, properly speaking, is a 'judge' who, in Muslim states such as existed in much of India before the coming of the British, presided over the ruler's court of judicature, deciding cases according to Islamic legal precepts. At the beginning of the 19th century, in the parts of India controlled by the British, these officials were divested of their former judicial authority, though some were retained as advisors on matters of Muslim law to British judges who had been brought in to administer justice to the 'native' populace in newly established British-style courts. In 1862, in conjunction with a major restructuring of the British–Indian judicial system, this role too was eliminated. Later, in response to community demands, the office of *qazi* was eventually resurrected in a new form with the passage of the Kazis Act of 1880.[8] In the present day, official *qazi*s are usually appointed by their respective state governments.[9] Their primary activities are to conduct wedding ceremonies (when invited to do so by the families concerned),[10] to write up and maintain records thereof, and to issue marriage certificates to the parties concerned. They may also register and maintain records of divorces (again, at the request of one or both the parties) and issue corresponding 'divorce certificates' (*talaqnama* or *khulᶜnama*) that clients can use as evidence that their marriage has been dissolved. Much of the other ongoing day-to-day work of the *qazi*'s office (*dar-ul-quzat*) involves looking up records needed by clients for one or another legal, career, travel, or other personal purpose. The *qazi* may also be called upon from time to time to answer the questions of clients about the minutiae of Muslim law with regard to marriage, divorce, child custody, inheritance, and the like. In addition, he often serves as an intermediary between husband and wife for those monetary transactions that may be associated with a marriage or a divorce, including the payment of *mehr* and *ᶜiddat* expenses and the return of dowry items to the wife after a marriage has been dissolved.

Given the *qazi*s' role as registrars of marriages and divorces, their records constitute valuable source materials for the study of the realities of Muslim divorce. Yet they have been little used by research scholars,[11] in part, no doubt, because of difficulty of access. Furthermore, there are limitations to their usefulness for some kinds of quantitative research. Since an individual wishing to get married or register a divorce can go to any *qazi* he wishes, the population covered by a particular *qazi*'s records is not geographically localised or bounded. Marriages solemnised by one *qazi* may be dissolved before another, making it extremely difficult for a researcher working in a large urban area, who does not have unlimited time at his or her disposal and the cooperation of all of the *qazi*s in the city, to trace individual marital careers. Furthermore, insofar as divorce is concerned, the individuals whose records are found in one or another *qazi*'s archives represent only a partial and quite selective sample of the larger population from which they are drawn. This is because, whereas most people call upon a *qazi* when they marry, not everyone does so when considering divorce. Since a *khul*ᶜ divorce is somewhat more complicated to effect on one's own than a *talaq*, a high proportion of those contemplating divorce through the former method consult a *qazi* or some other legal expert. In the case of *talaq*, only those who have (or think they may in the future have) some reason to require documentary proof of marital status are likely to bother with such formalities. Therefore the data on *talaq* that one finds in a *qazi*'s archives have a distinct class bias. The bulk of the *qazi*'s clients tend to be of at least lower-middle class status. They are likely to be possessed of some material assets, be regularly employed and / or aspire to travel abroad for educational or employment purposes. Those who find themselves involved in some kind of civil litigation may also require documents of the kind that the *qazi* can provide. The poor, while clearly predominant in the population, are less likely to have such needs and are consequently almost certainly under-represented in the *qazi*'s divorce registration records.

## *Qazis'* marriage records in Hyderabad

In Andhra Pradesh, seven 'chief' or *sadr qazis*[12] are appointed by the state Wakf Board, the government agency charged with supervising the operation of Muslim endowments.[13] The position is in practice, though not in law, virtually a hereditary one, passed down from father to son or other male heir.[14] Each *sadr qazi* serves within a particular loosely defined geographic area of the city.[15] He appoints his own assistants (*naib qazis*), who work under his general supervision in specific sub-areas of his larger jurisdiction. The *qazi*'s position is unpaid, although he is permitted to charge modest fees for the various services he provides. All the *qazis* I interviewed hold some other job as well. For example, one of the *sadr qazis* in Hyderabad who permitted me to examine a sample of his divorce records is a clerk in a state government office. His five-person office staff performs most of the day-to-day business of his *quzat*, though he reserves to himself and his *naib qazi*s the privilege of performing marriages.

When a couple marries, the *qazi* who presides over the ceremony enters the necessary details (in Urdu) onto a standard, printed form, called a *siyahnama*. At the top of the form is entered the date and place of the wedding. Next is noted whether the bride has been married before and, if so, how her prior marriage(s) ended.[16] The names and addresses of the bride and groom, their respective ages or dates of birth, occupation, 'nationality' (*qaum*—e.g., 'Hindustani'), 'community' (*firq*—e.g., 'Sheikh'), and school of Islamic law followed (*maslak*—e.g., 'Hanafi') are listed, along with the names of their respective parents and that of the bride's 'guardian' (*wali*—usually her father) and an 'agent' or 'representative' (*wakil*) and two official witnesses for each of the spouses, with their occupations and kinship relationship (if any) to the party they represent. Finally, the *qazi* notes down the amount of the *mehr* and whether it was paid 'promptly' or 'deferred'. Down the right side of the form is a row of spaces for the signatures or thumbprints of the bride and groom and each of the other official attendees. At the bottom, the officiating *qazi* and, if the marriage was performed by a *naib qazi*, the *sadr qazi* to whom he reports, affix their own signatures and official stamps. One copy of this form is retained for the *qazi*'s files, one each is given to the bride (or her *wali*) and the groom and another is transmitted to the Andhra Pradesh state Wakf Board. A fifth copy is, in theory at least, deposited in the Andhra Pradesh State Archives.[17]

## Divorce records

Whereas both the *sadr qazi*s whose records I examined in Hyderabad claim to have several hundred years of marriage records in their possession, passed down from ancestors who held the same post, they indicated that keeping records of divorces and issuing divorce certificates has become a common practice only within the last

30-40 years. They said that not only was divorce quite rare in the past but, when it did occur, there was little perceived need for documentation of the kind that they now are routinely asked to issue and, therefore, there was no need to go through the process of registration. Nowadays, divorces are registered on a form that is similar to, though briefer than, the standard marriage registration form. Here is noted the date and place of marriage, the type of divorce (*talaq* or *khul*ᶜ), the amount and type of *mehr*, and the names and signatures or thumbprints of each spouse and his and her two witnesses, and the amount of any payments made to the wife by way of a divorce settlement. The *mehr* and ᶜ*iddat* expenses, and any other monies that might have been transferred to the wife, are itemised separately. Sometimes further details about the divorce settlement or arrangements for the custody of children are noted. If it is a *khul*ᶜ divorce, then the terms of the agreement are outlined. There may also be a brief statement explaining why the marriage is being dissolved.

Each of the *qazi*s who permitted me to examine some of his divorce records has jurisdiction over an area in the predominantly Muslim 'old city' of Hyderabad. I will call them Qazi A and Qazi B.[18] The *dar-ul-quzat* overseen by Qazi A is staffed by a superintendent (who does most of the work involving direct dealings with clients) and two or three clerks. It is open daily, 11:00 a.m. to 4:00 p.m., except Fridays, and religious and civil holidays. Cupboards lining the wall of the large reception room contain cloth-wrapped bundles with individual files of all marriages performed (by the *qazi* himself or by one of his eleven *naib qazi*s) over the last several years. Similar bundles contain files of all divorces (both *talaq* and *khul*ᶜ) registered in his office—some at the time they took place, others afterwards. In other cupboards are the *qazi*'s marriage and divorce registers, later compilations of the most pertinent details from all of the individual case files accumulated during the past year: names of the parties, date of marriage (or divorce), amount of *mehr*, whether and how much was paid. Qazi A told me that, because of the pressure of work, it is difficult to keep these registers up to date. Indeed, when I visited his office in 1999, the clerks were several years behind in this.[19]

The 1993 divorce register that Qazi A allowed me to photocopy contained 407 entries, 391 of which pertained to an extrajudicial divorce registered in his office during 1993.[20] Fifty-three per cent of the divorces recorded in that register were *khulᶜ*, while only 47 per cent were *talaq*. The other set of documents I examined is a bound volume of original divorce forms filled out in the office of Qazi B during the *Hijri* year 1421 (from early April 2000 through March 2001).[21] There are 390 sheets in the volume but only 355 contain enough information to determine the type of divorce or even whether it went through at all. Here there was an even greater predominance of *khulᶜ* over *talaq*: 56 as against 44 per cent. Thus, in both these jurisdictions women appear to be consistently initiating more divorces than men, a rather surprising finding. There is reason to believe that one cannot take these figures entirely at face value, for reasons that I have mentioned above and will elaborate below, but they do testify to the undeniable significance, numerical and otherwise, of this form of divorce in contemporary India.

### What goes on in the *qazi's* office?

By the time a marriage has broken down to the extent that a *khulᶜ* is being contemplated, the couple is usually already living separately, the wife with her natal family and the husband in their former marital home or elsewhere. The usual first step is for the wife and one or more of her male relatives to go to their local *qazi*'s office. Typically, the *qazi* or a member of his staff listens to their story and, perhaps after asking the woman to consider reconciliation, explains how they should proceed.[22] He tells them that he will contact the husband on the wife's behalf, sending a registered letter, written on official letterhead, summoning him to come on a specified date and time to discuss the matter. If and when the husband appears, the *qazi* will try to get his version of the story and perhaps again suggest that the couple try to reconcile. If the husband is clearly averse to this suggestion, the *qazi* may propose that he simply divorce his wife by *talaq*. This way, the wife will be entitled to claim her outstanding *mehr* and other financial perquisites. If the husband refuses this also, the *qazi* will urge him to at least grant her the *khulᶜ* she desires, since she has clearly expressed her determination not to resume their conjugal life together. If he agrees, and the wife and the required number of witnesses are present on that occasion, the *qazi* will execute the necessary documents on the spot. Otherwise, he will set a time and date for both to return and complete the formalities.

In making an agreement for *khulᶜ*, the spouses are free to make any bargain they wish. However, most agreements follow a standard pattern: the wife offers to forfeit her *mehr* (or whatever portion of it is still outstanding at the time of the divorce) in exchange for her freedom. Since in the vast majority of cases the *mehr* was of the 'deferred' sort, and by the time negotiations for *khulᶜ* have begun it usually still remains unpaid,[23] the typical *khulᶜ* transaction is a purely paper one. No actual cash changes hands: the wife simply agrees to give up her right to claim what her husband promised at their wedding but never actually handed over to her. Occasionally a husband will drive a harder bargain, demanding additional compensation above and beyond his wife's waiver of *mehr*. He may, for example, ask for an amount in cash, gold, or consumer goods or he may demand that she give away her right to retain temporary custody (*hizanat*) of their young children or to receive child support while they are under her care.[24] Behaviour of this kind is legally permissible, though strongly discouraged by most religious authorities. In Hyderabad, at least according to the *qazi*s' records I examined, it does not appear to occur very frequently. However, it does seem to be standard practice there for the wife who initiates *khulᶜ* to forego, not only her *mehr*, but also her legitimate claim to be maintained during *ᶜiddat*.[25] In view of the fact that this waiver of *ᶜiddat* expenses occurs so consistently, it seems likely that the *qazi*s, perhaps under some misapprehension about what the law actually requires, routinely instruct their female clients to offer it.

### Reasons for divorce

There is little information in these documents about the reasons for divorce. Although the divorce registration form has ample space for 'comments', it is usually left blank or filled in with only one minimally informative sentence. Case narratives in family court petitions as well as my own interviews suggest that domestic violence, dowry disputes, and sexual jealousy are some of the major issues associated with marital breakdown in this society.[26] However, there is rarely any mention of any of these kinds of conflicts in the *qazi*s' divorce records. When I asked why they recorded so little information about the events leading up to the divorce, both *qazi*s responded that Islamic law does not require either party to provide a reason for wanting a divorce. Since what goes on between a married couple is a very private matter about which no outsider should enquire, they consider it both inappropriate and unwise to ask someone to justify his or her decision. If a man makes an allegation against his wife (or vice versa) and this is committed to writing, it could exacerbate the hard feelings between the spouses or new ones could be created, making future reconciliation impossible.[27] One *qazi* also mentioned the possibility of false allegations. If one party became aware that the other had made unfounded charges, he suggested, these might be used as a basis for a libel suit!

In any event, most of the 'reasons' that are provided in the files for pronouncing *talaq* or asking for *khul*ᶜ take a very repetitive and conventional form. This is understandable, since they are not written by the parties themselves but by the official who fills out the document. Though doubtless composed on the basis of the clients' oral statements, they are not a verbatim record. A typical statement goes like this: 'For some unavoidable reason it has become impossible for us to continue our married life and so I have given my wife *talaq* [on such-and-such date].' Occasionally a man makes more specific charges of 'disobedience' or other faults against his wife. For example, 'My wife is stubborn and her nature is opposite to mine. I have lost my mental peace. It is difficult to maintain our relationship and therefore we have separated.' Or, 'My wife is adamant about not wanting to live with my parents. She wants to live separately. So, as she wishes, she is living with her own parents.' Sometimes a statement hints at events that preceded the divorce. Thus in one case it is implied that the wife has filed criminal charges of some kind against the husband: 'Due to some unavoidable circumstances I was not able to manage my married life. I deposited Rs. 20,451 at the police station and handed over all the dowry items.' Only occasionally is the wife permitted to explain. For example, 'After marriage I immediately came back to live with my parents and until this day I am under their guardianship. Owing to these circumstances, my husband gave me *talaq* on 30th of March 2000 and we have separated.' In another statement, this time justifying a divorce by *khulᶜ*, the wife explains, 'I had three children from him, two daughters and a son. Now the son is four years old and is in my custody. Due to unavoidable circumstances we have been living separately for the past four years and my husband has married a second wife.'

## Granting *khulᶜ* vs. pronouncing *talaq*: Social considerations

From the man's point of view, granting *khulᶜ* has distinct advantages, both social and financial, over pronouncing *talaq*. One of the main costs of pronouncing *talaq* is the risk of social disapproval from his kin, peer group, community members and others in his social circle. Divorce is of course permitted in Islam and is even recommended if a couple finds it impossible to live in peace with one another. Yet, Muslims in India, unlike those in some Muslim-majority countries,[28] tend to share the high-caste Hindu idea that marriage is a life-long commitment, a bond that should not be broken no matter how unsuited the parties are to one another or how difficult it is for them to continue living together. Thus I was often told that while divorce is sometimes the only way out of an unbearable situation, it is one of the things that God most dislikes and should therefore be avoided if at all possible. The stigma of divorce generally falls more heavily upon the wife, as it tends to be assumed that a really good woman would be so obedient and amenable to her husband's wishes as to ensure domestic harmony. However, a man who has divorced his wife (unless it is well known that she was clearly at fault) cannot entirely escape social disapprobation. At the very least, questions will be raised about his character and his credentials as a good Muslim. From a more practical point of view, he may have difficulty persuading the parents of other young women that he is a suitable candidate for remarriage. However, if he can put the onus of initiating the break-up on his wife and cast himself as the innocent victim of an immoral woman who insisted he release her, he can largely avoid social opprobrium.

### Financial considerations

There is also, in theory at least, an obvious financial advantage for a man when the marriage is dissolved by *khul*ᶜ rather than by *talaq*: it frees him from the obligation to pay his ex-wife her *mehr* and perhaps also her allowance during ᶜ*iddat*. When men and women try to explain why a husband would pressure his wife to initiate a *khul*ᶜ divorce, they most often cite these monetary considerations. However, an exclusively economic explanation of the preference for *khul*ᶜ is not entirely convincing. In the first place, *mehr* amounts are often quite nominal.[29] Second, many women have been pressured to 'forgive' their husbands of the obligation to pay *mehr*, long before the question of divorce arose. Finally, even if a man divorces his wife by *talaq*, it is usually quite easy to evade the payment of *mehr* and ᶜ*iddat* expenses.[30] Most *talaq*s are pronounced in private, out of sight and hearing of any religious authority. If the man fails to pay his wife her *mehr*, he usually has little to fear beyond possible harassment from her natal family.[31] Only if he pronounces *talaq* in the presence of—or wishes to obtain a 'divorce certificate' from—a *qazi* or other religious authority who is committed to seeing that divorcers comply with the law, might he find it difficult to evade his financial obligations.

While, as I have noted, *qazis* have no enforcement powers, the ones I have interviewed (and whose work I have observed) in both Hyderabad and Tamil Nadu apparently do make some effort to see that men who divorce their wives by *talaq* pay whatever is due to them. To this end they use the only leverage they have, refusing to issue the desired divorce certificate until the man has handed the money over to the wife or has deposited it in the *dar-ul-quzat* for safekeeping. This suggests that class or economic standing may be a relevant factor in explaining why some men prefer *khul*ᶜ over *talaq*. Since men of the middle or upper classes are more likely to approach a *qazi* at the time of divorce, the financial benefits of pressing the unwanted wife for *khul*ᶜ rather than divorcing her by *talaq* are much more compelling for them than for the poor.

A few sociological studies have attempted to investigate the question of the extent to which women succeed in obtaining their *mehr* after *talaq*. All the samples surveyed in these studies are small, and in no case were the respondents randomly chosen, so the results are in no way statistically significant. However in the absence of any other more reliable or comprehensive quantitative data on the subject, their findings are worth citing. Not surprisingly, the overall pattern seems to be one of low compliance on the part of men. The most favourable outcomes are those reported by Munira Merchant, who interviewed 100 divorced women clients of various women's NGOs in Mumbai. As many as 66 per cent of those who had been divorced by *talaq* said that they had received what was due to them.[32] In sharp contrast, however, Moinuddin found that only two out of 128 divorced women surveyed in two rural Bengal districts had received their *mehr*.[33] Similarly, according to Zakiya Rafat, only three out of the 44 women divorced by *talaq* whom she interviewed in the town of Bijnor had received any monies at all from their ex-husbands. Some of these women had never made any effort to claim their *mehr*, either because they were determined to avoid any further dealings with their ex-husbands or because the amounts were so small that it was not worth their while to pursue the matter. Some women told the investigator that they did not even know how much *mehr* had been promised when they married or said that they had been persuaded, early on in their marriage, to 'forgive' it. Others said that, since their ex-husbands had no money, there was no point in trying to get them to pay up.[34] As for my own investigations in Chennai and Hyderabad, I too found that very few of the women I interviewed who had been divorced by *talaq* had received their *mehr* and *ᶜiddat* expenses. The only exceptions were those whose husbands had divorced them in the presence of (or had registered the divorce after the fact with) a *qazi*.

### *Mehr* in *qazi*s' divorce records

About two-thirds of all entries in the two sets of *qazi*s' divorce records I examined note both the amount of *mehr* and *ᶜiddat* expenses owed to the wife and the amount actually paid. The *qazi*'s usual procedure is to add to the *mehr* amount (which he verifies by consulting the client's *siyahnama*) whatever sum he considers sufficient to support the woman during her *ᶜiddat*. While one might expect that this amount would vary with the husband's economic standing and ability to pay, the documents indicate that this is not necessarily the case. For example, the 2001 divorce records of Qazi B show that, with very few exceptions, he consistently assessed the sum of Rs. 700/month for maintenance during *ᶜiddat*, whereas in 1993 Qazi A consistently considered Rs. 1,000 adequate for the entire period.

Usually, when a man comes to register a divorce or to pronounce *talaq* in the presence of the *qazi*, the wife is not with him. Even if she is present, he typically has not brought enough money to immediately pay her *mehr* and *ᶜiddat* allowance. In either case, the *qazi* will tell the husband what he owes and instruct him to come back as soon as possible with cash or a money order. Only then will the desired *talaqnama* be issued. The *qazi* then sends the woman a registered letter, notifying her that she has been divorced and instructing her to come and collect the funds for her *mehr* and *ᶜiddat* allowance that are being held in his office. Qazi B told me that, in order to ensure that the money does not fall into the wrong hands, he requires the divorcing husband to submit a photograph, which he keeps in the case file to use for identification purposes when the wife appears. All the pictures that he showed me appeared to have been cut out of the couple's wedding portrait, presumably to verify that it was really the man's ex-wife, not his mistress or some other woman, who was collecting the funds!

One cannot always tell from the records that I was allowed to see whether the woman has actually received her *mehr*. Ideally there is a signature or thumbprint as proof of receipt, but not infrequently the space in which the receipt is supposed to be entered is blank. This could mean either that the husband had never deposited the funds or that the wife had never collected them. Or it could simply mean that, for one reason or another, the register had not been presented to the wife for her signature when she came to get her money. In order to confirm whether or not the funds had been received, it would have been necessary to examine each individual case file, which I was not allowed to do. In any event, in 31 per cent of the *talaq* entries in Qazi A's divorce register there is no information at all about the payment of *mehr*. In 23 per cent, it is noted that the man had either handed over the amount owed to the wife in the presence of the *qazi* or had provided him with satisfactory documentation that he had already paid it on some earlier occasion. In another 30 per cent cases, it is indicated that the man had deposited the required amount, either with the *qazi* or with his advocate, for the wife to retrieve later. The remaining 16 per cent of men had simply signed an 'undertaking' or 'promise' to pay what they owed sometime in the future. For example, '*mehr* Rs. 1,100 prompt already paid in cash. Promised to pay Rs. 1,000 as *ᶜiddat* expenses of the lady and signed [by the husband]'. Or, 'Man has promised to pay through his advocate the *mehr* of Rs. 25,000 and Rs. 500 for the *ᶜiddat* expenses. Signed [by the husband] and recorded.' Thus, at least to the extent that this *qazi*'s records are to be relied upon, it seems likely that in at least half the cases of *talaq* that he registered, the wife did receive all or part of the *mehr* and $^{c}$*iddat* expenses due to her. This figure is much higher than is reported by most other researchers. However, it must be stressed again that those men who go through the process of registering their *talaq* with a *qazi* are a self-selected group, whose representativeness of the total population of divorcing men in the city is questionable.

### *Mehr* and other payments in cases of *khul*$^{c}$

As is to be expected, in most instances of *khul*$^{c}$ divorce the notation was made in the records that the wife is waiving the entire amount of 'deferred' *mehr* along with her $^{c}$*iddat* expenses. In these cases, no cash changed hands. Even in the few cases where the wife had been given 'prompt' *mehr* at the time of her marriage, there is no indication in the records that she was required to pay it back. In a few cases the husband paid some money to his wife. Such payments were rarely explained: they may have involved a return to the wife of money or goods that she had brought into the marriage as 'dowry'.

### *Khul*$^{c}$ initiated by the husband

When a couple is having severe marital problems there is usually an extended period of intense conflict between husband and wife.[35] At some point, the husband may simply pronounce 'triple *talaq*', but not infrequently there is a period of contestation between the two about how to go about ending the marriage, i.e., whether the man will pronounce *talaq* or the woman will ask for *khul*$^{c}$. I became aware of this first when examining case files in the Chennai family court. In several maintenance petitions or responses to petitions filed by men for 'restitution of conjugal rights', women described being threatened and psychologically and / or physically abused for refusing to approach the *qazi* for *khul*$^{c}$. Their husbands had no desire to remain married but hoped to avoid the necessity of pronouncing *talaq* by getting their wives to take the initiative instead. Some of the women wanted to preserve their marriage and were seeking some kind of compromise that would make it possible. Others were resigned to the dissolution of the marriage, but resisted the idea that they should assume the burden of initiating the divorce. It appeared from their testimonies that the women's motives were mainly social, not financial: they feared the loss of reputation that they would incur once it became known that they had been responsible for breaking up the marriage.

Jameela Nishat, likewise, calls attention to this phenomenon of 'male-initiated *khulᶜ*' in Hyderabad's Old City. She reports, as have I, that among all divorces registered with *qazi*s, *khulᶜ* divorces are more prevalent than *talaq*s, but she cautions that

> ... [t]hese figures disguise the fact that in many cases where the wife asked for a divorce, the reason might not be that she actually wanted to be free of the marriage bond. She may have been pressurised by her husband to ask for *khulᶜ*, as this would enable him to escape legal liabilities ... [or] the husband may have created a situation where the wife or her parents might have agreed to secure her freedom by agreeing to apply for a *khulᶜ*.[36]

Not surprisingly, none of the *qazi*s whom I asked about this would admit that it was a credible scenario. They insisted that—just as I had observed on more than one occasion in their office—they themselves always filled out the relevant forms and these had to be signed in person by both parties, in their presence or that of one of their office staff. Such protestations notwithstanding, a couple is in fact free under MPL to make their own private agreement for *khulᶜ*: the resulting divorce is considered valid, unless one party can demonstrate before the court that she (or he) has entered into it under duress or as a result of fraud. The practical likelihood of such a divorce being challenged by the victimised wife is, naturally, extremely small. So there is actually nothing except the *qazi*'s own conscience or sense of propriety to prevent a husband from bringing in an already signed agreement and asking that the necessary forms be filled out and a *khulᶜnama* issued.[37]

I asked each of the *qazi*s whom I interviewed what they would do if a woman came in asking for help in arranging a *khulᶜ* but the husband failed to appear when summoned or came but refused to cooperate. They all said that there was nothing further that they could do, pointing out that whereas in a society ruled by Islamic law it is possible for the *qazi* to dissolve a marriage even against the husband's wishes, assuming that he is persuaded of the legitimacy of the wife's grievance,[38] the Indian state does not grant them such powers. If a wife is determined to extricate herself from the marriage but the husband is adamantly opposed to releasing her, the *qazi* can only suggest that she turn to the civil courts for relief.

## The Dissolution of Muslim Marriages Act 1939

The Dissolution of Muslim Marriages Act was enacted in 1939 in response to pressure from the Muslim religious establishment, concerned about a perceived trend whereby Muslim women, desperate to extricate themselves from highly acrimonious or abusive marital relationships, were resorting to the stratagem of renouncing Islam and / or converting to another religion. At that time, the only way that a woman whose husband was unwilling to divorce her could free herself from the bonds of matrimony was by such an act of 'apostasy'. A group of prominent clerics drafted the Act in order to give such women a more acceptable way out of an unhappy marriage.[39]

There are nine grounds for divorce under DMMA. These include the husband's lengthy absence from the marital home, his failure to maintain his wife or 'to perform his marital obligations', his impotence, insanity or imprisonment for an extended period. Another legitimate ground for divorce is 'cruelty': under this rubric fall such offences as obstructing the wife's right to practice her religion, disposing of her property without her consent, falsely charging her with adultery or subjecting her to mental or physical abuse. In substance, this list of grounds overlaps in large part the grounds for divorce in the Hindu Marriage Act 1955, though there are some differences, one of which is that the DMMA does not provide for divorce by mutual consent, an option now available to Hindu couples under the Marriage (Amendment) Act 1976 (MAA). This omission is understandable, since the specific purpose of the DMMA is to meet the needs of *women whose husbands refuse consent* to a divorce or whose whereabouts are unknown. It assumes that, if the husband and wife both want to divorce one another, they will do so extrajudicially.

While I have not been able to find any published data on rates of resort to DMMA, my own research suggests that, at least in Hyderabad and Chennai, this statute is not availed of very extensively.[40] In all large cities marital suits are heard in specially constituted family courts, pursuant to central legislation passed in September 1984 as the Family Courts Act (FCA).[41] Hyderabad Family Court records for 1996 to 2001 show an annual average of 32.3 suits filed under the Act, while in Chennai, from 1988 to 1997, the comparable figure was only 6.3. However, Hyderabad has over four times as many Muslims as Chennai, so the difference in rates of resort was not large: an annual average of 2.3 suits per 1,00,000 Muslim inhabitants in Hyderabad, as against 1.9 in Chennai.[42]

One cannot conclude from these figures that Muslim women only seldom find themselves in the situation that the DMMA was designed to remedy. There are a number of reasons why, even if a woman is in dire marital distress, she may not choose to file for divorce under this Act. The first reason is the strong social stigma attached to divorce. Second, divorce almost always causes the woman serious economic difficulties. Few women have been gainfully employed during the marriage or possess sufficient education or job skills to be able to support themselves once they are on their own. So, if only for the sake of her reputation and her and her children's physical survival, an unhappily married woman will almost always choose to remain with an abusive or neglectful husband rather than initiate a divorce. Should her husband abandon her or eject her from their home, or if for some reason she feels compelled to leave of her own accord, she may well seek shelter with her parents or a brother. Even in this case, she may not feel that it is necessary or indeed in her best interests to file for a civil divorce.

Typically such a woman has suffered marital discord or abuse in silence for a long time before finally telling her natal family about her problems or, after some crisis event, seeking refuge with them. The family, especially its male members, usually takes charge of the situation then, rather than leaving it up to her to decide what she wants to do. In this matter, as in the negotiations leading up to her marriage, she will usually take a relatively passive role. Her parents may try negotiating with the husband and his parents, call in mediators from among their relatives or from their local mosque committee (*jamaat*) or consult an *imam* or the local *qazi* for advice. Often they send her back to her husband one or more times, with instructions to try harder to please him and his parents. Their usual goal is to try to preserve the marriage, both because they fear the stigma that will attach to their daughter and ultimately to them if she leaves her husband and because they are reluctant to assume moral and financial responsibility for her and her children for the foreseeable future. This is especially likely if they have recently made major outlays on her marriage for the accompanying ceremonial display, feasting, dowry and cash and other gifts to her groom and his relatives.[43] Eventually they may decide that the only solution is to take her back into their household. Unless they very much want to arrange another marriage for her, there may be no compelling reason to seek a formal dissolution of her marriage. It is easier and certainly more socially acceptable for her to remain legally married, even if she has no intention or hope of ever resuming conjugal relations with her husband.[44]

Finally, should such a woman (or her family) decide to seek an end to the marriage, they will not necessarily choose a 'court divorce'. Filing a civil suit is costly. Though the FCA specifies that litigants in family court do not have the right to be represented by an advocate (except with special permission),[45] it is in practice virtually impossible, even for an educated woman or her family, to navigate the system without legal assistance.[46] An advocate must be paid to write up the petition (in English) in the proper form and guide one through the subsequent lengthy bureaucratic process. There are also official court fees and unofficial, under-the-table, payments to be made to court staff if the case is to proceed in a smooth and timely fashion. Very few women are in a financial position to cover these expenses without assistance; their natal families may also lack the resources to help, even if they are supportive of the idea of her divorcing her husband.[47]

The requirement that litigants must personally attend every hearing in a family court—a corollary to the formal ban on third-party representation—is another severe imposition on the petitioner's pocketbook, her time and energy and that of her family members. It is especially hard for the poor, who must travel for long distances on public transportation or on foot, sometimes accompanied by their children, perhaps losing a day's wage in the process. They must then wait for hours, sitting on the bare floor in the hallway outside the courtroom—with no access to toilet facilities or drinking water—until their case is called and then, likely as not, continued for another month, either because their husband has not appeared, their advocate is nowhere to be found, or for some other bureaucratic reason whose nature they may not fully comprehend.[48]

Finally, pursuing a court divorce typically takes a very long time, during which the ultimate outcome may seem very uncertain. Many petitioners become discouraged in the process. From interviews I learned that women most often stopped attending court due to mounting legal expenses, the inconvenience of attending monthly court hearings, or they had come to believe that a favourable outcome was unlikely, whether because the husband was seriously contesting the divorce or he kept failing to appear, out of indifference or out of a desire to harass her by prolonging the process. In Chennai the average time from filing to disposal was one year and four months, but one contested case took three-and-a-half years. Less than fifty per cent of the 63 litigants stayed the course. With one exception, their suits succeeded. However, a spousal settlement financially disadvantageous to the wife was almost always attached to the decree.[49]

## Conclusion

I have presented here some of the findings of my research on how MPL is administered and how the provisions regarding divorce impact those women who are governed by that code of law. I have focused on woman-initiated divorce, something that has received little or no attention from other scholars. I have shown that, contrary to what most scholars and members of the general public imagine, this type of divorce is extremely common, at least in the parts of India where I have done research. My principal evidence for this is taken from divorce files maintained by Hyderabad *qazis*, in which cases of *khul*ᶜ clearly predominate over cases of *talaq*. This pattern is confirmed by interviews with other *qazis* I interviewed in both Hyderabad and Tamil Nadu who also agreed—while in those cases not providing any figures to support their assertions—that a majority of the divorces they handle are initiated by the wife. However, I have shown in the preceding analysis that, in fact, all appearances to the contrary, it would not be correct to conclude that most Muslim divorces, even in the cities where these figures were collected, are of the *khul*ᶜ variety. A majority of registered divorces may conform to this type, but since most *talaqs* are never registered, figures showing a predominance of *khul*ᶜ over *talaq* in *qazis'* records are misleading. Nevertheless, what these figures do demonstrate beyond any doubt is that this kind of divorce is very common and is therefore worthy of more scholarly attention than it has received to date.

How can we best explain the fact that *khul*ᶜ is as prevalent as it is in a society where unilateral divorce initiated by the man is so easy to effect and is allegedly so frequently and casually resorted to? What is the significance of these findings for our understanding of the position Muslim women occupy within marriage in India?

I have mentioned above that there are those who assert that man's right to give *talaq* and woman's to take *khul*ᶜ are equivalent, that the one balances the other. For example, the eminent Indian jurist, Tahir Mahmood writes:

> As regards divorce ... please do understand that in Islamic law men and women have absolutely the *same* right in respect of dissolution of marriage ... [It] makes available to either spouse the facility of extrajudicial divorce subject, *mutatis mutandis*, to the same conditions. The wife's right to *khul*ᶜ is legally analogous to man's right of *talaq* ... There is no inequality or inequity in this beautifully balanced law.[50]

In a later publication he reiterates and elaborates this point, saying,

> But where a wife insists on *khul*ᶜ ... it cannot be denied to her. The husband has to agree. And if ... not ..., third parties can intervene ... In no case will Muslim law keep an unwilling wife tied down to her unwanted husband.[51]

If the latter represents his own views on how the law relating to *khul*ᶜ ought to be interpreted by Indian jurists, then well and good.[52] However, this does not accord with the actual situation today, where a long-established precedent is clear on the point that for a woman to obtain *khul*ᶜ the husband's agreement is essential.[53] As Lucy Carroll puts it in a heated rejoinder to Mahmood's earlier article, equality can hardly be said to exist as long as a man can give *talaq* unilaterally whereas 'a woman cannot effect an extrajudicial *khul*ᶜ *unless her husband agrees to the divorce*' [italics in original].[54]

Aftab Hussain, in his book on the status of women in Islam, describes *khul*ᶜ in very much the same terms as Mahmood does. Although, unlike the latter, Hussain *does* see fit to mention that in order to have her marriage dissolved in this manner the wife must secure her husband's agreement, he goes on to minimise the significance of this qualification:

> The right of divorce conferred on man is counter-balanced by award [*sic*] to women of the right to seek dissolution of marriage and *khul*ᶜ,

> a right denied by other religions. Mutuality was thus maintained in matters of absolute separation too ... The right of the wife ... being subject ... to the consent of the husband ... [does] not impinge upon the concept of equality (Hussain 1987: 121–22).

Clearly both of these authorities are, intentionally or not, glossing over the crucial difference between men and women in respect of extrajudicial divorce: that the man can act entirely on his own initiative to dissolve the marriage, while the woman, though she can freely ask for *khul*ᶜ, can succeed in ending the marriage only if she can persuade her husband to act on her request.

Yet we might still ask whether the law of *khul*ᶜ, while clearly falling far short of conferring upon women equal rights with respect to divorce, nevertheless contributes in a positive way to women's 'agency', 'empowerment' or to their relative 'bargaining power' vis-à-vis their husbands within marriage. A number of scholars working on issues of law and society in the Middle East have framed the question in this way. In that part of the Muslim world—as in India today—there is, and has been in the past, a relatively high incidence of woman-initiated divorce. For example, Andrea Rugh reports on an Egyptian social survey conducted in the early 1970s, showing that one-third of all divorces were initiated, by women.[55] According to Judith Tucker, more than half of all divorces recorded in *shari'at* court records from the city of Nablus in Palestine in the eighteenth and nineteenth centuries were of the *khul*ᶜ variety.[56] These are figures very similar to those I found in Hyderabad *qazi*s' records in the 1990s. Madeleine Zilfi similarly found 'plentiful evidence ... regarding ... *hul*ʾ in her examination of marriage and divorce registers from eighteenth century Istanbul.[57]

It should be noted that, unlike in India today, matters of marriage and divorce were handled by religious courts where these scholars did their research. The petitioner was required to go before an Islamic judge to complain against her husband and the judge would make the determination as to whether or not she was justified. If so, he would order the marriage dissolved, regardless of the husband's feelings on the matter. In this sense the *khul*ᶜ was not an *extrajudicial* divorce at all, but was more analogous to a divorce granted under DMMA, though in the latter instance the judge is a civil, not a religious, judge.

Both Tucker and Zilfi, like some other scholars who have written on *khul*ᶜ in the Middle East, interpret their findings as indicating that the women who initiated this kind of divorce were not totally oppressed and passive in the face of marital distress. In taking advantage of the law's provisions they exerted independent agency to free themselves from unwanted entanglements. The right of a woman to initiate divorce, Zilfi says, 'validated the notion that women, too, deserved to be satisfied in their mates [and to that extent it] ... can be thought to have enhanced women's status'.[58]

However, Zilfi and other historians, to the extent that they are dependent entirely on documentary evidence, have not been in a position to look behind the scenes at the motivations of or the circumstances under which the women who brought the *khul*ᶜ cases they examined were operating. My research has some of the same limitations but I do have the advantage of having ethnographic evidence to supplement what I have found in the records. Personal interviews and observational data enable me to put my quantitative findings taken from *qazi*s' records on the incidence of *khul*ᶜ divorce into a broader social and cultural context. On this basis I argue that, although for many women the act of attempting to secure a *khul*ᶜ divorce may indeed represent a form of 'assertion of self', for many others it represents a last resort in a situation where other alternatives are lacking. Furthermore, my research suggests that to take *khul*ᶜ is not necessarily a woman's own choice at all. The decision to take this step is often one that she is pressured into by her natal family. In numerous other, even more sobering, cases, it is her husband who forces the decision upon her because, from his perspective, it is preferable to his pronouncing *talaq*.

Does the availability of extrajudicial *khul*ᶜ divorce provide those women locked in unhappy marriages a welcome and relatively easy way out? Does it empower them to exert independent agency and gain control over their lives or does it have a darker side? The answer, of course, is that both are true. There is no doubt that *khul*ᶜ meets the needs of many women who desire to divorce and are prepared to pay the price in financial insecurity and loss of social standing that accompany a marital break-up. There is no doubt that taking *khul*ᶜ is preferable in many respects to following the cumbersome and expensive route of filing a divorce suit in family court. And there is no doubt that, insofar as being able to obtain a relatively easy divorce is concerned, Muslim women have an advantage over most women of other religions. However, this provision of MPL is unfortunately open to a kind of manipulation that puts many women at a serious disadvantage. An indeterminate number of apparently 'woman-initiated' divorces are actually initiated by the husband. For many women, instead of providing the opportunity for female 'agency' in an otherwise oppressive situation, the law of *khul*ᶜ can end up subjecting her to increased force and compulsion. While the *qazi*s and other religious authorities that handle *khul*ᶜ divorces are quite aware of this problem, they are not disposed to take a very active interventionist role in trying to prevent it. Having in any case no power of enforcement, the most they feel obliged to do is to ask some questions and then, if they suspect wrongdoing, to try to use their powers of persuasion to convince the man to pronounce *talaq* instead. But a husband engaged in employing this tactic, motivated by the desire to gain financially and preserve his own reputation, is unlikely to be deterred at this point in the proceedings. For historians and anthropologists who are working with archival records, one lesson to be drawn from this research is the importance of looking beyond the written word when interpreting the significance of what the documents reveal. In relation to the specific issue of divorce under MPL today, it points to the urgent need for further detailed ethnographic investigation.

## Endnotes

[1] The original version of this paper was presented at the Annual Meeting of the Association for Asian Studies in April 2002, and was later expanded and revised for presentation at seminars at the Freie Universität, Berlin, and the universities of Köln, Heidelberg, Pittsburgh, Virginia, and Pennsylvania State. I am grateful to the organisers of each of these gatherings and to the various members of their audiences for their stimulating questions and constructive comments.

[2] See, for example, A.A.A. Fyzee, *Outlines of Mohamadan Law* (New Delhi: Oxford University Press, 1974), pp. 163–66; Syed Tahir Mahmood, *The Muslim Law of India* (Allahabad: Law Book Company, 1980), pp. 96–114; Syed Ameer Ali, *The Personal Law of the Mahommedans* (London: W.H. Allen & Co, 1980), pp. 354–73; M. Hidayatullah and A. Hidayatullah, *Mulla's Principles of Mahomedan Law* (Bombay: N.M. Tripathi Private Ltd., 1990), pp. 258–76.

[3] Tahir Mahmood, 'The Grandeur of Womanhood in Islam', *Islamic & Comparative Law Quarterly* 6(1) (1986): 11–12; and Aftab Hussain, *Status of Women* (Lahore: Law Publishing Company, 1987).

[4] Judith Tucker, 'Ties that Bound: Women and Family in Eighteenth and Nineteenth-Century Nablus', in N.R. Keddie and B. Baron, eds., *Women in Middle Eastern History* (New Haven: Yale University Press, 1991), p. 241 and *In the House of the Law: Gender and Islamic Law in Ottoman Syria and Palestine* (Berkeley: University of California Press, 1998), pp. 95–100; Madeline C. Zilfi, '"We Don't Get Along": Women and *Hul* Divorce in the Eighteenth Century', in M.C. Zilfi, ed., *Women in the Ottoman Empire* (Leiden: Brill, 1997), p. 271.

[5] The situation is different in Pakistan, as it is also in many Middle Eastern countries that have undergone law reform in recent years. See Lucy Carroll, 'Qur'an 2:229 "A Charter Granted to the Wife"? Judicial Khul' in Pakistan', *Islamic Law and Society* 3 (1) (1996): 91–126; Livia Holden, 'Divorce at the Woman's Initiative in South Asia and in the Diasporas' in R. Mehdi, W. Menski & J.C. Nielsen, eds., *Interpreting Divorce Laws in Islam* (Copenhagen: DJØF, 2012).

[6] I thank Werner Menski for pointing out that this statement is not entirely accurate. While *most* Hindu women must go to a civil court to obtain a divorce, the HMA makes an exception for those who belong to a locality, a tribe or community that has for a long time continuously followed customary procedures for severing the marital bond. Such a woman can divorce her husband by, for example, presenting her case before a village or caste council and/or compensating him financially for the loss of her company and services. See sections 29(2) and 3(a) of the HMA.

[7] *Mubarat* is divorce by mutual consent. Either party can initiate it and, as with *khul'*, its terms are negotiated by the spouses themselves. While recognised as a valid option in MPL, it is, as far as I have been able to determine, rarely resorted to in India.

[8] The Kazis Act explicitly refrains from conferring any administrative or judicial powers on *qazis*, and makes no mention of remuneration: see D.V. Chitaley and S. Appu Rao, *The A.I.R. Manual: Unrepealed Central Acts [Civil and Criminal]*, vol. 12 (Bombay: The All India Reporter Ltd, 1971). Some individual states have since enacted their own laws pertaining to the appointment and responsibilities of *qazis*; in their broad outlines these all follow the model of the Central Act. When it was enacted, the Kazis Act was, of course, meant to apply only in British India. Hyderabad city was at that time still under the administration of the Nizam of Hyderabad, in whose own system of Islamic jurisprudence *qazis* presided over *shari'at* courts, as well as conducting marriages and authorising divorces. That system was dismantled after the state was incorporated into the Indian Union in 1948. Note that, with regard to the spelling of this Act, it has long been the convention in India to represent the letter *qaf* with a K, rather than the more accurate Q, when transliterating Urdu words into Roman script. Similarly the word *waqf* is usually rendered as 'wakf', as in Wakf Board.

[9] There are, in addition, all over India, large numbers of non-official *qazis*, some independent and self-appointed, others connected with religious organisations or institutions, who play roles similar to the ones I describe here with respect to marriage and divorce among Muslims.

[10] It is not legally required that a Muslim cleric—or any other outside authority—be called to preside over the wedding ceremony but, in practice, the services of such an individual are almost always used.

[11] Jameela Nishat has consulted the divorce records of one Hyderabad *qazi* which she analyses in 'A Long Way to Go: Divorce Practices among Muslim Families of Hyderabad City', in I. Ahmad, ed., *Divorce and Remarriage among Muslims in India* (New Delhi: Manohar 2003), pp. 303–15. Frank Fanselow has also used mosque records to document changing patterns of Muslim marriage over several decades ('Law and Custom Reconsidered: A Comparative Study of Hindu and Muslim Inheritance Laws and Practices in Southern Tamil Nadu', unpublished paper).

[12] Although I interviewed the chief qazi of Tamil Nadu in Chennai and another *qazi* in the district town of Vaniyambadi and was able to briefly observe their modes of operation, it was only in Hyderabad that I was able to personally examine *qazis*' records.

[13] The principal responsibility of this body is, as its name implies, to oversee the financial affairs of Muslim endowments. However two decades ago, in

the wake of the infamous Shah Bano decision (*Mohd. Ahmed Khan v. Shah Bano Begum and Others*, AIR 1985 SC 945), it was charged with an additional responsibility, namely the maintenance of destitute divorced Muslim women. Thus, the 1986 Muslim Women (Protection of Rights on Divorce) Act 1986 provides that a divorcée with no earnings of her own and no adult child or other close relative financially capable of supporting her, can file suit for a maintenance award against her local Wakf Board. Although in 2001 I was told by one employee of the Andhra Pradesh State Wakf Board that it had been called upon on numerous occasions to come to the aid of such women, I was unable to obtain any details about how often this had occurred or how much had actually been paid out in this connection since the MWA was passed. However, in December 2005 a news report revealed that, up to that time, only four women were currently in receipt of maintenance stipends from the Board (*The Times of India* [Hyderabad], 'Not Many Divorcées Avail Wakf Board Scheme', 12 December 2005). This was confirmed in an interview with the Board's Law Officer, Shaik Saleem Basha, on 9 January 2006. Since that time the number of women being supported by the A.P. Wakf Board has greatly increased, doubtless because this announcement brought the availability of the option to the attention of local advocates, who almost immediately began using it to obtain financial support for their indigent divorced women clients. For more details see Ch. 8 this volume.

[14] For some years the issue of succession to the post of *qazi* has been the subject of litigation in the Andhra Pradesh High Court. The dispute, in its broad outlines, is over whether the post should be given to the 'most qualified' individual or (as has been the longstanding practice) should go automatically to a relative of the deceased or retiring office holder.

[15] Nishat says there are six ('A Long Way to Go', p. 305). In fact, in the course of my interviews I found that even the *qazi*s often differed among themselves about such seemingly straightforward matters as the number of officially recognised *sadr qazi*s in the city, their respective jurisdictions, the hierarchy of authority among them and the way in which succession to the post was handled.

[16] The *qazi* does not ask whether the *groom* has been previously married or currently has another wife, presumably because his marital history, unlike the bride's, does not affect his eligibility for marriage.

[17] In practice, this latter requirement seems not to be taken very seriously by the various *qazi*s in the city, as I discovered to my dismay when I attempted to examine the pertinent records in the Andhra Pradesh State Archives in Hyderabad. I am very grateful to the staff of the Archives for locating and making available to me such recent marriage records as they did have on hand.

[18] I would like to express my gratitude to both these individuals for their gracious cooperation with my research. For their assistance with interviews and for copying the relevant data from the documents, I thank Mr. Muhammad Ayyub and Ms. H. Rayees Fathima.

[19] The individual files of marriages and divorces are arranged in chronological order by Hijri year. However the annual marriage and divorce registers are kept according to A.D. year, perhaps because this is the calendar under which the Wakf Board operates.

[20] Of the entries, sixteen were incomplete or pertained to something other than an extrajudicial divorce by *talaq* or *khul*ᶜ. Thus three entries record the 'cancellation' of a divorce, and two recorded divorces awarded to women under the DMMA.

[21] Qazi B allowed my research assistant to hand-copy the relevant information from these forms. In order to avoid privacy issues, I chose not to have her copy any information, such as names or addresses, that would enable the parties to be identified later.

[22] According to my observations, women do not usually hesitate to speak their mind in front of the *qazi*, nor are they necessarily constrained by considerations of *purdah* to keep their faces covered before him. Even women accustomed to wearing a full *burqa* in public places frequently cast the veil aside when called up to the *qazi*'s desk to present their case.

[23] It is not unusual, very shortly after the wedding, for a man or his parents to urge—or even compel—his young bride to 'excuse' him (*mo*ᶜ*af karna*) from the obligation of making good on his promise of *mehr*. Even if she has not formally waived her rights in this way, it is still considered very bad form, indeed as unwifely behaviour in the extreme, for a married woman to demand that her husband pay what he owes her.

[24] Under Hanafi law, followed by most Indian Sunni Muslims, a divorced mother is entitled to retain custody of a son until age seven, and of a daughter until puberty, after which the father may claim them (see Fyzee, *Outlines*, p. 198). In practice, if the child is very young at the time of the divorce (which is usually the case), the father is unlikely to reclaim him, probably because, by the time the child is old enough to return to the father, the latter has remarried and started a new family and is not highly motivated to take on responsibility for a child whom he may not even have seen for many years. If the father does sue for custody, the courts may nevertheless decide that it is in the best interests of the child to remain with the mother. In practice, most such cases are dealt with outside the judicial system, but the fact that the husband *may* legally claim the child and not infrequently subject his ex-wife to repeated threats to do so, is the cause of much pain and distress for divorced young mothers.

A divorced Muslim woman can still file (under Section 125 of the Criminal Procedure Code) for an award of maintenance from their father on behalf of any minor children in her custody, though she is not entitled to claim maintenance for herself.

[25] Since passage of the MWA in 1986, there has been much controversy and a number of conflicting High Court decisions over the issue of whether a divorcing husband can be required to provide financially for his former wife even beyond the *ᶜiddat* period (cf. Flavia Agnes, *Judgement Call: An Insight into Muslim Women's Right to Maintenance* [Mumbai: Majlis, 2001]). In 2001 this question was answered in the affirmative by the Supreme Court in *Danial Latifi v. Union of India* (AIR 2001 SC 3958). However, it is not yet known how much difference this has made for the average Muslim divorced woman or even for those who have actually approached the lower courts to demand that their husbands provide for them over the longer term. In order to shed some light on this, I have collected data from the Hyderabad magistrate's court on suits filed by divorced women under the MWA since 1995. Many of these women have asked for—and in numerous cases have received—lump sum payments as 'reasonable and fair provision' for their future. See my 'Maintenance for Divorced Muslim Women' in this volume.

[26] Sylvia Vatuk, 'Domestic Violence and Marital Breakdown in India: A View from the Family Courts', in Lina Fruzzetti and Sirpa Tenhunen, eds., *Culture, Power, and Agency: Gender in Indian Ethnography* (Calcutta: Stree, 2006), pp. 204–26.

[27] The logic of this is unclear, since with few exceptions the divorces being registered are described as 'irrevocable' (*talaq-ul bain*), after which reconciliation would be impossible in any case. However, it does seem that there is considerable confusion in the minds of all of the Hyderabad *qazis* whom I interviewed about the true meaning of the phrase *talaq-ul bain.* Whereas in Arabic its literal meaning, as I have noted, is 'irrevocable divorce', the *qazis* whose records I examined insisted that it signifies a *single* divorce! One of them further explained that he always tells clients to say *talaq-ul bain*, rather than 'triple *talaq*' or 'three times *talaq*', *in order to ensure that, if they later change their minds, they can revoke it*! They firmly dismissed my feeble attempts to correct them. The professional local translator whom I employed to render Qazi A's divorce register into English made a similar but not identical error, translating *talaq-ul bain* not as 'single' but as 'twice' *talaq*!

For a long time I was at a loss to explain this inconsistency, which clearly has important implications for how one interprets the documentary evidence on *talaq* found in their records. Later, however, I accidentally found in a mid-nineteenth century work on Muslim law, a passage suggesting that this particular 'misperception' has a very long history in southern India. In an appendix entitled 'Divorce, According to Ordinary Custom', the author cites to that effect an 1832 account of marriage and divorce practices in the Deccan which 'does not profess to treat of *legal* subjects, but ... is held in high repute as an authority on Mahomedan *customs*' (italics in original) (W.H. Macnaghten, *Principles and Precedents of Moohummudan Law...*, 2nd ed. (Madras: Higginbotham & Co, 1890), p. 395.

The work to which Macnaghten refers is Jaffur Shurreef's *Qanoon-e-Islam*, or *Customs of the Moosulmans of India; Comprising a Full and Exact Account of Their Various Rites and Ceremonies from the Moment of Birth till the Hour of Death*, translated by G.A. Herklots (London: Parbury, Allen, and Co., 1832). See also my 'Shurreef, Herklots, Crooke, and Qanoon-E-Islam: Constructing an Ethnography of "the Moosulmans of India"', *South Asia Research* 19(1) (1999): 5–28. According to Shurreef, there are three forms of 'divorce by repudiation'. If the phrase 'I divorce you' is spoken only once, the divorce is called '*tulaq-e-byn*'. The husband may retract this divorce and the couple resume married life without any ceremony within the wife's subsequent three menstrual periods. After a second *talaq*, Shurreef's '*tulaq-e-rujaee* [*rajai*]', the couple must renew their marriage vows before resuming conjugal relations. But after a third pronouncement of *talaq* ('*tulaq-e-mootuluqqa* [*mutalaqa*]') the divorce becomes irrevocable (*Qanoon-e-Islam*, pp. 146–47).

[28] This is true of Egypt, for example. See Andrea Rugh, *Family in Contemporary Egypt* (Syracuse: Syracuse University Press, 1984), pp. 175–82. In countries where divorce is not strongly disapproved of, both divorce rates and rates of remarriage for both sexes tend to be correspondingly relatively high, though still much lower than in western countries. In Egypt in 1994, for example, there were 1.55 divorces each year per 1,000 population, in comparison with 0.46 in Turkey and 4.57 in the United States (Rita J. Simon & Howard Altstein. *Global Perspectives on Social Issues: Marriage and Divorce* [Lanham, MD: Lexington Books, 2003], pp. 23–24).

[29] For example, in my sample of 260 marriages registered in 1990–91 by Qazi A, the amounts ranged from Rs. 500 to Rs. 51,000, with a mean of Rs. 8,200. Half of the women sampled had been promised less than Rs. 5,000. Ten years later the mean amount of *mehr* had almost doubled. However, in order to properly assess the significance of this increase it would, of course, be necessary to take into account the rate of inflation during the period.

[30] A third option, if one wants to avoid paying the *mehr*, is to simply abandon the wife or expel her from the marital home without giving her a formal divorce. This way of freeing oneself from an unwanted wife is extremely common, perhaps more so than the 'triple *talaq*', especially among the poor and less well-educated.

[31] It should be noted that a Muslim woman is entitled to sue under the MWA or in a civil court for her unpaid *mehr*, but unless the amount sought is substantial it is rarely worth her while to do so.

[32] Thirty-eight women in her sample had initiated their own divorce, 35 of them through a *qazi* or 'marriage council'. Thus, of the 62 women *who could legitimately have claimed their mehr*, almost two-thirds (i.e., 40 women) *did in fact receive it* (Munira Merchant, 'Divorce Among Indian Muslims: Survey Report from Bombay and Pune', *Manushi* 77 [1993]: 9–12). Indeed, the actual success rate for those eligible to obtain their *mehr* may have been even higher than this, inasmuch as some of those who did not get it may have already 'forgiven' it earlier in the marriage and therefore no longer had a valid claim.

[33] S.A.H. Moinuddin, *Divorce and Muslim Women* (Jaipur: Rawat Publications, 2000), p. 146, and 'Divorce and Separation among Muslims in West Bengal', in I. Ahmad, ed., *Divorce and Remarriage among Muslims in India* op. cit., pp. 161–78.

[34] Zakiya Rafat, 'Muslim Women's Divorce and Remarriage in a Town of Western Uttar Pradesh', in I. Ahmad, op. cit., pp. 89–92.

[35] Contrary to the popular stereotype, my investigations suggest that most divorces are not pronounced on the spur of the moment on an unsuspecting wife who is still living together with her husband. In most cases there has been a lengthy period of persistent marital discord, into which other members of the family, and often community leaders, the caste panchayat, the *jamaᶜat* of the local mosque, social workers, and even the police may be drawn to mediate. By the time the man has decided to pronounce *talaq*, the couple is often already informally separated.

[36] Jameela Nishat, 'A Long Way to Go', pp. 305–6.

[37] In fact, in 2012 a case of this very kind came before the Madras high court. *S. Basheria vs. The State of Tamil Nadu* was a writ petition, brought by a woman who charged the Chief Qazi of Tamil Nadu with affixing his signature and stamp to a *khulᶜnama* that bore her forged signature. Her husband has written it, without her knowledge, had two witnesses sign it, and brought it to the *dar-ul-quzat* to be registered. The court agreed that the document was fraudulent but dismissed her petition pending the outcome of her husband's trial for forgery in a separate criminal case.

[38] This procedure is called *faskh*. In Hyderabad and Chennai there was unanimous agreement among the *qazis* I spoke to that they do not have the authority to dissolve a marriage in this way. But the procedure is apparently used by *qazis* elsewhere in India, including those associated with the *Imarat Shariah*, an institution established in Bihar in 1921 and since spread to some other states, for the purpose of providing a religious venue for the settlement of Muslim disputes outside the state-run judicial system. Its officers settle

cases involving issues of personal law according to what they consider the 'original Islamic juridical' principles. See Sabiha Hussain, 'Male Privilege, Female Anguish: Divorce and Remarriage among Muslims in Bihar', in I. Ahmad, ed. op. cit., pp. 263–89.

In August 2005, the existence and legitimacy of this and other so-called 'shari'at courts' was challenged by a public interest petition submitted to the Supreme Court of India. See 'India: Supreme Court to Rule on Religious Courts', *New York Times*, 18 August 2005, p. A12; Sharat Pradhan, 'Supreme Court Notice on Religious Courts Draws Flak', *Indo-Asian News Service,* 17 August 2005, http://www.eians.com/stories/2005/08/17/17sup.shtml (last accessed 17 September 2005).

In July 2014, the Supreme Court finally issued a ruling in this case, *Vishwa Lochan Madan vs Union of India & Ors* (http://indiankanoon.org/doc/22464727 [last accessed 28 August 2015]). The two-judge bench refused to ban *shari'at* courts, while also emphasising—as did the All India Muslim Personal Law Board itself in its testimony opposing the writ petition—that the decisions of such bodies have no legal standing and are not enforceable, either by themselves or by the state. For reactions to the decision by some of the concerned parties, see 'India rejects ban on Islamic courts', 7 July 2014, http://aljazeera.com/news/asia/2014/07/india-rejects-ban-islamic-courts-2014779525449676.html (last accessed 28 August 2015).

[39] For further details about the events and controversies leading up to the passage of the DMMA, see Syed Tahir Mahmood, *Muslim Personal Law: Role of the State in the Indian Subcontinent* (Bombay: The All India Reporter Ltd., 1983); Shahida Lateef, *Muslim Women in India: Political and Private Realities: 1890s-1980s* (New Delhi: Kali for Women, 1989); Muhammad Khalid Masud, 'Apostasy and Judicial Separation in India', in M.K. Masud, B. Messick and D.S. Powers, eds., *Islamic Legal Interpretation: Muftis and Their Fatwas* (Cambridge, MA: Harvard University Press, 1996), pp. 193–203; Gail Minault, 'Women, Legal Reform, and Muslim Identity', *Comparative Studies of South Asia, Africa and the Middle East* 17(2) (1997): 1–10; Rohit De, 'Mumtaz Bibi's Broken Heart: The Many Lives of the Dissolution of Muslim Marriages Act, 1939,' *Indian Economic and Social History Review* 28(4) (2009): 105–130 and 'The Two Husbands of Vera Tiscenko: Apostasy, Conversion and Divorce in Late Colonial India', *Law and History Review* 28(4) (2010): 1011–1041.

[40] It would be fruitful to explore the question of how rates of resort to DMMA compare with those to the IDA, HMA and SMA. Due to time constraints, I was not able to gather the data for such a comparative analysis. I did, however, randomly select the year 1992 for recording some basic information on every divorce suit filed by a woman in Chennai family courts. In that year only six suits were filed (by Muslim women) under DMMA, while 197 suits

(excluding suits for divorce by mutual consent) were filed, under one of the three other relevant divorce laws, by women of other religions. This works out to 1.8 divorce suits initiated by women per 1,00,000 Muslim inhabitants of the city as against 5.5 per 1,00,000 inhabitants of other religions. These figures strongly suggest that, at least in this city, non-Muslim women file for divorce more frequently than do Muslim women. The factors contributing to this disparity in rates of resort to the civil statutes governing divorce are complex and varied and cannot be adequately explored here.

41 See Devendra Kumar Tiwari and Mahmood Zaidi, *Commentaries on the Family Courts Act, 1984* (Allahabad: Alia Law Agency, 1997). By 1994 there were 50 such courts in operation (*Justice Delivery through Family Courts. Proceedings of the National Conference* [New Delhi: National Commission for Women, 1994], p. 19). According to the most recent data available, the number had risen to only 153 by 2009 and several states had not even begun to implement the FCA by that time (Namita Singh Jamwal, 'Have Family Courts Lived Up to Expectations?' *Mainstream* 47[12] [2009], http://mainstreamweekly.net/article1205.html (last accessed 27 August 2015). The first family court in Delhi was not set up until May that year, though by 2012 a total of nine courtrooms in four different locations throughout the city were adjudicating family law suits exclusively (http://delhifamilycourts.gov.in/history.html [last accessed 27 August 2015]).

42 In 1991, there were 14,02,973 Muslims in Hyderabad, whereas the Muslim population of Chennai was only 3,33,672.

43 While Islamic law neither requires nor condones giving a 'dowry' to the daughter when she marries, the practice is very widespread among Indian Muslims. In Hyderabad a cash gift to the groom, presented under the guise of covering the cost of his wedding outfit (*jore ki raqm* or *ghora jora*), has acquired increasing importance in recent years. See my 'The "Cancer of Dowry" in Indian Muslim Marriages: Themes in the Popular Rhetoric from the South Indian Muslim Press', in M. Hasan, ed., *Living with Secularism: The Destiny of India's Muslims* (New Delhi: Manohar Publishers and Distributors, 2006), pp. 155–76 (reprinted in this volume. See Ch. 3).

44 My research suggests that, contrary to popular stereotypes, Muslim divorcées rarely remarry. For example, in only four percent of the 3,515 marriages conducted by Qazi A in 1990–91 and 2001 had the bride been married before. Of these, only a third were divorcées; the rest were widows.

Unless a divorcée is very young and has no children, her chances of remarriage are very poor. She will not attract a groom with the most sought-after qualifications and will probably have to settle for a man who is himself divorced or widowed, considerably older than her and possibly with children of his own for whom he needs a caretaker. Furthermore, few prospective husbands are willing to accept into their home a child from a woman's previous marriage and women are usually unwilling to give up their children in exchange for the questionable security of a second marriage. For further discussion of this matter see my 'Muslim Women and Personal Law,' in R. Menon and Z. Hasan, eds., *In a Minority: Essays on Muslim Women in India* (New Delhi: Oxford University Press, 2005), pp. 18–68 (reprinted in this volume, see ch. 2).

[45] See FCA, Chapter IV, 13: 'Notwithstanding anything contained in any law, no party to a suit or proceeding before a family court shall be entitled, as of right, to be represented by a legal practitioner: Provided that if the family court considers it necessary in the interest of justice, it may seek the assistance of a legal expert as *amicus curiae*'. However, in 1991 the Bombay High Court ruled that barring lawyers from representing clients in family court proceedings presents a severe handicap to litigants, particularly to those who are poor and uneducated. Since then a number of other High Courts have issued similar judgments and in most family courts today lawyers are routinely allowed to appear on behalf of litigants, much as they do in any other civil court (see Flavia Agnes, *Family Law, Volume II: Marriage, Divorce, and Matrimonial Litigation* [New Delhi: Oxford University Press, 2011], pp. 294–299).

[46] In rural areas or in cities and towns that lack specialised family courts, the regular civil courts, where different rules about legal representation apply, handle divorce suits.

[47] Some limited financial assistance is available to impoverished women in the form of state-funded legal aid programmes. See Roma Mukherjee, *Women, Law and Free Legal Aid in India* (New Delhi: Deep & Deep Publications, 1998).

[48] I base this description mainly on my 1998–99 observations in the Chennai family court (see my *Muslim Women*). Conditions and facilities are somewhat better in other places and may well have also improved in Chennai since I was there last.

[49] Before passage of the Family Courts Act in 1984 all personal law cases were handled in the regular civil courts, where the backlog often made the wait for a divorce interminable. One of the main goals of the Act's original proponents was to shorten the time which disputing couples would have to spend waiting for a judgment. Anecdotal evidence suggests that the situation has improved somewhat, though statistics on the matter are lacking.

[50] Mahmood, 'The Grandeur', pp. 11–12.

[51] Syed Tahir Mahmood, *Statute Law Relating to Muslims in India: A Study of Constitutional and Islamic Perspectives* (New Delhi: Institute of Objective Studies, 1995), p. 136.

[52] To be fair to Mahmood, I should point out that, replying to Lucy Carroll's 'Rejoinder' (in *Islamic and Comparative Law Quarterly* 6[4] [1986]: 295–305),

to his assertion (in 'The Grandeur') that *in Islam* women have the same rights as men to dissolve an unhappy marriage, he insists that in that essay he had only intended to outline 'the *theory* of Islamic teachings on women's rights', not to address questions of the actual practice in the Indian subcontinent, which, he acknowledged, often deviates greatly from what the religion prescribes (see p. 305).

[53] *Marium Bibi v. Nur Mahommad*, (1882) All. 83.

[54] Lucy Carroll, 'Rejoinder', p. 296. In so effectively disposing of the question of putative 'gender equality' under the Islamic law of *khul*ᶜ and *talaq*, Carroll leaves open the question of whether the availability of *khul*ᶜ in MPL might not still contribute to the relative bargaining power of wives versus husbands in Muslim marriages. In a personal communication Carroll has raised the question of to what extent an extrajudicial *khul*ᶜ divorce would be recognised as valid by the courts if, for example, upon her remarriage it were to be challenged by her first husband. I have not yet had the opportunity to carefully study the relevant case law on this point. However, a cursory online search for the words '*khul*', '*khula*' or '*khoola*' among high court and Supreme Court decisions cited in the *indiankanoon.org* database reveals that they occur very seldom. Furthermore, wherever they *do* occur, the issue at hand is not whether a woman who obtained a *khul*ᶜ is legally divorced: the judiciary appears to take this for granted. Instead, most such cases revolve around questions of whether, at what point in time, or how and by whom a *khul*ᶜ contract was signed or agreed to, what its terms were and whether or not the parties have fulfilled them.

[55] Andrea B. Rugh, *Family in Contemporary Egypt* (Syracuse: Syracuse University Press, 1984), p. 177.

[56] Tucker, 'Ties that Bound', pp. 240–41.

[57] *Hul* is the Turkish spelling of the Arabic *khul*ᶜ.

[58] Zilfi, '"We Don't Get Along"', p. 295.

# 5.
# Islamic Feminism in India
## Muslim women activists and the reform of Muslim Personal Law[1]

### Introduction
In recent years, growing numbers of Muslim women have been publicly calling for the reform of Muslim Personal Law (MPL), justifying their demands for gender equity with religious arguments, referring to the authority of the Qur'an rather than to the Indian Constitution or to universal principles of human rights that have long guided secular feminists in their campaigns for a gender-neutral uniform civil code. These women are part of a trend observable all over the Muslim world, in which 'a new breed of Muslim women scholar-activists'[2] is seriously and critically studying the foundational texts of their religion. They are

> challeng[ing] conventional histories and canonical texts ... pointing to the openness of the Qur'an and Sunna to *ijtihad* ... looking at the context in which the Qur'an was revealed ... [and] applying this understanding to the present so as to question the ways in which Islamic knowledge has been produced.[3]

Scholars of the Middle East began to use the term 'Islamic feminism' in the 1990s for movements then gaining prominence in Egypt, Iran and elsewhere, in which women were attempting, 'through a rereading of the Qur'an and early Islamic history' to 'reclaim their religion ... [and] undermine both Islamist patriarchal distortions and Western stereotypes of Islam as backward and terroristic'.[4] While the goals of these Islamic feminists—to achieve greater gender equity under the law and in society more generally—are similar to those pursued by secular feminists, their understanding of the sources of male bias in Muslim societies and many of the remedies they propose to combat it, are different.

Many scholars have questioned whether those whose aim is to get women their Qur'anic rights can be called 'feminists' at all, and the related issue of whether an 'Islamic approach' to gender justice is in any way viable, has aroused strenuous scholarly debate.[5] Moghissi, for example, sees a real risk that if Iranian women are pushed into accepting an 'Islamic feminist' approach as 'the *only* "culturally suitable" or workable' one, any chances of achieving true gender equity will be foreclosed.[6] Muslim women activists in India do not have to contend with the force of an authoritarian Islamic state, but their adversary, a well-entrenched and widely influential male religious establishment, is only slightly less intimidating. Insofar as they choose to confine themselves to 'changing MPL from within', rely on the Qur'an for guidance and side with the *ᶜulama* in their rejection of state intervention, they risk having to scale back their aspirations for gender equity under the law.

Nair has a slightly different but related fear. 'It may be too early', she says, 'for feminists to take heart' from the growth of Islamic feminism in India, because blatant challenges to the authority of the *ᶜulama* may have 'the unfortunate consequence of providing a rallying point for a new patriarchal unity',[7] leading to renewed attempts to make women give priority to community solidarity over the pursuit of their own interests as women. I am somewhat more optimistic than Nair on this point. It seems unlikely to me that the women whose activities I will describe here will allow themselves to be distracted by religious identity-based appeals of this kind. This is especially true of those among them who are already more-or-less openly calling for taking the next step, working to get women their Islamic rights but preparing them to 'go beyond *shari'at*' to obtain those that the Qur'an does not provide. There is little sign that these women can be made to stop and reverse direction anytime soon.

Realistically speaking, there is, for a variety of political reasons, slim prospect that either a UCC or any new legislation within MPL will be enacted in the foreseeable future. Under these circumstances, an 'Islamic feminist' approach holds considerable promise, at least in the short run, for improving the legal lot of Muslim women. The movement may make some concrete progress towards remedying the consistent failure of the religious authorities to implement those provisions of Islamic law that were originally designed to protect women but are widely ignored in practice today. More importantly, as these activists' voices become louder and more persistent, making the Muslim community—clerical and lay alike— increasingly aware of the issues and the remedies they propose, some amount of change is inevitable. Clearly, an approach that merely seeks to obtain for women those rights provided to them in the Qur'an will not lead to complete equality of the sexes, but it is nevertheless a promising beginning.

### An Islamic feminist 'movement'?

Islamic feminist activism in India is not yet an organised 'social movement', in the strict sense of that term. It is being pursued by a rather amorphous assortment of individuals and groups, all engaged in avid discussion and debate about the negative impact of MPL on women but only loosely organised in terms of action.[8] These women share similar goals—to spread awareness of 'the correct teachings of Islam' about women's rights (*huquq-e-niswan*) and find ways to help women gain practical access to them. They employ similar arguments to justify their calls for legal reform.

Though most work quite independently or in small groups, they are well aware of one another, and even those living in distant places find or create periodic opportunities to meet and exchange ideas. Sometimes they join together, often in cooperation with sympathetic secular feminist organisations, to call a press conference, draw up and submit a petition, or demonstrate publicly against some perceived threat—whether from the state or from orthodox religious forces—to Muslim women's welfare.

How many are involved in this nascent movement is impossible to gauge. There are a few prominent activists in each of the major cities and in certain other second-tier urban centres like Lucknow, Ahmedabad, and Calicut. Some run small to medium-sized NGOs with associated staff and have a significant local 'grassroots' following. But, even if one includes the latter in the reckoning, they are far fewer than the numbers associated with 'women's wings' of Islamist reform organisations like the Tablighi Jama'at (TJ) or Jama'at-i Islami Hind (JIH).

## The All India Muslim Women's Personal Law Board

In March 2005, the formation of an All India Muslim Women's Personal Law Board (AIMWPLB) drew national and even some international media attention.[9] The organisation was conceived by a small group of prominent women who had gathered in Lucknow for a wedding. They cited as the motive for their action the failure of the mainly male All India Muslim Personal Law Board (AIMPLB)[10] to seriously come to grips with women's concerns: 'Despite prattling about working for the *rights* of the women, the men-dominated boards took no account of the *voice* of women' (emphasis mine).[11] They assembled 35 women, representing the major sects and schools of Islamic jurisprudence, including a few Hindus. They got off to a good start towards the end of February 2005, convening a mahila adalat (women's court), at which 166 cases of unilateral divorce and 'atrocities related to dowry' were registered. The alleged offenders were summoned to appear two months later to answer the charges.[12]

The AIMWPLB was greeted by condemnation and derision from members of the AIMPLB, who denied its legitimacy and questioned the women's scholarly credentials and political motives.[13] However the latter body was already becoming increasingly sensitive to charges—from both within and outside the community—of failing to address women's problems. It had begun to pay more attention to such issues at its annual meetings, and in 2001 organised a national conference to which it invited some of its more prominent female critics. Earlier, in 2000 the Board was enlarged and the number of slots reserved for 'lady members' was increased,[14] but women still represent only 12 per cent of its membership. Even if they voted as a bloc they could not seriously influence the outcome of the Board's deliberations. Some observers complain that these women do little to promote women's causes in any case, either because they genuinely share the conservative outlook of the male majority or because

> they are simply too scared to speak out against [the Board's] patently patriarchal biases ... They fear that if they do they might be accused of dividing the community or challenging the authority of the *mullahs*.[15]

In all fairness, it should be noted that several of these women have taken strong pro-woman positions during the Board's deliberations in recent years, though so far they have little to show for their efforts.[16]

Neither the women behind the Lucknow initiative nor other women's rights activists are asking that MPL be abolished or secularised, nor do most of them favour passage of a UCC. By and large they identify themselves as devout Muslims and many affirm their willingness to be governed entirely by Muslim law in the realm of family relations. But they resist being told by the AIMPLB or any other male clerical organisation what that law consists of. They insist that MPL is not 'a true reflection of the intention of the Qur'an'.[17] They consider that text to be supportive of the principle of gender equality but claim that over the centuries it has been subjected to highly 'patriarchal' readings, leading to women being deprived of many of their God-given rights. As one activist explained: 'According to most people's understanding of Islam, all of the rights belong to men, all of the duties to women!'[18] Another told me:

> There are so many rights given to women in the Qur'an that are not found in the books of any other religion, but the religious authorities mislead people, they misuse their position ... The *ʿulama* are an almost entirely male group. They give everything a patriarchal interpretation ... interpreting the texts to suit their own interests.[19]

Muslim women's rights activists assert their right to read the Qur'an for themselves and interpret it in a woman-friendly way. They point to God's command that all believers read and study the Holy Book, using their own reasoning abilities to understand it, rather than relying on intermediaries:

> The Qur'an clearly says that there is no clergy. So the *ᶜulama* have no right to tell me anything. Their job is to tell women to read the Qur'an, not to tell women what the Qur'an says![20]

In thus insisting on going back to the foundational Islamic text for guidance, they are reclaiming the right to *ijtihad* that the Sunni establishment maintains was foreclosed many centuries ago.[21]

These women also reject the notion, so often put forward by clerics to justify their opposition to state-initiated legal reform, that MPL is divinely given and therefore unalterable—they point out that MPL was created during the colonial period. Though based on Islamic law (*shari'at*), it has been modified by judicial precedent and by several legislative enactments that in each case, ironically, were initiated by representatives of the *ᶜulama.*[22] So why, they ask, cannot further changes now be introduced to benefit women?

Notwithstanding their insistence on the need for legal reform, these activists are always at pains to emphasise that neither their religion nor their personal law are ultimately responsible for Indian Muslim women's oppressed condition:

> Our women's problems are largely economic, caused by poverty, lack of education, lack of job opportunities. It is the media and the general public that always blames their problems on religion.[23]

Nevertheless, they believe that better enforcement of MPL's more woman-friendly provisions, and implementation of others in ways that enhance and safeguard women's interests, would go a long way towards easing the difficulties that so many confront as mothers, daughters, wives, co-wives, divorcées, and widows living under Muslim law.

## Muslim women's NGOs

Muslim-led women's NGOs began to make an appearance in the late 1980s. While Muslims predominate among their staff and clientele, like other feminist NGOs they welcome women of all religions, considering it antithetical to their purpose of promoting gender equality to make sectarian distinctions among themselves or among those they serve. For some, the fact that they came into being in times of heightened communal unrest reinforces their commitment to 'communal harmony'.[24] The main focus of most of these NGOs is similar: aiding and 'empowering' poor, illiterate, abandoned, and otherwise marginalised women, especially victims of domestic violence, while 'raising their consciousness' about the sharp gender inequities that exist in their society and the need to strive to overcome them. Their concern with larger issues of legal reform is usually an outgrowth of these more service-oriented activities.

### Awaaz-e-Niswaan

One of the oldest, largest and most well-established Muslim-led women's NGOs is the Mumbai-based Awaaz-e-Niswaan (AeN, 'women's voice'), founded in 1987. In 2005 it occupied several rooms on the first floor of a seven-storey walk-up building, a former Jain school in the heavily Muslim neighbourhood of Dongri. The organisation offers literacy classes and teaches work skills to poor women, giving them the tools to both support themselves financially and deal self-confidently and effectively with the larger world around them. It also provides once-a-week marital 'counselling' sessions, run by peer counsellors who, in some cases, initially came to AeN seeking assistance with their own problems and then stayed on to use what they had learned to help others.

These sessions follow a pattern familiar in the world of the Indian feminist mahila mandal (women's circle). Women gather at an appointed time, often accompanied by a close relative or neighbour and frequently carrying small children in their arms.

Each new 'case' is registered in a large ledger and is called upon to tell her story, to speak out, to hold nothing back. The counsellors listen attentively and usually sympathetically, only occasionally expressing irritation when someone wanders off the point or gets overly excited or hysterical. There are frequent interruptions as the narrator's supporters contribute additional information, make corrections and offer their own opinions. Audience members, those waiting to present their own tales of woe, listen avidly, sometimes expressing sympathy or offering unsolicited suggestions. The counsellors probe for further details before conferring as a group to consider possible courses of action.

The next step is usually to summon the husband for a hearing. Should he fail to appear, a delegation may be sent to fetch him. AeN prefers, if possible, to reconcile the couple or at least broker a settlement agreeable to both parties, but the ultimate outcome of many of these disputes is a separation or divorce. Sometimes AeN calls upon a sympathetic religious functionary for help. Aisha, for example, had returned to her parents' home after suffering physical abuse from her husband for four years. 'I wanted to be rid of him', she told me. 'I didn't want to have his name, to be known as Rashid ki bibi (Rashid's wife)'. Her family pleaded with him to divorce her but he refused, saying that divorce was not customary in his family. So AeN persuaded a local cleric to dissolve the marriage without his consent by *faskh-e-nikah.*[25] Aisha then completed high school and found a job: 'Now that I can earn myself, I don't want to be dependent on anyone. I am very happy, living a free life!' While she could now legally remarry, she is reluctant to risk becoming trapped in another unhappy marriage.

When a husband proves recalcitrant, AeN sometimes resorts to veiled (or even not-so-veiled) threats. They may indicate to him that if he refuses to listen to reason they will assist his wife in filing for a maintenance award, or will go with her to the police station to file a charge of cruelty or dowry harassment under Section 498A of the Indian Penal Code. Farzana came to AeN when her husband married a second time and moved out, leaving her and her children behind in his parents' home. A delegation from AeN went to see her husband's uncle who owned the house in which they were living. He was sympathetic to Farzana's plight and agreed to set her up in a small house of her own, but her husband refused to contribute to her living expenses, claiming that he could not afford to support two families. So AeN took her to the 'legal centre' of Majlis, a secular women's NGO with whom they have a cooperative relationship, and with their help Farzana obtained a maintenance order against him.[26]

AeN also brings women together for regularly scheduled informal gatherings where they socialise, share personal experiences, sing uplifting songs and lend one another moral support in times of domestic crisis. In 1999, these meetings were being held in a small rented room, up some rickety stairs, above the Laxmi Beer Bar. One day ten women had gathered, including AeN's coordinator, Hasina Khan, and two other staff members. They sat sociably in a circle on the floor, discussing recent happenings in the neighbourhood and in their lives, filling me in on the background of their own involvement with AeN. Just as one woman was winding up her tale of dowry harassment at the hands of her husband and in-laws, a youngish man burst into the room and thrust a plastic folder into Hasina's hands. It transpired that a few weeks earlier he had been summoned to AeN because his wife had come there seeking help in filing for divorce. They had been married for four years but, according to her, he was impotent and the marriage had not been consummated. He had denied his wife's allegations that day and now had come to deliver the results of a medical examination that he claimed would prove that he was capable of sexual intercourse. He was alternately deferential and belligerent. He insisted that not only was he not impotent, but that he had had sex with his wife 50 times in the early weeks of marriage, 'not only at night but in the daytime too!' At this, all of the women in the room began to giggle; Hasina tried to maintain her composure but soon started laughing as well. He was clearly embarrassed but would not drop the subject. 'It is a matter of her word against mine. If she will place her hand on the Qur'an and swear that we never had intercourse, I will accept it.' Hasina protested: 'Here we don't do any swearing on the Qur'an. If you want to do that, do it in your own home or somewhere outside, not here.' She agreed to find a physician to interpret his medical reports and promised to contact him again. After he left they all had a good laugh at his expense and at Hasina's as well, for having been unable to retain a more professional demeanour during the encounter.

For special events AeN can assemble an even larger number of women. Two months prior to the meeting I attended, members of AeN and other women's NGOs had plastered the city with posters protesting the Shiv Sena's attempts to suppress showings of the Deepa Mehta film, *Fire.* A few years later, in July of 2005, they mustered a 100-strong group, 'many of them wearing burqas ... carrying roughly made cut-outs of maulanas with their faces crossed out', to shout provocative slogans against attempts by the Tablighi Jama'at, in one heavily Muslim neighbourhood of the city, to suppress the singing and ceremonies customarily performed by women at weddings.[27]

## Muslim women's networks

A number of 'networks' or 'coalitions' of Muslim women's organisations have also come into existence in recent years. Two of the earliest of these were the Muslim Women's Forum (MWF) in Delhi and the Federation of Muslim Women of Bangalore (FEMWOB). Rather than help individual women, they strive to develop a dialogue—among themselves, with the clerical establishment and within the larger community—on women's issues. To this end they hold conferences at which resolutions are passed and issued to the press, and organise rallies, often in conjunction with secular women's organisations. They run 'legal awareness camps' for poor women in rural areas and urban slums and occasionally investigate and even intervene when an 'anti-woman *fatwa*' issued by clerics somewhere in the country draws widespread public attention.[28]

*Muslim Women's Rights Network*

The most successful and longest surviving coalition, and the one that until 2007 had the most national reach, is the All India Muslim Women's Rights Network (MWRN). It was started in 1999 in Mumbai by leaders from Women's Research and Action Group (WRAG) and AeN. Their first conference was attended by approximately 250 women, including a few Hindus, from 25 different organisations. Issues of child custody, guardianship and adoption, women's rights in the marital home, compulsory registration of marriage and divorce, *mehr*, a proposed model *nikahnama*, and the need for a ban on 'instantaneous divorce' were on the agenda.[29] Thereafter they began meeting once or twice a year, each time in a different city. The November 2005 gathering, for example, attended by 300 women and a few men, was held in Lucknow. On the agenda were sessions on the role of the state in protecting women's rights, the threat posed by 'anti-woman *fatwas*', the impact of communal violence on Muslim women and the challenges ahead for Muslim women's activism.[30]

*Bharatiya Muslim Mahila Andolan*

In 2007, a new national organisation dedicated to voicing the concerns of Muslim women was inaugurated at a meeting in New Delhi that was attended by more than 350 Muslim women from across the country, along with many academics, social activists, and government officials, many of them non-Muslim. Prior to this convention, according to one of its founding members, there had been much discussion about what to call the new organisation. The final choice was made in accordance with the group's desire to emphasise among themselves and convey to outsiders that they were a national 'movement' comprised of 'women' who identify as both 'Indian' and 'Muslim': hence the name Bharatiya Muslim Mahila Andolan (BMMA, 'Indian Muslim Women's Movement').[31] At that time the organisation claimed to have already enrolled 5,000 members from throughout the country; its membership had reportedly grown to 23,000 by 2011, 42,000 in 2013[32] and, according to a recent news report, now numbers 'over 70,000 members'.[33]

As these numbers suggest, the BMMA has a very different organisational structure from that of the MWRN and other earlier Muslim women's rights networks. Rather than being a coalition of like-minded NGOs, the BMMA is a mass organisation, enrolling individuals as members. Like most other Muslim-led NGOs and networks, it welcomes non-Muslims to join its organisation: in 2011 they made up 10 per cent of the total. It enrolls some men as well, but the BMMA has a specific policy of reserving its leadership roles and 70 per cent of its membership for Muslim women. This is based on their belief that the mainstream women's movement in India has historically been so dominated by upper-caste/class Hindu women that the concerns of Muslim women have never been given the attention they deserve.[34]

The BMMA has branches in 15 states, all guided by its core values of democracy, secularism, equality, non-violence, human rights, and justice, 'as enshrined in the Constitution of India'.[35] Each branch initiates and carries out its own projects to ameliorate the overall conditions of the local Muslim community—in particular, its women—while also helping the latter 'to raise [their] voice at the national level'.[36] The main foci of these projects are those that the movement has identified as particularly critical for the Muslim community, namely education, livelihood, health, social security and law reform—areas in which Muslims are (in the Andolan's own words) known to be 'extremely backward'.

Thus, for example, efforts have been instituted in various states to enable girl dropouts to gain re-admission to their former schools, in some cases providing books and special coaching classes as well.

Other BMMA state units run general education classes and literacy instruction for adult Muslim learners, provide scholarships for female college students, and so on. The Tamil Nadu branch of the BMMA has focused upon increasing awareness of, and facilitating access, by Muslims to various government welfare schemes for which they are eligible but have not previously taken advantage of in significant numbers. BMMA activists in Maharashtra have directed their efforts towards the economic betterment of the community, for example by targeting corrupt practices in the distribution of food rations to the poor. In other states, local branches have emphasised vocational training for Muslim women and worked to enhance their access to small business loans.[37]

Legal reform is thus only one of several items on the BMMA agenda, but it appears—at least if its media coverage is any indication—to be the one that the national headquarters is most directly and actively involved in. In line with its commitment to equality and democratic decision-making within the organisation, a number of 'state consultations' were held to discuss issues of Muslim Personal Law before the leadership began its long-term project of designing and working for the codification of a more 'woman-friendly' set of family laws for Indian Muslims. At these meetings, participants were encouraged to identify those aspects of the present code that affect them most negatively, to prioritise their concerns and to suggest specific reform measures. To date, the organisation's main concrete accomplishment in this area has been to draw up a 'model *nikahnama*' that, since it was issued in 2008, is said to have been used by 40 marrying couples in Mumbai and in 200 group marriages in one district of Gujarat.[38]

Since publishing its *nikahnama*, the BMMA has not only grown in terms of membership but, through its many branches all over India, has actively pursued its agenda of 'empowering Muslim women...to ensure their social, economic, political, civil, legal, and religious rights'.[39] Among its most noteworthy accomplishments have been the establishment in 2013 of four 'women's *shari'at* courts'—in Pune, Ahmedabad, Mumbai and Dindigul (Tamil Nadu).[40] Then, in June 2014 it released a draft Muslim Marriage and Divorce Act, 'based on the values and principles of the Qur'an', with provisions favouring women's interests, to replace provisions in the uncodified MPL that are biased towards men.[41] In addition, the organisation has conducted and published the findings of a national survey of 4,710 mostly poor Muslim women in ten states, concerning both their current personal situations and their views about the desirability of reforming MPL, particularly with regard to its provisions on the minimum marriage age for girls, *mehr*, polygamy, 'triple *talaq*', and inheritance. Not surprisingly, they found that, in each of these areas, between 75 to 93 per cent of those surveyed agreed on the need for significant changes in the relevant laws, which currently greatly favour men over their female counterparts.[42]

## Women leaders

Muslim women's rights activists are quite diverse in terms of such variables as social class, sectarian affiliation, educational background, the amount of time they commit to the cause, and the degree of Islamic expertise they command. Some come from the same elite, *sharif* Muslim families that produced the early twentieth century women reformers.[43] However, the class origins of most of the current leadership are more modest. While almost all whom I interviewed have degrees from English-medium colleges, many were raised in lower-middle class, non-English-speaking homes and are among the first women in their families to have been educated to this level.

Several of the activist leaders were inspired by personal hardship to devote themselves to bettering the lives of others. The father of Hasina Khan was reportedly an alcoholic, sometimes violent, who 'gambled away the family's money', forcing her mother to work as a maid and seamstress. Her brother went to work in the Gulf to help support the family, but he later squandered all that they had saved from his earnings and turned to a life of crime. Hasina struggled to remain in school and work her way through college, experiences that led her 'to recognise the injustices of patriarchy'.[44]

Sharifa Khanam is founder of an NGO called STEPS in Pudukkottai, Tamil Nadu, that aids victims of domestic violence. She spearheaded a controversial and widely publicised campaign to build an all-women mosque. Born 'the tenth child of a poor rural family ... [she] grew up without a father'. Due to their poverty, her family was never able to arrange her marriage and she has remained single to this day. It is perhaps for this reason that she regards the custom of 'dowry' as one of the most serious problems facing Muslim women today.[45]

Rehana Sultana, Director of the Centre for Women's Studies at Hyderabad's Maulana Azad Urdu University, is another well-known spokeswoman for Muslim women's legal rights, who was impelled by personal adversity to dedicate her life to empowering Muslim women. Raised in a stable, religiously observant, middle-class home, she was married while still in high school. The marriage was not a happy one and soon ended in divorce. Though her natal family gave her little financial or moral support, she was determined to finish her education; eventually she completed high school, a BA, MA, PhD, and a law degree. In addition to her university job, she runs a school for girls in a building adjoining her home in a Muslim-dominated area of the old city and devotes her weekends to a small NGO, Bazm-e-Shama-e-Niswan, that provides marriage counselling and legal advice to troubled women. After what she has suffered, she says, she wants to save others from a similar fate.[46]

## Legal reform priorities

Close to the top of most activists' list of priorities is the issue of male-initiated, extrajudicial, unilateral divorce, especially the infamous instantaneous divorce by 'triple *talaq*'. The women do not usually speak out against extrajudicial divorce *per se*, in as much as it is clearly allowed by Islamic law, but they insist that if a man wishes to divorce his wife he should be required to do so in a 'phased' manner, pronouncing one *talaq*, then waiting for a month before uttering a second. In the meantime the two should try to reconcile their differences, with help from their respective families. Only if, after another month has passed, it is clear that their problems are irresolvable, should the man be permitted to utter the third, irrevocable *talaq*.[47]

Indeed, when pressed on the point, most clerics[48] also express disapproval of triple *talaq*, and the AIMPLB has gone on record as 'recommending' the more gradual procedure just described. In the English version of their new model *nikahnama*, the husband is '*instructed*' to '*avoid* declaring "*talaq*" thrice at a time' [italics mine], but the Board is unwilling to go any further than this, insisting that instantaneous divorce is a 'social evil', not a 'legal' one. They say they cannot either ban or invalidate divorces effected in this manner, but can only endeavour to make the faithful aware that to pronounce a 'triple *talaq*' is a morally undesirable act.[49]

Most activists would also like to make extrajudicial divorce more readily available to women. The 1939 Dissolution of Muslim Marriages Act provides a generous list of grounds on which a woman can file suit for divorce, but a 'court divorce' is expensive and time-consuming and a woman who resorts to it risks social disapproval. An extrajudicial *khul*$^{c}$ divorce is simply arranged and inexpensive, but it requires the husband's consent. Activists want religious functionaries to respond more sympathetically to women's applications for *khul*$^{c}$, even if their husbands refuse to cooperate or cannot be located. Alternatively, they want the *faskh-e-nikah* option to be more liberally employed. However male clerics do not generally favour making it easier for women to initiate divorce, reasoning that to do so would cause an unacceptable rise in the divorce rate. As the Secretary of the AIMPLB told me, 'We are in the business of preserving Muslim families, not contributing to their breakup!' He explained that women are too emotional to be given the privilege of divorcing on demand. If allowed to do so, they would begin divorcing their husbands on the slightest of pretexts; the result would be social chaos.[50]

Islam obliges a man to give his bride a 'dower' (*mehr*) in cash or other valuables when they marry. The amount must be recorded in every marriage contract but need not be paid immediately; in India its payment is usually deferred indefinitely. Upon pronouncing an irrevocable *talaq*, however, the man is required to hand over the full amount. In theory, this provides a woman with some insurance against hasty divorce. Should her husband divorce her anyway, the *mehr* serves as a nest-egg with which she can start a new life, but as there is no legal mechanism to enforce its payment, in practice few women ever receive it.

*Mehr* amounts are in any case often quite minimal. Women's rights activists propose that the cleric presiding over the marriage (the *nikahkhwan*) insist that the groom pledge more than a token amount and either pay it in full or fix it in terms of some material asset (like gold) whose value will rise with inflation. They also want clerics to speak out against the common practices whereby the husband persuades his new bride to waive her claim to *mehr*, or the in-laws convince a widow that if she claims her legal right to be paid her *mehr* before her deceased husband's estate is distributed among the heirs, he will suffer greatly in the afterlife. Clerics, of course, readily acknowledge that every wife is entitled to her *mehr*, if not during the marriage then certainly upon divorce or widowhood. Some even go so far as to declare it a sin to force a bride or widow to forego it, but few are prepared to take any firm measures to ensure that women actually benefit from this provision of the law.[51]

Restrictions on polygamy are also high on the agendas of Muslim women's rights activists. They contend that the Qur'anic injunction to treat multiple wives equally is clearly impossible either to comply with or to enforce; therefore, a man should be allowed to marry another wife only under very special circumstances, such as the inability of the first to bear children.[52] In that case he should be required to get his current wife's permission and the *nikahkhwan* should be required to ascertain that he has done so before proceeding with the wedding. Again, neither the AIMPLB nor other clerical bodies have shown any inclination to discourage multiple marriages by instituting such procedures.

*The model nikahnama*

In the 1990s, Muslim women activists began trying to make the community aware that the law permits a woman to specify in the marriage contract the conditions under which she is giving her assent to the match: for example, that she will be allowed to continue her education or that her husband will not take another wife during her lifetime.[53] She may even require him to agree that, should he fail to fulfil the conditions she has set, she may dissolve the marriage herself, by a procedure called *talaq-i tafweez* (delegated divorce).[54] A Mumbai group that included several lawyers, academics, and NGO leaders began drafting a model *nikahnama* that clearly presents these options. However, they found it difficult to reach unanimity on its wording. One of the main sticking points has been whether to include a mention of *talaq-i tafweez* and, if so, how. In 1994, some of the group presented a version to the AIMPLB for its consideration.[55] It tackled the problem of polygamy by including a declaration by the bridegroom as to his current marital status. If married, he is asked to affirm that his first wife is aware that he is marrying again, that he has set up a separate household for her and has made provisions for her maintenance. The document also outlines some conditions under which he may later take another wife.

Not surprisingly, the AIMPLB did not embrace this document, but it did take note of the issue, and after years of discussion and debate issued its own model *nikahnama* in April 2005.[56] While some activists welcomed this as a step in the right direction, most were extremely critical.[57] They complained that the model contract fails to address several matters of vital importance to women's interests. For example, whereas the *nikahkhwan* is instructed to establish whether the couple is eligible to marry—in terms of the prohibited degrees of kinship relationship and the woman's marital status—nowhere is he instructed to verify that they are old enough, under Indian law, to do so![58] Nowhere is it mentioned that the bride may specify the conditions under which she is marrying, nor is space provided on the form for her to set them down. There is also no mention of the option of *khul*ᶜ, by which the wife can initiate dissolution of a marriage that she considers untenable. And the only mention of polygamy is contained in instructions for the *nikahkhwan*, who is merely told to ascertain that, if the groom already has one wife, he will follow the Qur'anic injunction to treat both wives equally. How he is to determine this is not explained.

In addition to these omissions, there are a number of clauses that activists found to be highly objectionable. For example, in the list of 'guidelines' (*hidayat*) for the couple, outlining their respective marital obligations, the wife is told that it is her duty to obey her husband and never to leave the house without his permission. Activists point out that such injunctions make a mockery of the concept of gender equity.

Shortly after the AIMPLB *nikahnama* was unveiled, a group from AeN took part in a protest demonstration at which a young woman in a black burqa was photographed in the act of tearing it up.[59] The MWRN soon released a *nikahnama* of their own devising which, they claimed, would better 'protect the rights of women in times of marriage, divorce, custody, and maintenance'.[60] The AIMWPLB then issued its own sharp critique of the AIMPLB document and in January 2006 announced the formation of a 30-member committee to develop 'a set of marriage laws, which ... will safeguard [women's] interests'[61] by, among other things, specifying that the *mehr* be paid before or at the time of the *nikah*, prohibiting 'triple *talaq*', and removing the *halala* rule that requires a divorced woman who wishes to remarry her former husband to first marry and be divorced by another man.[62]

In March 2008, the AIMWPLB's new four-page 'model *nikahnama*', published in both Hindi and Urdu, was released in

Lucknow at a special meeting of the organisation. In addition to making it more difficult for a man to divorce his wife unilaterally by so-called 'triple *talaq*' and/or via modern means of communication such as instant messaging, e-mail, telephone or video conferencing, the marriage contract requires him to pay his divorced wife's *mehr* and make other financial provisions for her and their children. It also affirms the woman's right to seek an extrajudicial divorce (by *khulᶜ*) under certain conditions.[63] Other clauses require that both bride and groom have reached the legal age for marriage under Indian law and that the marriage be registered with the appropriate civil authorities.[64] Predictably, the reaction of the religious establishment to the AIMWPLB document was generally hostile. The *ᶜulama* especially objected to the latter two clauses that, if enforced would, in the view of some, seriously infringe upon Islamic law. Even the sole woman on the executive committee of the AIMPLB at that time—Begum Naseem Iqtedar Ali of Lucknow, the seat of the AIMWPLB—opined publicly that the new marriage contract simply distracts attention from more pressing issues facing the Muslim community.[65]

What is rarely openly acknowledged by those campaigning for a revised model *nikahnama*—though they are of course well aware of it—is that in actual practice few women ever have the chance even to examine their marriage contract, never mind add any stipulations to it. Negotiations over its terms are essentially limited to the question of how much is to be offered as *mehr,* and they are handled entirely by the bride's father, with no input from her. Although during the wedding ceremony she is asked to consent to the marriage, she is seldom if ever given a chance to peruse the contract at that time. So even if the clauses desired by the women activists were inserted into the AIMPLB *nikahnama*, there is little guarantee that any but a very few adult, highly educated, and personally assertive brides would be able to lay down conditions of their own choosing. Without the active cooperation, not only of the clerical establishment but of all the men who are arranging their daughters' marriages, a revised *nikahnama* would not alter the marital ground rules for the vast majority of women.

*Shari'at courts*

The AIMPLB has been trying for some time to persuade Muslims experiencing marital difficulties to approach *shari'at* courts (*dar-ul-quzat*) rather than resort to the state-sponsored judiciary. Muslim women's rights activists oppose this, as they believe that these exclusively male-run religio-legal bodies are biased against women. But they themselves are not entirely satisfied with the way the civil and criminal justice systems operate, in terms of providing solutions for women's marital and other problems. Recent moves to set up special 'women's courts' in various parts of the country reflect this attitude.[66] However, their scepticism about the law's efficacy does not prevent Muslim women's NGOs from assisting their clients to make use of the courts when alternative measures have failed.

## Ideological divisions

Whereas all of those involved in fighting for Muslim women's rights say that their goal is to achieve gender equity under the law, there are some important differences of opinion among them. The most crucial question is whether and to what extent to go beyond the boundaries set by *shari'at* in seeking equal rights for women. Noorjehan Safia Niaz, a co-director of WRAG, told me that, since there are some areas of Islamic law that are inherently biased against women, her group advocates taking what is relevant from the Qur'an while at the same time pressuring the state to codify Muslim law anew.[67] An AeN volunteer likewise told me that, while Islam gives some rights to women, there are others that are unavailable in *shari'at*. 'So we need to go outside it to provide women those rights as well. This is not to say that religious law should not be followed, but it is not enough.'[68]

The question naturally arises whether all of those who use religious arguments in arguing for gender equity are truly convinced that Islam—when interpreted 'correctly'—can provide everything that women need. The choice of an Islamic discourse can be 'both genuine—an expression of ... religious convictions—and a strategic attempt to acquire legitimacy that also serves to broaden the base of support for women's rights'.[69] Here Moghadam's distinction between 'Islamic' and 'Muslim' feminists is relevant: the latter are 'believing women who agree that Islamisation has been detrimental ... to women' and approach issues of legal reform from that perspective *but also* 'often use familiar cultural concepts and religious phrases' in order to promote their reformist goals more effectively to a Muslim audience.[70] There is reason to believe that at least some of the women whose ideas and work I have been discussing here would fall into this category.

However, there is little doubt that others sincerely believe that Islam already provides women all the rights they could possibly require. Noorjahan Begum, who runs 'women's empowerment' programmes for the Hyderabad-based COVA,[71] acknowledged that her organisation has some differences with AeN over this issue: 'They say we need to go beyond the *shari'at*, but we don't agree.' Her co-worker, Qamar, continued: 'We feel that it is enough if women get the rights that they are given by Islam.'[72] It was mainly because of their discomfort with the position taken by the leadership of MWRN on this question that they and some other groups decided to withdraw from the network a few years ago, though COVA has since returned to the fold. Divergence of opinion on this point has made it somewhat difficult for MWRN to keep its membership rolls intact, and to present a united front to the male religious establishment that most regard as their principal adversary in the battle for legal reform. But thus far it has not led to a permanent cleavage. All of those involved seem to believe that more is to be gained from continuing to work together than from allowing their differences to derail the larger effort.

That said, it may be noted that differences on this issue were at least partly responsible for the fact that in 2007 some of the groups that were formerly involved with MWRN (among them, most notably, WRAG) left that network to go on to form the BMMA. As one observer puts it: '[T]he MWRN...is tolerant but not celebratory of religion, [while] the BMMA actively engages with Islamic texts as part of their strategy.'[73] The same could also be said of the AIMWPLB, though, as Tschalaer shows in her comparative analysis of their respective *nikahnamas*, the latter organisation's use of Islamic discourse seems to be more than a purely strategic device.[74]

Whereas those who resist going beyond *shari'at* are naturally averse to state intervention in the reform of MPL, they do not necessarily rule out supporting pro-woman legislation that impinges only indirectly upon their code of personal law. For example, none of the activists to whom I spoke oppose—as does the AIMPLB and some other clerics—the application to Muslims of the Prohibition of Child Marriage Act 2006 (PCMA). Many have expressly called for the compulsory registration of marriages, though most clerics regard government attempts to institute such a requirement as interference in their personal law. They also argue that it is anyway unnecessary for Muslims, since the officiating *imam* or *qazi* already keeps a record of every marriage he performs.[75]

*Relations with the ʿulama*

There are also differences of opinion about whether and how to work with the *ʿulama* on issues of personal law. Most Muslim-led women's NGOs do maintain contacts with local *qazi*s or the *imam*s of nearby mosques and, as I have noted, regularly seek the cooperation of the more sympathetic among them when trying to help the women who come to them with marital or other problems. Some spend considerable time and effort trying to develop relationships with and keep open lines of communication with the local religious authorities. However they are often frustrated by these men's frequent reluctance or refusal to heed their recommendations when dealing with issues that affect women's well-being.

All the Muslim women's networks have also at some time or

other entered into dialogue with the higher clerical leadership, in particular with the AIMPLB. Those who are themselves members of this Board naturally believe in working closely with the *ᶜulama*, exerting whatever influence they can from within, rather than opposing them from outside. As one told me, 'One should be positive in one's approach, not confrontational.'[76] Another pointed out that, since the masses have great respect for the *ᶜulama*, it is counter-productive to tell women not to heed what they say. It is much better to show that one is willing to give them proper deference and work with them to the extent possible.[77]

The MWRN and some of the smaller coalitions, positioned well outside the AIMPLB and not so averse to confrontation, have on different occasions invited members of the Board and other prominent clerics to discuss issues of women and the law. Though there is still a large gap between what most women activists would like to see the AIMPLB do and the steps that it has actually taken, there are clear signs that the reformist women's voices are being heard by the members of this body and are even having some impact—though hardly a dramatic one—on their decision-making. Some women are pleased by the results of their efforts to exchange ideas with the Board, while others are discouraged by what they perceive as an absence of positive outcomes. Thus one of the leaders of WRAG is quoted as saying,

> For a long time we did try to dialogue with [the AIMPLB] but with each of their declarations, they haven't done enough. They had a golden opportunity to do so much [in their new *nikahnama*]. How long can we direct our energies at them? It's like banging one's head against the wall.[78]

*Presenting a public image*

Activists in the movement for Muslim women's rights often find themselves in a position of having to defend themselves against both direct attacks and more subtle, insidious insinuations from the religious leadership and from members of the wider community, including members (especially men) of their own families. The activities they engage in often preclude their conforming strictly to orthodox standards of seclusion and Islamic femininity. They are also vulnerable to criticism for putting their interests as women ahead of the community's need to maintain a united front against the communal forces rampant in society at large. Since so many Indian women's NGOs rely heavily on funding from foreign aid agencies, they are sometimes the target of suspicion on that front. Even aside from questions about the *sources* of their funding, they risk being accused of being 'in it only for the money', instead of genuinely concerned about the welfare of poor women.

The strength of their loyalty to the community is often questioned as well, especially if they also belong to non-sectarian women's organisations or to Muslim organisations that work closely with secular ones on controversial issues of current concern to Muslims. The same is true if they are closely associated with one of the secular political parties. In this case they may be suspected either of knowingly allowing themselves to be used by politicians (perhaps for personal gain) or of being unwittingly duped into participating in dubious activities harmful to the community.[79]

Women activists' Islamic credentials are routinely questioned. Even those who succeed in presenting themselves as devout Muslims can be dismissed as lacking in scholarly qualifications when they begin to cite the Qur'an or other religious sources to support their demands for gender justice. Although growing numbers of young women are being educated in women's *madrasas*, some even earning the title of *ᶜalima* (female scholar), few of them have shown an inclination to involve themselves publicly in fighting for women's rights. Activists argue that one doesn't need to be a highly-trained religious expert in order to read the Qur'an and discover for oneself that Indian Muslim women today are not being given their God-given rights. But the fact that very few of them have had a rigorous religious education makes it easy for the *ᶜulama* to dismiss them and their ideas out of hand.

*To be or not to be a feminist*

Muslim women who are pressing for social and legal change in pursuit of gender equity always have to concern themselves about 'framing' the issue of women's rights in such a way that they are not 'put on the defensive and made to prove that they are not spouting alien and western concepts'.[80] Uzma Naheed, a granddaughter of the founder of the Deoband *madrasa*, is one of the few prominent Muslim women's rights activists who has earned advanced Islamic qualifications. When I met her in her office, she was wearing a long-sleeved salwar-kameez with a headscarf tied so as to completely cover her hair and shoulders. Her husband was seated at an adjoining desk but did not take any part in our conversation. When I asked about relationships between women activists and the clergy, she said that she was able to remain on good terms with the AIMPLB leadership because,

> [A]lthough they know I am working for women, they know that I am not a feminist. It is because our religion has given us rights that I am doing this... It is important, if we want them to listen to us, that we show that we are good Muslims. By not wearing a sari, by covering our heads and so on.[81]

Hasina Khan similarly used the phrase 'not strongly feminist' when explaining to me AeN's approach to raising the consciousness of their mostly poor and uneducated women clients.[82] The reluctance that these and other activist women display to openly claim a 'feminist' identity—at least when campaigning for women's rights before a Muslim audience—is understandable, since the term has quite negative connotations, not only within this community but in India more generally. It calls up images of an excessively westernised woman, unfeminine, aggressive, antagonistic towards men, immodest, sexually loose, and careless of domestic and family responsibilities. Thus, despite sharing with self-identified feminists 'a theoretical perspective and a practice that criticises social and gender inequalities, aims at women's empowerment, and seeks to transform knowledge',[83] they shy away from adopting the label for themselves.[84]

From the other side, these women are often suspect in the eyes of their secular sisters, who tend to view them as either suffering from false consciousness or using a misplaced rhetoric as a convenient, even cynical, strategy. Even those secular feminists who recognise the difficulty of confronting an entrenched male religious establishment from within the community, and are therefore prepared to give Islamic feminists credit for standing up to be counted on the issue of Muslim women's rights, are often dubious about what they can actually accomplish. Yet, forced as these women are to operate within the contemporary context, wherein a more radical secular feminist approach is certain to attract strong community antagonism, an Islamic feminist approach may indeed be the most effective choice.

## Conclusion

I have sketched here in very broad outlines the growth and development of a nascent Islamic feminist movement in India, wherein a relatively small cohort of young to middle-aged, middle-class, college-educated Muslim women, spread throughout the country in various large and medium-sized cities, many of them long engaged in providing adult education and various kinds of social services to poor and otherwise marginalised women, have begun to campaign for changes in the way MPL is interpreted and applied, with the aim of achieving a greater degree of parity for the sexes under the law. To support their arguments for legal reform they refer chiefly to the authority of the Qur'an, which, they say, gives women many rights and benefits that are denied to them in practice.

The most immediate roots of this movement can be traced to the 1985 Supreme Court judgment in the Shah Bano case and the subsequent successful campaign by the Muslim clerical leadership to enact the MWA, making divorced Muslim women no longer eligible to sue their husbands for maintenance under the relevant provision of the Criminal Procedure Code.[85] However the broader context of its emergence lies in the process of 'fragmentation of religious authority' in the contemporary globalising Muslim world that is related to such developments as the spread of mass education, the coming of new forms of media and transport, and the growth of a mobile, worldwide labour market.[86]

With respect to issues of MPL in particular, while the *ᶜulama* continue to claim exclusive rights to interpret *shari'at*, the arenas in which it is now being discussed are opening up. Those who formerly followed clerical authorities unquestioningly are raising their independent voices and demanding to be heard. A variety of 'new people', including western-educated Muslims who lack religious credentials of the traditional sort, are participating in these conversations. Robinson has argued that in India this process began with the widespread adoption of lithographic print technology by Urdu-speaking Muslims in early nineteenth century, a process that intensified in the early twentieth century.[87] For centuries, manuscripts of the classic texts of Islam were reproduced by hand and were consequently in scarce supply. This gave religious scholars a firm monopoly on religious knowledge. The only way to study these texts was by sitting at the feet of someone to whom the knowledge they contained had been passed down orally through a long line of earlier teachers. Now they could be reproduced, in the original language or in translation, in thousands of copies. Any literate person could read them for him or herself. There was no longer any need to rely on an intermediary to explain their meaning or to give one permission (*ijazat*) to pass on what one had learned to others.

Ironically, although the *ᶜulama* themselves exploited this technology because it enabled them to disseminate religious knowledge more widely, it ultimately eroded their authority as exclusively qualified interpreters of Islam. A wide variety of competing sectarian groups soon sprang up, each with its own religious vision. In time, newer media technologies were developed—first the radio, then television, audio and video cassettes, CD-ROM and the Internet—and were enthusiastically received and utilised by such groups as well as by individual self-styled Islamic experts. In the case of the sound and visual media, the ever-expanding audience for new religious ideas included many who lack the literacy skills required to absorb them from the printed page. Even though literacy is spreading at a rapid pace throughout the Muslim world, in a country like India the number of Muslims—especially women—who are still unable to read remains high. By whatever means they are exposed to new religious ideas, members of the modern audience are not simply passively taking them in. They are forming their own opinions, avidly discussing and debating them, and trying to bring others around to their way of thinking. This means trying to follow—and persuade others of the importance of their following—new standards of virtuous Muslim behaviour.[88]

Women are becoming increasingly prominent participants in this 'new Muslim public sphere'.[89] Female voices were previously virtually absent from scholarly religious discourse; today women increasingly feel in a position to develop and promote competing views on these subjects and are making themselves heard through a wide variety of media forms, both old and new. The women's rights activists about whom I have written here are part of this worldwide trend. They make ample use of the media, experiencing little difficulty in obtaining newspaper or television coverage for their activities: images of black-robed women raising a ruckus against the male clerical establishment can always be counted on to attract readers—or viewers, as the case may be. Their opinions are also regularly sought by journalists, whenever incidents occur in which Muslim women are mistreated by their menfolk, by community elders, or by clerical authorities. Yet they are highly ambivalent about the media's role in relation to their cause, criticising it for habitually playing up such incidents in ways that reinforce existing negative stereotypes of Muslims. Here they echo the concerns of the clerical leadership, which likewise perceives the 'secular' media to be overly inclined to sensationalist reportage that helps to stir up anti-Muslim sentiments among the general public.[90]

## Muslim women's rights activism and Islamic reform

In many ways the 'movement' I have been describing fits uneasily within current discussions of Islamic reform movements, either historically or in the contemporary Muslim world. The politics of gender have been central to reformist discourse in India from the nineteenth century onwards, though its specific manifestations were varied and changed over time. Women began to be called upon to assume the role of symbolic representatives of their larger community of faith:[91] this process accelerated after Independence, with pressure from both outside and within the Muslim fold. As Metcalf suggests, there has been

> a shift in the boundaries of public and private from an ideal long held in Islamic societies: women are, ironically, now part of public life... [and] talk about women ... fills public space.[92]

Contemporary Islamic reform movements are of course many and varied, both ideologically and in the specific practices that they endeavour to promote; but insofar as their discourse on women is concerned, they all tend to share a preoccupation with the need for women to conform to Islamically prescribed norms (however these may be defined) of 'modest' behaviour and appearance.[93] Traditional maternal and domestic roles are usually valorised as well; if, due to economic or other exigencies of modern life, women must also assume other roles, their priorities are supposed to remain with home and family. Islamist women's movements also strongly emphasise the importance of self-disciplining the mind and body through regular prayer, the study of the Qur'an and other religious texts and the conscious emulation of ideal feminine models from the Islamic past.[94]

In these respects, 'Islamist' women, 'less concerned with the advancement of women's rights than with the advancement of Islamisation', seem to have little in common with the Islamic feminist activists whose ideas and work I have discussed here.[95] That is not to say the some of the individuals involved in women's rights activism may not also hold 'Islamist' views and be engaged in promoting these (for themselves and others) in their personal capacities or as members of religious organisations that share such an orientation. But the Muslim women's rights 'movement', *per se*, is not concerned with identifying or enforcing particular standards of dress or deportment, teaching women how to become better Muslims or encouraging them to pray more regularly. Its leaders are indeed outspokenly critical of—and, as I have mentioned above, have at times publicly protested against—reformers' attempts to control women's behaviour. Although I never heard it explicitly verbalised in this way, their attitude seems to reflect a conception of religion that is very far from that of the Islamists, one that sees religious faith and modes of observance as private matters, to be negotiated by each individual between herself and God.

Notwithstanding my assertion that a considerable gap exists between Muslim women's rights activists and Islamist women in India and elsewhere, there are recent indications that even the women's wing of the Indian branch of the Jama'at-i Islami Hind may be moving in an incipiently Islamic feminist direction on issues of marriage, family life, and personal law. Whereas in 1998, 75,000 JIH women gathered in Kerala to discuss girls' education, the right to worship in mosques, abolition of dowry and 'protecting the right to live with modesty and dignity',[96] at a February 2006 meeting of the same organisation in Hyderabad, attended by 30,000 people from around the country, women's legal rights were prominently highlighted and the state chief of the JIH women's wing, Nasira Khanum, was quoted as saying,

> Islam advocates protection of women rights [*sic*] but men-dominated society hides the facts. Women themselves should know about their rights and learn to snatch them if denied![97]

Whether this meeting really heralds a new direction for the JIH remains to be seen, but it is certainly an encouraging sign when the leader of a religiously orthodox Islamist mass organisation of this kind essentially echoes what the leaders of so many much smaller organisations, with longstanding and serious commitment to the pursuit of feminist goals, have been striving for two decades to communicate to the Muslim clerical establishment and the Muslim community at large.

## Endnotes

[1] This essay is a slightly revised version of an earlier article, in Filippo Osella and Caroline Osella, eds., *Islamic Reform in South Asia* [Cambridge: Cambridge University Press, 2013], pp. 346–382). That article was itself a revision of an earlier one with the same title, published in 2008 in a special double issue of *Modern Asian Studies* 42(2–3): 489–518. I have sought here to bring the essay more up-to-date, mainly by adding to the endnotes information on recent developments in the movement. I thank Filippo and Caroline Osella for giving me a reason to think more seriously and systematically about the movement I discuss here and for their careful reading and critiques of earlier drafts. Geraldine Forbes, Karen Leonard, and Andrea Rugh have also provided valuable inputs. In revising and updating this essay for republication, I have greatly benefitted from correspondence with Mengia Hong-Tschalaer and from recent discussions with Nadja-Christina Schneider, Nida Kirmani, and other participants in the workshop 'New Approaches to Gender and Islam: Translocal and Local Feminist Networking in South and Southeast Asia' (Humboldt University, Berlin, 29–30 April 2011). I am especially grateful to Yoginder Sikand for initially calling my attention to the phenomenon of Muslim women's rights activism in India. I am indebted to the following women who, at various times between 1998 and 2011, kindly made time in their busy schedules to allow me to observe their ongoing activities, talk about their ideas, their goals, their past and current activities and their future plans: Haseena Hashia, Sona Khan, Sughra Mehdi, Terry Rogers, and Suraiya Tabassum in New Delhi; Nigar Ataulla, Zakia Soman, and Hasnath Mansur in Bangalore; Flavia Agnes, Neelofar Akhtar, Farhat, Nasreen Fazalbhoy, Hasina Khan, Khatun Begum, Uzma Naheed, Naseem, Noorjehan Safia Niaz,

and Yasmin in Mumbai; Jameela Nishat, Noorjahan Begum, and Rehana Sultana in Hyderabad; and Badr Sayeed in Chennai. Finally, I thank the following religious authorities for discussing their work and sharing their perspectives on women's rights and duties under MPL: Mohammed Abdul Rahim Qureshi, Secretary of the All India Muslim Personal Law Board; Muhammad Khwaja Sharif, Dean of the Department of Hadis at Jamia Nizamia and Qazis Anjam Arifi, Mir Muhammad Qadar Ali, and Najamuddin Husain Shah in Hyderabad; Qazi Salahuddin Muhammad Ayyub in Chennai; Qazi Muhammad Waliullah in Vaniyambadi; Syed Jalaluddin Umari, Vice-President of the Jamaat-i Islami Hind, and Qazi Maulana Kamil, presiding officer of the AIMPLB's *dar-ul-quzat*, in New Delhi.

[2] Yoginder Sikand, 'The Muslim Personal Law Debate: Need to Listen to Alternative Voices', 5 May 2005, http://www.islaminterfaith.org (last accessed 7 May 2005).

[3] Miriam Cooke, *Women Claim Islam: Creating Islamic Feminism through Literature* (New York: Routledge, 2001), p. 62.

[4] Valentine M. Moghadam, 'Towards Gender Equality in the Arab/Middle East Region: Islam, Culture, and Feminist Activism', *HDR Office Occasional Paper* (New York: UNDP, 2004), p. 53.

[5] Haideh Moghissi, *Feminism and Islamic Fundamentalism: The Limits of Post-Modern Analysis* (Karachi: Oxford University Press, 1999); Valentine M. Moghadam, 'Islamic Feminism and its Discontents: Toward a Resolution of the Debate', *Signs* 27(4) (2002): 1135–71; Margot Badran, *Feminism Beyond East and West: New Gender Talk and Practice in Global Islam* (New Delhi: Global Media Publications, 2007).

[6] Moghissi, *Feminism*, p. 10. Cf. Moghadam, *Islamic Feminism* and Ziba Mir-Hosseini, *Islam and Gender: The Religious Debate in Contemporary Iran* (Princeton, NJ: Princeton University Press, 1999).

[7] Janaki Nair, 'Doing it Their Way', *The Telegraph* (Calcutta, 9 February 2005), http://india.indymedia.org/en/2005/02/210101.shtml (last accessed 14 October 2005).

[8] Badran, for example, contends that in the Egyptian context it is inappropriate to speak of a 'feminist movement', because gender activism there 'is mainly pragmatic rather than political in the more highly-organised or self-conscious sense' ('Gender Activism: Feminists and Islamists in Egypt', in Valentine M. Moghadam, ed., *Identity Politics and Women: Cultural Reassertions and Feminisms in International Perspective* [Boulder: Westview Press, 1994], p. 203). Al-Ali, on the other hand, is prepared to define the term 'movement' more broadly (Nadje Sadig Al-Ali, *Secularism, Gender and the State in the Middle East: The Egyptian Women's Movement* [Cambridge: Cambridge University Press, 2000], pp. 3–8). Similar issues are discussed with reference

to India by Nadja-Christina Schneider ('Islamic Feminism and Muslim Women's Rights Activism in India: From Transnational Discourse to Local Movement—or Vice Versa?' *Journal of International Women's Studies* 11[1] [2009]: 56–70).

[9] Tarannum Manjul, 'Four Law Boards: Will Muslim Women Find a "Masiha"?' 7 February 2005, http://www.sawf.org/newedit/edit02072005/index.asp (last accessed 5 May 2005).

[10] This self-appointed body was established in 1972 'to protect the Muslim Personal Law in India' (All India Muslim Personal Law Board, 'Aims and Objectives' (http://aimplboard.in/objectives.php [last accessed 31 December 2015]). It originally had a membership of 151, made up of many of the country's leading clerics, representing all the major Islamic sects found in India. From time to time the board has added to its membership and in March 2010 (the most recent date for which I have been able to find information) its numbers totalled 251. ('Nadvi Re-elected Muslim Personal Law Board President', *Zee News*, 20 March 2010, http://zeenews.india.com/news/uttar-pradesh/nadvi-re-elected-muslim-personal-law-board-president_612857.html (last accessed 31 December 2015). The organisation has no real authority to set legal policy for the Muslim community but it is very vocal and exercises a great deal of public influence on matters related to MPL.

[11] Manjul, 'Four Law Boards'.

[12] *The Hindu*, 'Muslim Women [sic] Board Registers 166 Cases', 12 February 2005, http://www.hindu.com/2005/02/27/stories/2005022702101100.htm (last accessed 25 April 2006).

[13] *The Muslim News*, 'Muslim Women's Board is a Joke', 3 February 2005, http://www.muslimnews.co.uk/news.php?article=8786 (last accessed 14 October 2005).

[14] Originally, 15 seats (ten per cent) were reserved for women. In 2003, their numbers were increased to 25 and one of them was appointed to the 41 member executive committee (All India Muslim Personal Law Board 2003). At the March 2010 meeting of the Board, four additional women members were elected to serve on the executive committee. The Board's constitution was amended to increase that committee's size from 41 to 51 members, and a number of new men and three women were nominated to serve on the Board, raising its total membership to 251. See Virendra Bhatt, 'Muslim Personal Law Board Gets More Women Members', *Indian Express*, 21 March 2010, http://www.indianexpress.com/news/muslim-personal-law-board-gets-more-women-members/593504 (last accessed 13 August 2011); Farzand Ahmed, 'AIMPLB Begins a New Journey from Lucknow', *India Today*, 21 March 2010, http://220.226.193.37/site/story/AIMPLB+begins+a+new+journey+from+Lucknow/1/89212.html (last accessed 13 August 2011).

[15] Yoginder Sikand, 'Interview: Hasnath Mansur on Muslim Women and the All India Muslim Personal Law Board', 12 February 2005, http://www.islaminterfaith.org (last accessed 8 March 2005).

[16] For example, when a new AIMPLB *nikahnama* was being drafted, Begum Naseem Iqtedar Ali, then the sole woman on the executive committee, tried unsuccessfully to insert therein a provision for 'delegated divorce' (*see below*). See S. Anand et al., 'Muslim Personal Law: Amend, Amend, Amend!', *Outlook India*, 19 July 2004.

[17] Yoginder Sikand, 'Islam and Gender Justice: Interview with Suraiya Tabassum', 6 December 2004, http://www.islaminterfaith.org (last accessed 8 March 2005).

[18] Interview, Noorjahan Begum, 3 January 2006.

[19] Interview, Neelofar Akhtar, 30 November 2005.

[20] Interview, Hasnath Mansur, 25 November 2005.

[21] The vast majority of Indian Muslims are Sunni, followers of the Hanafi school of law. Muslim women activists are quite diverse in terms of their sectarian affiliation, though most are also of Sunni background, but in their legal rights work they generally try to avoid identifying themselves or the issues they deal with in sectarian terms.

[22] The laws referred to are the Wakf Validating Act 1913, Shariat Application Act 1937 (SAA), Dissolution of Muslim Marriages Act 1939, and Muslim Women (Protection of Rights on Divorce) Act 1986.

[23] Interview, Hasnath Mansur, 25 November 2005.

[24] This is true, for example, of Shaheen and of Aman Shanti (a Christian-sponsored NGO), both working among low-income Muslim and Hindu women in the old city of Hyderabad. The Mumbai-based Women's Research and Action Group (WRAG), founded in 1993 in the aftermath of riots following the demolition of the Babri Masjid, has also been deeply involved in efforts to bring about Hindu-Muslim understanding.

[25] Many clerics refuse to use this procedure, but others are willing to accommodate women who have been abandoned or severely abused by husbands who refuse to agree to *khul*ᶜ or cannot be located (see Sabiha Hussain, 'Male Privilege, Female Anguish: Divorce and Remarriage among Muslims in Bihar', in I. Ahmad, ed., *Divorce and Remarriage among Muslims in India* [New Delhi: Manohar, 2003], pp. 263–89).

[26] Majlis' founder is the prominent lawyer and legal scholar, Flavia Agnes (see her *My Story... Our Story of Building Broken Lives,* 4th edition [Mumbai: Majlis, 2004]); 'Ashoka Fellow Profile—Flavia Agnes', 1986, http://www.ashoka.org/fellows/viewprofile3.cfm?reid=128049 [last accessed 4 April 2006]).

[27] See Sashi Menon, 'Protest by Mumbai Muslim Women', 29 July 2005, http://www.mailarchive.com/sapac_chicago@yahoogroups.com/msg01038.html

(last accessed 31 July 2006). Women's customary rites have been key targets for Islamic reformers at least as far back as the early 19th century and continue to be so today.

[28] For example, the 2005 'Imrana case', involving a rural UP woman allegedly raped by her father-in-law (see Sheela Reddy, 'Imrana, Her Story', 18 July 2005, http://outlookindia.com/full.asp?fodname=20050718&fname=Imrana+%28F%29&sid=1 (last accessed 17 April 2006). For an analysis of public responses to this occurrence see Barbara D. Metcalf, 'Imrana: Rape, Islam and Law in India', *Islamic Studies,* 45(3) (2006): 389–412.

[29] Awaaz-e-Niswaan, *Muslim Personal Law and Women: A Report of the National Conference* (Mumbai: Awaaz-e-Niswaan, 1999); Interview, Farhat, Yasmin, and Naseem, 30 November 2005.

[30] National Consultation on Muslim Women by All India Muslim Women's Rights Network, 21–23 November 2005, 'Tentative Schedule' (Lucknow, 20 October 2005).

[31] Interview, Zakia Soman, 6 January 2011.

[32] 'Muslim Women Pull Together for Education, Livelihoods, Health and Harmony', http://www.actionaidindia.org/Muslim_women_pull_together_for_education_livelihoods_health_harmony.htm (last accessed 11 August 2011); Bharatiya Muslim Mahila Andolan, 'BMMA Annual Reports: 2007–2013', https://bmmaindia.com/publications (last accessed 14 July 2016).

[33] Eram Agha, 'Muslim Women Write to PM Modi on Reforms Needed in Personal Law', 27 November 2015, http://economictimes.indiatimes.com/news/politics-and-nation/Muslim-women-write-to-PM-Modi-on-reforms-needed-in-personal-law/articleshow/49945009.cms (last accessed 31 December 2015).

[34] Interview, Zakia Soman, 6 January 2011; Nida Kirmani, 'Claiming Their Space: Muslim Women-led Networks and the Women's Movement in India', *Journal of International Women's Studies* 11(1) (2009): 81–82 and *'Beyond the Religious Impasse: Mobilizing for Muslim Women's Rights in India'*, Religions and Development Research Programme Working Paper 35, International Development Department, University of Birmingham, 2009, http://www.religionsanddevelopment.org/files/resourcesmodule/@random454f80f60b3f4/1267021364_ working_paper_35_for_the_web.pdf (last accessed 13 April 2011).

[35] Bharatiya Muslim Mahila Andolan, 'About BMMA', http://bmmaindia.com/about (last accessed 3 January 2016).

[36] 'About BMMA'.

[37] 'About BMMA'.

[38] For a detailed discussion and analysis of this document, see Mengia Hong-Tschalaer, '*Nikhanama [sic]-Politics in Lucknow: The Interlegality of Islamic*

*Family Laws in Post-Colonial India*'. Unpublished paper presented at the Annual Meeting of the Law and Society Association (San Francisco, CA, June 2011). See also Yoginder Sikand, 'The BMMA's Muslim Marriage Contract: Championing Women's Rights in the Absence of Legal Reform', http://bmmaindia.com/2016/01/03/the-bmmas-muslim-marriage-contract-championing-muslim-womens-rights-in-the-absence-of-legal-reform (last accessed 3 January 2016).

[39] 'About BMMA' and 'BMMA Annual Reports'.

[40] Bharatiya Muslim Mahila Andolan, *An Overview of BMMA's Women* [sic] *Sharia Court* (Dindigul: Mantham Trust, 2013), https://drive.google.com/file/d/0B620GpkWZ9-UT1Jlak5zTnhpbHc/edit (last accessed 3 January 2016).

[41] This draft has been amended three times—most recently in 2015. See Bharatiya Muslim Mahila Andolan, *The Muslim Family Act—3rd Amendment Prepared by Bharatiya Muslim Mahila Andolan,* 27 March 2015, http://bmmaindia.com/2015/03/27/the-muslim-family-act-3rd-amendment-prepared-by-bharatiya-muslim-mahila-andolan/ (last accessed 3 January 2015).

[42] Noorjehan Safia Niaz & Zakia Soman, *Seeking Justice Within Family* [sic]: *A National Study on Muslim Women's Views on Reforms in Muslim Personal Law* (Belgaum: Omega Publications, 2015), https://drive.google.com/file/d/0B620GpkWZ9-UQmx1T212WHpWelE/view (last accessed 3 January 2016).

[43] These women belonged, for the most part, to families whose male members held Islamic modernist views and were themselves engaged in social reform efforts. They were mainly concerned with promoting female education and achieving enhanced mobility for women through relaxation of the more stringent forms of female seclusion. See Minault, *Secluded Scholars* and 'Women, Legal Reform, and Muslim Identity', *Comparative Studies of South Asia, Africa and the Middle East* 17(1) (1997): 1–10.

[44] 'Ashoka Profile: Hasina Khan'. 2000, http://www.ashoka.org/fellows/viewprofile3.cfm?reid=976532 (last accessed 4 April 2002).

[45] Vanessa Baird, 'Making Waves: Interview with Daud Sharifa Khanam', *New Internationalist* 367, May 2004, http://newint.org/issue367/waves.htm (last accessed 4 April 2006). The dowry custom is of Hindu origin and has no sanction in Islam but is widely practiced by Indian Muslims today. See my 'The "Cancer of Dowry" in Indian Muslim Marriages: Themes in the Popular Rhetoric from the South Indian Muslim Press', in this volume.

[46] Interview, Rehana Sultana, 18 March 1999.

[47] In 2002, the Supreme Court of India—in the case of *Shamim Ara v. State of U.P. and Anr.*—decreed that an irrevocable *talaq* can only be given for 'a

reasonable cause' and must be preceded by 'an attempt of reconciliation' by relatives from each side (http://indiankanoon.org/doc/332673 [last accessed 31 December 2015]). This and other similar decisions notwithstanding, instantaneous divorces by 'triple *talaq*' continue unabated.

48 It is, of course, impossible to validly generalise about 'clerical opinion' on any particular matter of MPL. Tens of thousands of men in India are assigned—or claim—the label of *ᶜalim* (plural *ᶜulama*). They in no way constitute a unified group, either ideologically or organisationally. They are divided by sect and within each sect into many distinct schools of thought and, in addition, each individual cleric has personal views on specific points of law, on which he may differ even from his closest peers.

49 AIMPLB, *Nikahnama* (New Delhi, 2005).

50 Interview, Mohammed Abdul Rahim Qureshi, 31 January 2006. The Board's views have not changed since then. In September 2015 a group of Muslim clerics, the Sunni Ulema Council, wrote to the AIMPLB and two other clerical organisations to call their attention to the serious social problems caused by the practice of instantaneous divorce by triple *talaq* and to seek their agreement to henceforth require that three months must pass before such a divorce becomes final ('Clerics Urge Muslim Bodies for Reforms in "Triple Talaq"', 1 September 2015, http://zeenews.india.com/news/india/clerics-urge-muslim-bodies-for-reforms-in-triple-talaq_1665715.html [last accessed 15 September 2015]). Almost immediately, however, the same *ᶜalim* whom I interviewed in 2006 issued, in his capacity as official spokesman for the AIMPLB, a statement strongly rejecting the Council's proposal, arguing that although, 'as per Quran and Hadith' the procedure is 'a crime', it results, nevertheless, in an irrevocable end to the marriage (Press Trust of India, 'Maulana Abdul Raheem Qureshi: No Scope of Change in Triple Talaq System', 4 September 2015, http://www.india.com/news/india/maulana-abdul-raheem-qureshi-no-scope-of-change-in-triple-talaq-system-533733 (last accessed 15 September 2015).

51 Some *qazi*s insist that, if a man wants to formally 'register' his divorce in their office and receive a signed and stamped 'divorce certificate' (*talaqnama*), he must first deposit the full amount of his wife's *mehr*. However a man is not legally required to register his divorce and most do not.

52 These same arguments were put forward in an anti-polygamy campaign conducted by the Anjuman-e-Khawatin-e-Islam (All India Muslim Ladies Conference) in 1918 (Gail Minault, *Secluded Scholars: Women's Education and Muslim Social Reform in Colonial India* [New Delhi: Oxford University Press, 1998], pp. 145–46, 289–90).

53 For a useful discussion of the debates surrounding these issues see A. Suneetha, 'Muslim Women and Marriage Laws: Debating the Model *Nikahnama*',

*Economic & Political Weekly* 47(43) (27 October 2012): 40–48.

[54] Lucy Carroll, '*Talaq-i-Tafwid* and Stipulations in a Muslim Marriage Contract: Important Means of Protecting the Position of the South Asian Muslim Wife', *Modern Asian Studies* 16(2) (1982): 277–309. Already in the late 1930s a 'model *nikahnama*' containing such a clause was promulgated—under the leadership of its Muslim president—by the non-sectarian All India Women's Conference (see Minault, *Secluded Scholars*, p. 299).

[55] Its authors were Uzma Naheed, Flavia Agnes, Nasreen Fazalbhoy, and Neelofar Akhtar, assisted by Maulanas Mohammed Shoeb Koti and Abdul Waheed Wahid Fayazi.

[56] AIMPLB, *Nikahnama*.

[57] Geeta Seshu, 'Nikaahnama: Time for a Gender-Just Model', June 2005, http://humanscape.org/humanscape/2005/june/nikah/php (last accessed 26 April 2006).

[58] Under the Prohibition of Child Marriage Act 2006, which applies to all Indians, regardless of religion, the minimum legal marriage age for women is now 18, for men it is 21, but a large proportion of Muslim brides are younger than this.

[59] Anupama Katakam, 'Reluctant Reform', *Frontline* 22(11) (21 May–3 June 2005, http://frontlineonnet.com/fl2211/stories/20050603003303600.htm (last accessed 14 October 2005).

[60] Seshu, 'Nikaahnama'.

[61] Manjari Mishra, 'Muslim Women to Pen "Nikahnama"', *The Times of India* (New Delhi), 31 January 2006.

[62] In April 2006, the Supreme Court ordered the state of Orissa to provide police protection to a couple who, in defiance of a *fatwa* issued by local clerics, had resumed conjugal relations after the man, in a drunken rage, had pronounced triple *talaq*. This decision may encourage future courts to refuse to enforce the *halala* rule (J. Venkatesan, 'Protect Fatwa-Separated Couple: Court', *The Hindu*, 22 April 2006, http://www.thehindu.com/2006/04/22/stories/2006042206591100.htm [last accessed 18 May 2007]).

[63] Tschalaer ('*Nikahnama*') usefully compares the AIMWPLB *nikahnama* with those drafted by, respectively, the AIMPLB in 2005, the All India Shia Personal Law Board (AISPLB) in 2006, and the BMMA in 2008.

[64] These two stipulations do no more than conform to existing Indian law. The Prohibition of Child Marriage Act, 2006, prohibits the marriage of males under 21 years of age and of females under 18, regardless of their religion. Furthermore, on 25 October 2007, the Supreme Court of India ruled that every state must enact, within three months, legislation making registration compulsory for all marriages. Whether all states have actually passed such laws and, if so, whether they are being effectively enforced, is another question.

[65] For other reactions to the document, see Venkitesh Ramakrishnan, 'Women's

Charter', *Frontline*, 11 April 2008, http://www.frontlineonnet.com/fl2504/stories/20080411230702800.htm (last accessed 11 August 2011).

[66] The Tamil Nadu Muslim Women's Jama'at, established by Daud Sharifa Khanum's NGO called STEPS in the town of Pudukkottai, is one such example. See her interview at http://groups.yahoo.com/group/saldwr/message/1669 (last accessed 12 August 2011). As noted above, the BMMA has recently set up four such courts in different parts of the country and more are in the planning stages. For a general description and discussion of the structure and functioning of bodies of this kind, as operating in India today, see my 'The Women's Court in India: An Alternative Dispute Resolution Body for Women in Distress', *The Journal of Legal Pluralism and Unofficial Law* 45(1) (2013): 76–103.

[67] Interview, Noorjehan Safia Niaz, 28 November 2005. The BMMA's recently released Muslim Marriage and Divorce Act (BMMA, *The Muslim Family*) is a major first step in this direction.

[68] Interview, Farhat, 30 November 2005.

[69] Valentine M. Moghadam, 'Islamic Feminism and its Discontents', op.cit.

[70] Moghadam, 'Towards Gender Equality', p. 53.

[71] COVA is not a women's organisation as such, rather an umbrella group of over a hundred community-based organisations. It was formed in 1994 when a number of Hindu and Muslim groups joined together to work for communal harmony, and only later broadened its mandate to include issues of specific relevance to women.

[72] Interview, 3 January 2006.

[73] Kirmani, 'Claiming Their Space', p. 77.

[74] Tschalaer, '*Nikahnama*'.

[75] In February of 2006 the Supreme Court (in *Smt. Seema v. Ashwani Kumar* [2006] [2] SCC 578, http://indiankanoon.org/doc/1037437 [last accessed 31 December 2015]) ordered all states to institute such procedures. They are already on the books in several states, though not yet actually implemented in all of them. See J. Venkatesan, 'Registration of Marriages Must: Court', *The Hindu*, 15 February 2006, http://www.thehindu.com/2006/02/25/stories/0060215139301.htm (last accessed 23 April 2006).

[76] Interview, Haseena Hashia, 14 October 2005.

[77] Interview, Neelofar Akhtar, 30 November 2005.

[78] Seshu, 'Nikaahnama'.

[79] For example, the fact that the Founder President of the AIMWPLB is 'a long time secretary of the Rashtrawadi Communist Party' has been raised by at least one of its prominent clerical critics (Puja Awasthi, 'Our Own Personal Law Board', http://www.indiatogether.org/2006/sep/wom-aimwplb.htm [last accessed 23 April 2006]).

[80] Moghadam, 'Towards Gender Equality', p. 51.

[81] Interview, 28 November 2005. Though some activists do wear saris, most wear the salwar-kameez, draping a dupatta over their chest and shoulders when outdoors. Assuming this dress is not necessarily a religious statement, it is nowadays de rigeur among college-educated young women of all religions. Some activists wear a black burqa when in public, either the older style two-piece garment with attached face veil or the newer long coat with a separate square of cloth covering the head, neck, and shoulders and sometimes pulled tightly across the face in such a way as to leave only the eyes visible.

[82] Interview, 18 February 1999.

[83] Moghadam, 'Islamic Feminism', p. 1165.

[84] For this reason, some scholars question the appropriateness of using the term in their own writings (cf. Cooke, *Women Claim Islam*, p. ix).

[85] Asghar Ali Engineer, ed., *The Shah Bano Controversy* (Hyderabad: Orient Longman, 1987).

[86] Dale F. Eickelman & James Piscatori, *Muslim Politics* (Princeton, NJ: Princeton University Press, 1996), pp. 68–79, 131–35.

[87] Francis Robinson, 'Technology and Religious Change: Islam and the Impact of Print', *Modern Asian Studies* 27(1) (1993): 244–51.

[88] See Charles Hirschkind's discussion of how the wide circulation of religious cassette tapes in modern day Cairo has contributed to the creation of a new and diverse 'Islamic counterpublic' there ('Civic Virtue and Religious Reason: An Islamic Counterpublic', *Cultural Anthropology* 16(1) (2001): 3–34.

[89] Dale F. Eickelman & Jon W. Anderson, 'Defining Muslim Publics', in D.F. Eickelman & J.W. Anderson, eds, *New Media in the Muslim World* (Bloomington, IN: Indiana University Press, 2003), pp. 10–11.

[90] As Syed Jalaluddin Umari, a founding member of the AIMPLB and Vice-President of the JIH, remarked to me, 'The Imrana case was very bad but such things [incest and rape] also happen among Hindus. The media is biased. If something happens, one case, they make a big hullaballoo about it. One Hindu journalist said to me, "Then you should make your views known in the media". I said "How? The media are in your hands!"' (Interview, 25 October 2005).

[91] See Faisal Fatehali Devji, 'Gender and the Politics of Space: The Movement for Women's Reform in Muslim India, 1857–1900', *South Asia 14*(2)(1991): 141–53; Barbara D. Metcalf, 'Reading and Writing about Muslim Women in British India', in Z. Hasan, ed., *Forging Identities: Gender, Communities and the State* (New Delhi: Kali for Women, 1994), pp. 1–21 and 'Women and Men in a Contemporary Pietist Movement: The Case of the Tablighi Jama'at', in P. Jeffery & A. Basu, eds., *Resisting the Sacred and the Secular: Women's Activism and Politicised Religion in South Asia* (New Delhi: Kali for Women,

1999), pp. 107–22. A similar theme was present in the nationalist discourse on women's education that was directed largely at the need for reform of Hindu tradition (see Partha Chatterjee, 'The Nationalist Resolution of the Women's Question', in K. Sangari & S. Vaid, eds., *Recasting Women: Essays in Indian Colonial History* (New Delhi: Kali for Women, 1989), pp. 233–253.

92 Metcalf, 'Reading and Writing', p. 102.

93 I do not mean to suggest that men in these movements are not also expected to adhere to norms of proper Islamic behaviour, but I am specifically concerned here with the way these movements construct the ideal Muslim woman.

94 See Saba Mahmood's description of a women's piety movement in Cairo (*Politics of Piety: The Islamic Revival and the Feminist Subject* [Princeton, NJ: Princeton University Press, 2005]). For some South Asian examples, see Elora Shehabuddin, 'Beware the Bed of Fire: Gender, Democracy, and the Jama'at-i Islami', *Journal of Women's History* 10(4) (1999): 148–71, and 'Jamaat-i-Islami in Bangladesh: Women, Democracy, and the Transformation of Islamist Politics' in F. Osella and C. Osella, eds., *Islamic Reform in South Asia* op. cit., pp. 445–471; Maimuna Huq, 'Reading the Qur'an in Bangladesh: The Politics of "Belief" amongst Islamist Women' in F. Osella and C. Osella, eds., op. cit., pp. 283–316; Metcalf, 'Women and Men'.

95 Moghadam, 'Towards Gender Equality', p. 53.

96 'Reformist Drive Spreads among Muslim Women in Kerala', Rediff on the Net, 13 June 1998, http://www.rediff.com/news/1998/jun/13muslim.htm (last accessed 1 May 2012).

97 'Women's Meet Blazes a New Trail' *The Hindu,* 12 February 2006, http://www.thehindu.com/2006/02/12/stories/2006021220060500.htm (last accessed 29 May 2007); 'Fight Injustice, Jama'at Tells Muslim Women' *The Times of India,* 13 February 2006, http://timesofindia.indiatimes.com/article show/msid-1411793 curpg-1.cms (last accessed 12 April 2006).

# 6.

# Change and Continuity in Marital Alliance Patterns

## Muslims in south India, 1800–2012

### Introduction

This chapter will address two questions about changing marriage patterns in contemporary South Asia that were raised by the organisers of the conference for which the original paper was written. First, to what extent are South Asians moving away from traditional systems of parentally arranged marriage and moving towards a system of personal choice? Second, how are the criteria for evaluating the suitability of a match—whether for oneself or for one's son or daughter—changing? Are traditional rules of endogamy (e.g., of the caste, linguistic region, or kin-group), exogamy (e.g., of the village, *gotra*, or kindred) being adhered to or being relaxed? Is the frequency of customary preferential marriages (such as for Dravidian-type cross-cousin and uncle-niece marriages among Hindus or for consanguineal kin marriages among Muslims) declining?

There is indeed considerable evidence from South Asia of an increasing prevalence, especially among urban, western-educated young people, of the so-called 'arranged love marriage', in which parents allow themselves to be persuaded to approve their children's choice of a mate and then proceed to put on a wedding that resembles in every other respect the one they would have organised had they themselves made the match in the 'traditional' manner. Even in families where the parents continue to take the primary initiative in choosing mates for their children, both daughters and sons are being allowed to provide more input into and exercise more control over the choice of a spouse.[1] These new practices have been associated with declining birth and death rates, rising ages at marriage, higher levels of education for both sexes, greater economic prosperity (for some groups within the population), a growing middle class, the increased entry of women into the labour force, and widespread internal and international migration associated with a globalising economy.

Although some researchers have noted that in certain social settings marriages of personal choice are becoming increasingly prevalent,[2] the notion that marriages based solely or primarily on romantic attraction between young people of the opposite sex are replacing on a significant scale those arranged by parents (except perhaps among a very small minority of South Asians) does not appear to be well-supported by the available evidence. The very concept of the so-called 'love marriage' still carries considerable negative valence for most people in the region. It suggests to many the likelihood that illicit sexual intimacy has occurred and implies that the union was entered into against the wishes of one or both sets of parents. Therefore, couples who have married 'for love' will typically try to downplay or conceal this aspect of their personal history when speaking about their marriage. If the pair belongs to different castes or religious communities, parental consent to the match is indeed unlikely and the couple may be ostracised—or worse—by their families, kin, and caste community.[3] Furthermore, because most people still regard romantic attraction as providing a weak foundation for a long and stable marital relationship, 'love marriages' are widely believed to be at high risk of failure. This belief may become a self-fulfilling prophecy, since such couples typically lack the kind of social support that those whose marriages were arranged can call upon when problems of adjustment or economic difficulties arise.

## Marriage in a south Indian Muslim family

Most scholars agree on the general direction of change in marriage patterns in today's globalising world, that is, towards more participation by young people in the choice of their own spouses and some widening of the pool within which mates are being sought, through a relaxation, though not complete abandonment, of earlier limits on eligibility for marriage; but observers have noted wide variation within the South Asian population insofar as the specific nature and extent of the changes taking place is concerned. I will examine the issue here with reference to the experience of members of a large extended family of south Indian Sunni Muslims of the Nawwayat *qaum*.[4]

In 1801 the founding ancestor of this *khandan* became diwan in the court of the Nawab of the Carnatic in Madras (now Chennai). After 1855 the Carnatic Nawwabi was dismantled by the British and some of the *khandan* founder's descendants left Madras to seek employment in Hyderabad. After the partition of India a few men of the extended family joined the Muslim exodus to Pakistan and others followed later, forming the core of what is now a substantial settlement of *khandan* members in that country. In the 1970s, several young men left India and Pakistan to study and/or work in Great Britain, North America, and the Middle East, and thereafter the rate of emigration rapidly increased. Those who settled abroad brought parents, siblings ,and other close kin to join them.[5] Today, *khandan* members—who now probably number somewhere between 1,000 and 2,000 persons—are found in many parts of the world. Yet they maintain a high degree of social unity, through frequent travel back to their home countries and by the use of modern forms of communication such as cell phones, instant messaging, e-mail, webcams, and social networking sites such as Facebook.

I have been engaged for many years in a long-term study of the past nine or ten generations of this family.[6] My sources include genealogical records (*shajre*) that document their ancestry at least as far back as the fourteenth century.[7] Their family archives also contain daily journals, letters, and biographies of deceased *khandan* members, both published and unpublished. Many of the latter were written in the mid-twentieth century for family magazines that also contain many essays about the *khandan's* history and about current social and political events and issues.

In 1983–84, I carried out ethnographic research among members of this family in Hyderabad. In 1988, 1989, and 1992 I made brief visits to Chennai and spent nine months there in 1998–99. On two research trips to Hyderabad, in 2001 and in 2005–06, I was able to reconnect with members of the family living there. Over the years I have also been in contact by letter and in person with some *khandan* members living in India and in the United States, and in this way have obtained considerable information about their and their relatives' marriages, migration patterns, educational attainments, and occupational choices, though not in a systematic manner. Though the more recent information is not as complete and detailed as the archival and ethnographic data collected in the 1980s, it is sufficient to enable me to make some generalisations about continuity and change in marriage alliance patterns within the *khandan*, to suggest some of the possible reasons for those patterns, and to compare my findings with the observations of scholars who have studied marriage alliance patterns among other South Asian Muslim immigrant groups in the United States and Great Britain.

I will show that while the manner in which marriages are arranged have undergone considerable change over the past thirty or forty years, with young people of both sexes now being given somewhat more opportunity for input into the choice of a life's partner than they were in the past, there is no evidence that the system of arranged marriage is being rapidly replaced by one in which they choose their own mates. One does find occasional examples of 'arranged love marriages', in which an educated daughter or son finds someone of appropriate religious and social background whom they would like to marry, and are able to persuade their parents to agree to the match. As far as adherence to traditional preferences for close kin marriages is concerned, here again the extent of change is minimal. *Khandan* endogamy is still widely practiced. Many parents continue to make efforts to match their children with cousins or other close relatives, rather than actively looking outside the extended family into the wider Muslim community for suitable spouses.

## Marriage arrangements in the past

Marriage alliance strategies have always played an important role in this *khandan*, as parents tried to ensure not only that their children attained full adult status and continued the family line, but that existing social and kinship networks were strengthened and sometimes extended outward, often with an eye towards possible concrete benefits for the young people involved, the parents themselves and the *khandan* as a whole. In the past, young people were not considered capable of making their own choice of a life's partner or even of participating in the deliberations leading up to it. The practice of early betrothal and the customary segregation of potentially marriageable young people of the opposite sex, even within the extended family household, once they reached puberty, ensured furthermore that in most cases they would neither have any basis upon which to choose their own life's partner nor be even tempted to try. Parents and grandparents took full responsibility for identifying a potential mate and negotiating the terms of the marriage, typically without even discussing the matter with the son or daughter concerned.

Occasionally, according to family lore, a young man did make his wishes known in the matter of his marriage. It is said of one prominent *khandan* ancestor that when he was in his early teens a daughter was born to one of his aunts. As soon as he saw the new baby he said that he wanted her to become his wife when she grew up; that wish was eventually realised and they are remembered as having been a devoted couple. More often, however, if a young man expressed a desire to marry a particular cousin, his wishes were disregarded and he was married to someone else instead. Sometimes the bride chosen by his father is said to have won the young man's heart and they lived happily ever after. Other marriages begun in this manner were less successful. Similar issues rarely, if ever, arose where a daughter was concerned. For a girl to show an interest in marrying a particular man—or even to display an overt interest in the progress of the search for a suitable husband—would have been regarded as shamefully immodest. Should the knowledge of their daughter's attraction to a man she had seen or met have come to the notice of her parents, it would be hushed up immediately, even if he were a close relative, and another match would be quickly arranged, thus forestalling the possibility of a family scandal and the destruction of her reputation.

### The Muslim preference for close kin marriage

Among Muslims, marriageability is determined in terms of a two-fold classification of all members of the opposite sex into the categories *mahram* and *namahram* (from the Arabic *haram*: 'sacred' or 'forbidden'). Their significance is related to customary patterns of the gendered allocation of space. *Mahram* are those men with whom a respectable Muslim woman may freely associate and who may enter the private female space within her home. They include her closest consanguineal male relatives: father (and other direct ascendants), brother, son (and other male descendants), parents' brother and sibling's son. None of them may marry or have sexual relations with her.[8]

The *namahram* category is a residual one, encompassing all other persons of the opposite sex, whether relative or stranger. Direct contact between a woman and any *namahram* is carefully limited and controlled, if not avoided altogether, in order to preserve her privacy and ensure her chastity. It is from among some carefully delimited segment of a woman's *namahram* that a suitable husband will be sought for her.[9]

In the Middle East, marriage to close kin is very common and is indeed preferred by most Muslims, even though it is not specifically prescribed by their religion.[10] Several ethnographic studies of South Asian Muslim communities have also reported a preference for marriage to consanguineal relatives.[11] A recent analysis of National

Family Health Survey data on almost 10,000 Indian Muslim women found that 22 per cent were married to relatives within the second cousin range,[12] while two large-scale surveys of a total of 7,600 women in Pakistan show an even higher rate of close kin marriage: 60 per cent of the sample were married to relatives and 80 per cent of those couples were first cousins.[13]

The practice of marrying almost exclusively within a relatively small circle of close relatives is also characteristic of this *khandan*. Family genealogies confirm that in the past the *khandan* was practically a closed, endogamous group. Marriages to first cousins (of all kinds) as well as to second and more distant cousins were very common. Marital alliances frequently reflected arrangements made by siblings or first cousins years ahead of time to join their respective children or grandchildren in marriage, or to marry the child of one to the grandchild of the other. Such agreements were sometimes made when the proposed couple was very young; sometimes the prospective bride was still an infant.

Much of the theoretical literature on Muslim marriage in the Middle East focuses on trying to explain the preference for patrilateral parallel cousin marriage—that is, marriage to the father's brother's daughter.[14] In this *khandan* marriage to the patrilateral parallel cousin is rarely cited as a specific preference and such marriages, while not uncommon, do not constitute a significant percentage of all unions. Some do feel that, if their relative ages are appropriate,[15] a man seeking a wife for his son should first consider his own brother's daughter. To put it another way, brothers are felt to have a special obligation to one another with regard to the marriage of their respective offspring. This is not so much a matter of a young man's right to be given his father's brother's daughter (*cacazad bahen*) in marriage, but rather the idea that he has a 'duty' to offer to marry her, especially if she does not have other suitors, in order to avoid the possibility that she will remain unmarried or that her marriage will be unduly delayed.[16]

This notion that it is incumbent upon the parents of sons to see that the daughters of their close kin (and of their siblings in particular) are suitably married before they seek elsewhere for a daughter-in-law is generalised beyond the set of brothers and other sibling pairs, though it naturally has somewhat greater force for them than for more distant kinsmen. The argument is sometimes made explicitly in discussions about the pros and cons of young men of the *khandan* marrying unrelated, 'outsider' (*ghair khandan)* women: 'if "our boys" don't marry "our girls", who else will do so?' Thus, instead of expressing their marriage preferences in terms of specific relationships—*cacazad bahen*, for example—a quasi-spatial metaphor is employed: to marry 'within' the *khandan* rather than 'outside it.' The possessive adjective *zati*, meaning 'one's own', is also sometimes used, as in the phrase *zati larka*, 'one of our own boys', in contrast to *bahar ka larka*, 'an outside boy'.

## Marrying 'outside'

In earlier generations arranged marriages rarely joined a *khandan* man or woman to a non-relative,[17] and almost never was a marriage arranged with someone outside of the Nawwayat fold. According to a 1904 book written by a Nawwayat of a related *khandan*, and considered by contemporary members of the family to be the definitive work on Nawwayat social organisation and customs, the Nawwayat (or Nait) observed *qaum* endogamy very strictly. He writes (my translation):

> ... adherence to the principle of equality (*kufu*[18] *ki pabandi*) in marriage is this *qaum's* chief characteristic... [T]he way in which the Nait *qaum* adheres to [this principle] is not seen in any other *qaum* in Hindustan... However wealthy or however noble the ancestry of the other party, if he is not of the Nait *qaum*, then under no circumstances will a girl be given to him nor taken from him. This has the fortunate consequence that up to the present day the [pure] pedigree (*nasal*) of the *qaum* has been maintained.[19]

Note that the author speaks as if the entire Nawwayat *qaum* constituted the relevant endogamous unit, although in fact most marriages (in his own extended family as well as in the *khandan* of which I am speaking here) were in practice confined to a very much smaller circle of close kin.

I should qualify this by saying that whereas marriages were almost never *arranged* between a *khandan* member and a non-Nawwayat man or woman, occasionally a man whose first, *khandani,* wife had died, chose a non-Nawwayat woman (in what would today be termed a 'love marriage') as his second wife. Polygynous unions were very rare in this *khandan*: there are no examples of a man married to two *khandani* women at the same time. Occasionally a married man might contract a second, polygynous marriage with a non-Nawwayat woman while his first wife was still alive. In most cases such second wives came from Muslim families of lower social class or were of Hindu background, converted to Islam in order to marry the Muslim man. Although there were some exceptions, the 'outsider' wife in a polygynous marriage was not usually accepted into the family fold as a social equal. She was typically set up in a separate household from that occupied by the first wife and had little interaction, not only with the latter but with other *khandan* women as well. Genealogies confirm that the children of such women seldom married full-blooded *khandani* young men or women. Instead, they married others of mixed descent or *ghair khandan* relatives of their non-Nawwayat mother. Their descendants, in turn—in part, no doubt, as a result of not having frequent intimate contact with members of the *khandan*—usually disappear from family records after a generation or two. By thus excluding the offspring of such 'irregular' unions from marriage relations (in practice, if not through the operation of a stated 'rule') and by defining membership in the *khandan* in terms of 'pure' descent, the *khandan* ensured that their 'blood' and 'pedigree' would indeed remain unsullied, while at the same time providing an avenue for that minority of men who were so inclined to establish unsanctioned unions with 'outsider' women.

The second decade of the twentieth century saw some loosening of *khandan* endogamy, for a variety of reasons that I do not have space to go into here. In this period several marriages were arranged between young men of the family and *ghair khandan* women. The first marriage of this kind took place in Hyderabad in 1914. In the following decade the marriages of two or three other men were arranged outside of the *khandan*, but it was not until the next generation that arranged first marriages with *ghair khandan* women began to occur with some frequency. By attending and participating in the associated wedding festivities, and by interacting with the couple thereafter on the same basis as they did with other married couples, members of the *khandan* gave social recognition and approval to unions with 'outsiders' in a way that their ancestors had not done back in the nineteenth century. These new brides were not subject to the same social marginalisation that was formerly imposed upon 'outsider' women brought into the family as second wives. This was largely due to the fact that the marriages concerned had been arranged by or—in a few cases where the young man himself chose his bride—took place with the agreement and cooperation of the young man's parents. Furthermore, these brides invariably came from 'respectable' (*sharif*) Muslim families whose social status was at least comparable to the groom's own. This distinguished them from the *ghair khandan* women taken as second wives in the nineteenth and early twentieth centuries, whose family backgrounds were either somewhat obscure or known to be clearly inferior or at least too different from the groom's own. However, the change also reflected changing *khandan* attitudes towards relations with outsiders. By this time the *khandan* had become much less exclusive and insular a social group in other ways as well, a process that both accelerated the decline of the former practice of strict endogamy in first marriages and was facilitated by it.

The idea of giving a girl in marriage to an 'outsider' boy took somewhat longer to gain acceptance. It was not until 1934 that the first arranged marriage of this type took place; another was celebrated in 1937. However, in both cases the men belonged to the

Nawwayat *qaum* and the second man was not a complete 'outsider', as he was descended from the *khandan* founder's younger brother who had married an unrelated Nawwayat woman back in the late eighteenth century. In the 1950s a few *khandan* daughters were given in marriage to men from 'respectable', non-Nawwayat, families. Such matches continue to be made with increasing frequency, especially among families living outside India, in Pakistan, Great Britain or North America.

## Marriage arrangement in the *khandan* today

Today ages at marriage within the *khandan*—as among middle-class Indians more generally—are significantly higher than in the past. Few young people, female or male, get married before reaching their twenties, and most brides and grooms have at least a high school, if not a college, education and perhaps further professional training. Consequently, young people today are generally kept informed as the process of matchmaking proceeds and are usually given the opportunity to express their views and perhaps even reject candidates that their parents are considering. Sons are able to take a more active role than daughters, as it is still thought inappropriate for a girl to show excessive interest in the matter of her marriage. She is certainly not expected to be too outspoken in expressing her opinion about the men who have been suggested as possible husbands for her, but there are indirect ways by which a girl can make her views known. Should she be strongly opposed to a particular match, her feelings are likely to be honoured. Although young people certainly participate to a far greater degree than in the past in the search for a mate and are more able to discuss with their parents what kind of qualifications they would prefer their future spouse to have, marriages based primarily on personal choice are still not the usual pattern.

Sometimes cousins or other close kin who have encountered each other at family gatherings, such as weddings, or when visiting one another's homes with their parents, are attracted to one another, though usually without having had much opportunity to interact privately. One of the pair, usually the man, may get up the courage to mention his feelings to a sister or to his mother, who will then tactfully make it known to his father and, if the parents have no strong objections to the match, they will try to determine the inclinations of the girl's family, usually in an indirect way, so as to forestall the risk of embarrassment if the overture is rejected. Assuming that the latter indicate a willingness to give their consent, a formal proposal of marriage may follow.

There have also been occasional 'arranged love marriages' that came about when a young man or woman became acquainted with a *ghair khandan* classmate or with someone from their workplace, and then proposed to their parents that they be allowed to marry. The family of one young woman, then living in India, agreed to her marrying a young man whom she had met in college. He happens to be a descendant of one of the former Carnatic Nawwabs—a family that many generations ago came from north India and with whom her ancestors had never had any previous marital connections. Soon after the wedding she came to the United States for graduate study and he joined her a year later. They are currently working and raising their children there. Two other young women whom I know, both brought up in North America, had 'arranged love marriages' to young Muslim men of South Asian background whom they met in high school or college. Neither man is a Nawwayat but both come from educated families and, like their wives, grew up abroad. I have also heard of two or three young men of whom it is said that they married the sister of a friend—presumably one whom they had met (or seen) at the friend's home or at a wedding. But I know of no case in which a young couple fell in love and married without securing their parents' permission. Nor am I aware of any marriages contracted with non-Muslims. 'Love marriage' in that sense of the term, has so far not made inroads in this *khandan*.

## A continued preference for close kin marriage

There is some evidence that in India today many communities that formerly practiced caste endogamy, village exogamy, or preferential kin marriage and the like, have begun to expand their marriage networks, as new criteria for mate choice begin to replace old ones. Fuller and Narasimhan, for example, find that Tamil Brahmans, who formerly practiced cross-cousin marriage, today generally *prefer* to seek mates among unrelated families, though they still adhere in most marriages to caste endogamy and descent group exogamy and care is still taken to match the prospective couples' horoscopes.[20] Educational and occupational qualifications now play a larger role than they did in the past when assessing the relative desirability of prospective candidates for marriage. Young people of both sexes, but especially boys, are concerned about a potential mate's physical appearance, something that was never taken into consideration in former times. The desire to obtain overseas employment for one's son through the influence of a prospective bride's father, or to obtain a green card by marrying a woman who is a U.S. citizen may also enter into the calculations when a prospective match is being considered. It stands to reason that one has a better chance of finding someone with the desired qualifications if one is willing to expand the pool of eligible candidates, rather than confine oneself to a small number of persons closely related in a particular way.

In this *khandan*, however, the long-standing preference for marrying close relatives persists up to the present day, most *khandan* families still seeming to prefer to make an endogamous match for their child, if at all possible.[21] This is a particular concern for some of those living in Canada and the United States or other western countries, who are concerned that their children will be overly influenced by western ways, will wish to date members of the opposite sex, and will eventually want to select their own spouses. So far they have been able to forestall such possibilities by paying careful attention to the socialisation of their offspring and sometimes by arranging their children's, especially their daughters', marriages at a fairly young age, often with close relatives living in India, Pakistan or Saudi Arabia. One such marriage joined a young woman born and raised in New Jersey and just graduated from high school, to her father's brother's son, a college graduate from Chennai. After the wedding, which was held in India, he applied for a spousal visa to come to the United States. At first they lived with her family. She attended a nearby college and did exceptionally well, despite giving birth to a child within two years. Later her parents arranged the marriage of her younger brother with another Chennai relative, who soon joined him in the United States. The last time I saw them they were living with the husband's parents.

Since that time, another set of Chennai brothers and their wives have managed to arrange marriages for several of their offspring to relatives from within their immediate kindred. The brothers are the offspring of a pair of cousins; their respective wives are from two different *khandani* families from Hyderabad. A few years ago the son of one of these couples married the daughter of a woman from Hyderabad whose sister and mother's sister were both married to brothers of the groom's father. On the same occasion, the two families celebrated the engagement of two of the bride's mother's sisters' daughters to two father's brother's sons of the groom. Calculating the relationship in the most direct way, the two fiancées and the bride were second cousins of the men they were to marry. Due to the complicated pattern of intermarriage that had already taken place between these families over many generations, they were, like most *khandan* men and women, related in a multitude of other ways as well.

There seem to be a number of reasons for the persistence of close kin marriage in this *khandan*. First, there is a feeling that a marriage to an outsider is more risky than marriage within the family. There is felt to be a greater chance that a couple coming from different backgrounds and lacking shared values and outlook on life will fail to adjust to one another. Although there have been very few cases of separation or divorce resulting from 'outside' marriages—and at least one between spouses who were close relatives—this notion persists and contributes to the reluctance among some *khandan* members to risk making an alliance with an unrelated family. The danger of marital maladjustment and discord is seen to be greatest when the man comes from India to marry a woman brought up in North America, whether she is a relative or an 'outsider'. About twenty years ago, a marriage between a *khandan* man and a Muslim woman raised in America—whose parents had advertised for a groom in a Hyderabad newspaper—ended in divorce. He was later encouraged by relatives to marry a second cousin. They are now happily married, living in the United States.

Other reasons to prefer *khandan* endogamy relate to the relative ease of finding a suitable candidate, arranging a match and negotiating the financial and other details of the agreement, and subsequent celebration of the wedding when both spouses belong to the *khandan*. In such a case the parents already know or can easily find out all that they need to know about the prospective spouse's education, occupation and earnings, personal abilities, temperament, and habits. These matters typically require extensive research when an unrelated candidate is being considered and often, even then, the most careful inquiries fail to turn up the most damaging facts!

The financial transactions that accompany a Muslim marriage in India, as they do among most South Asian Muslims in the diaspora, also favour close kin marriage. The first of these transactions is the *mehr*. In this *khandan*, it has long been customary for the *mehr* to be a small, standard amount, usually Rs. 640, whereas many Muslims of equivalent social and economic stratum are accustomed to offer several thousand rupees or more.[22] Although among Indian Muslims the *mehr* is almost always stated in the marriage contract as 'deferred' (*mu'wajjal*), rather than promptly paid up front (*mu'ajjal*) and it is rare for any part of it to be handed over at the time of the wedding, it is nevertheless considered a debt that the wife may claim at any time during the marriage and that must, in any event, be paid to her upon divorce or widowhood. Since divorce is generally considered to be much more likely if the partners are unrelated, a man taking a *ghair khandan* bride may be compelled by her elders to commit himself to a much larger *mehr* than he would normally be obliged to offer if he married a cousin.

A few years ago the engagement of a Nawwayat man (of a different *khandan* from this one) to a young Hyderabadi Pathan woman brought up in America was broken off at the initiative of the bride's family, because of a serious disagreement over the *mehr*. His family insisted on a token amount, in line with their customary practice, whereas her parents demanded $25,000, on the grounds that, in case of a divorce, she should have enough money to maintain herself for at least one year.

The other significant material transaction associated with a marriage—one that has even more serious implications for parents contemplating a *ghair khandan* match for their daughter— is the dowry. Muslim law does not require the bride's parents to make any substantial gifts to the groom and his family, but the originally Hindu custom of giving an elaborate dowry has become widespread among South Asian Muslims. The amounts being paid, often in response to demands from the groom's side, have also been increasing in recent decades.[23] However this *khandan* has not adopted the practice, at least in *khandan*-endogamous marriages, where the only expected gift for the groom is a ring and a set of clothes to be worn at the wedding ceremony, or a cash amount sufficient to purchase such an outfit. If a girl is given to an 'outsider', on the other hand, her parents may be subjected to demands for cash, jewellery, household goods, appliances and even motorised vehicles.

There are other perceived disadvantages to arranging a marriage with an 'outside' family or allowing a son or daughter to marry an 'outsider' whom he or she has chosen. If it is the daughter who may be marrying out, it might mean that she will be under pressure to become fully incorporated into her husband's family and will not be able to maintain as close a relationship as they, and she, would like her to have with her natal family. This becomes an issue even if the couple lives in the same city, because a woman's husband and in-laws, even under the best of circumstances, are understood to have the right to determine how much time a daughter-in-law may spend with her natal relatives. They may limit her opportunities to communicate with or visit her parents, both because they need her labour for housework, cooking, and eventually childcare, and because they want her to adjust as quickly as possible to their way of living and to shift her loyalties accordingly.

There is also a perceived risk that a daughter who is married to an outsider may not be treated well by her husband and in-laws. Should that happen, she may find it difficult or impossible to communicate her problems to her parents and seek their help. If the husband is a cousin, it is believed that the likelihood of mistreatment is minimal. Furthermore, it is not customary within the *khandan* to place restrictions upon a young married woman's access to her parents, siblings or other natal relatives. So, even if problems arise in a daughter's or sister's marriage, keeping an eye out for her welfare is a relatively simple matter. The fact that so large a proportion of marriages nowadays involve emigration for the bride or the groom, or both, further increases the risk of marrying one's daughter outside of the *khandan*. It makes it more difficult or even impossible for parents back in India or Pakistan to learn what is happening in her marital home or to intervene on her behalf if they discover that she is having difficulties with her husband or in-laws. I was told about one such case, in which a Pakistani girl came to the U.S. to join her *ghair khandani* husband and his parents, all of whom soon began to physically and psychologically abuse her. Relatives living in the same city became aware of the situation, but felt unable to intervene or even to maintain frequent direct contact with her, for fear of inciting her in-laws' anger and aggravating her situation even further. If a young woman is married to a relative, on the other hand, even if she has to move abroad, there are enough *khandan* members who are in regular contact with her and in frequent communication with the family back in India and can keep her parents abreast of her domestic situation.

Having drawn attention to all the purely practical and instrumental motivations for the persistence of the practice of close kin marriage, it would be a mistake to discount the force of the ideology of purity of blood which has always played such an important role in determining marriage choices for members of this *khandan.* Among those who claim descent from their founding ancestor, it is a mark of distinction to be able to trace the connection to him through *all* ancestral lines. The term 'noble on both sides' (*najib -uttarfain*) is sometimes used to describe those who have no outside ancestry, whose descent line is therefore 'pure' (*khalis*). They also sometimes speak of their 'pedigree' (*nasal*) having been 'preserved' (*mahfuz*) for many generations, kept free of admixture and 'separate' (*alag*) from all 'outside' lines of descent. Those who are *najib -uttarfain* share the same 'blood' (*khun*), and are believed to share also certain transmitted 'qualities' (*khassiat, khisal*) that can be lost or diluted through marriage with outsiders. Among the many good qualities that they consider their *khandan* to possess are 'moral' ones (such as honesty, simplicity, religiosity, and self-respect), as well as abilities (such as intellectual prowess) and physical traits (such as fair skin).

Those who are of 'pure' descent in this sense constitute, in a substantive as well as a symbolic sense, the core of the *khandan.* They sometimes refer to themselves, or are referred to by others whose ancestry is mixed to some degree, as *khas khandan ke log*, the 'real', 'particular', 'special', or 'genuine' *khandan* people. Today, most, though not all, of those who boast such ancestry have spouses whose ancestry is similarly 'unsullied' and have arranged—or intend to arrange—their children's marriages within the same core group. By doing so they enact the most crucial behavioural sign of loyalty and commitment to the preservation of the *khandan* as a distinctive and viable social and cultural unit.

The issue of the transmission of qualities through a bloodline has become a somewhat sensitive one in recent decades. At a time when many social forces have been propelling a move towards a more extensive network of marital alliances, 'scientific knowledge' about the presumed deleterious effects of close-kin marriage has also been spreading. Indeed, a genetic study of the *khandan* conducted by a local university team back in the 1960s became very controversial within the *khandan,* contributing to feelings of unease among certain of its members about the possibly deleterious consequences of *khandan* endogamy. The question, of course, usually arises not in the abstract but in connection with discussions about the advisability of particular matches. Some use quasi-genetic arguments to support their opinion that close kin marriage is harmful. Some young men, in particular, have been known to use such arguments to justify their expressed preference for an unrelated girl, a more exciting and mysterious choice in their eyes than a cousin one has known all one's life.

Others hotly contest this genetic argument. They deny, on the one hand, that their traditional practice could lead (or has led) to genetic defects; or they point out that, if genetic principles do in fact operate in the way that they are said to do, then it is better to keep on marrying endogamously so as to continue to replicate the family's desirable traits! If this also means that some hereditary defects will be passed on, it is better that these be the relatively mild defects that are already known to be carried within the family (such as poor eyesight). It is risky, they contend, to begin engaging in marital exchange with *khandans* of whose bad qualities one is unaware.

## Other South Asian Muslims in the diaspora

Since the largest number of *khandan* members living outside South Asia reside in North America, and since these are also the people with whom I am most familiar, it would be useful to try to compare this *khandan* with other Muslims of South Asian origin living in the United States and Canada. Are they a unique case in continuing to practice close kin marriage, or is this marriage pattern typical of others in the larger community of South Asian Muslims in the diaspora? Regrettably, data on this subject are scarce. There are a number of published studies of Muslims in the United States[24] and two that deal specifically with *South Asian* Muslims.[25] There is also a growing number of sociological and anthropological monographs on South Asians more generally in North America.[26] However, none of these works discusses issues of family and marriage in any detail.

There is more information on marriage patterns among South Asian Muslims in Great Britain, and several researchers have reported a high incidence of close kin marriage among Pakistani immigrants there.[27] Shaw, for example, found that 76 per cent of the couples in her sample of 70 marriages in the Pakistani Muslim community of Oxford were consanguineally related to one another, and 59 per cent were first cousins. Interestingly, she also found that young Pakistani immigrants were even more likely than their parents or grandparents to have married a first cousin, suggesting that in the diaspora consanguineous marriages, rather than declining in frequency, may be on the rise.[28] The reasons that Shaw and the other scholars I have cited give for the persistence of consanguineous marriage among Pakistanis, and for its apparent rise in frequency among immigrant families, are very similar to those that I have put forward to account for the patterns observed in the Nawwayat *khandan* about which I have written here.

## Conclusion

I have shown here how patterns of marital alliance have changed over several centuries in one Muslim family from southern India, and have linked these changes with corresponding changes in the social and economic situation in which the family has found itself in different times and places. Throughout its history there has been a strong and recurring tendency to favour marriage to close kin, rather than people outside one's own family circle, however that circle may be defined or conceptually bounded at any given point in time. Even today, when so many forces of change seem to favour the development of extensive social networks rather than inwardly oriented repetitions of earlier established marital alliances, many members of this *khandan* continue to find cousin marriage safe, congenial, useful, convenient, and ideologically satisfying, as they make their way in the global world that they have now come to occupy.

**Endnotes**

1 Henrike Donner, '"One's Own Marriage": Love Marriages in a Calcutta Neighbourhood', *South Asia Research*, 22 (1) (2002): 79–94; and *Domestic Goddesses: Maternity, Globalization and Middle-class Identity in Contemporary India* (Aldershot: Ashgate, 2008).

2 See, for example, Jonathan Parry, 'Ankalu's Errant Wife: Sex, Marriage and Industry in Contemporary Chhattisgarh', *Modern Asian Studies* 35 (2001): 783-820.

3 Cf. Prem Chowdhry, 'Enforcing Cultural Codes: Gender and Violence in Northern India', *Economic & Political Weekly* 32 (1997): 1019–1028; Perveez Mody, *The Intimate State: Love-Marriage and the Law in Delhi* (London: Routledge, 2008); Isabelle Clark-Decès, *The Right Spouse: Preferential Marriages in Tamil Nadu* (Berkeley: University of California Press, 2005); and 'The Decline of Dravidian Kinship in Local Perspectives', in I. Clark-Decès, ed., *A Companion to the Anthropology of India* (Oxford: Wiley-Blackwell, 2011), pp. 517–535; U. Kalpagam, '"America Varan" Marriages among Tamil Brahmans: Preferences, Strategies and Outcomes', *Indian Journal of Gender Studies* 12 (2–3) (2005): 189–215.

4 Victor D'Souza, *The Navayats of Kanara: A Study in Culture Contact* (Dharwar: Kannada Research Institute, 1955); and Aziz Jang Wala, *Tarikh-un Nawwayat*, 2nd ed. (Hyderabad: Wala Akadami, 1976 [1904]).

5 This is not possible for most of those working in the Middle East, since those countries allow very few foreign workers to bring family members with them and, in any case, require them to return home once their terms of employment have ended.

6 Sylvia Vatuk, 'The Cultural Construction of Shared Identity: A South Indian Muslim Family History', *Social Analysis* 28 (1990): 114-131; 'Schooling for What? The Cultural and Social Context of Women's Education in a South Indian Muslim Family', in C.C. Mukhopadhyay and S. Seymour, eds., *Women, Education, and Family Structure in India* (Boulder: Westview Press, 1994), pp. 135-164; 'Identity and Difference or Equality and Inequality in South Asian Muslim Society', in C. Fuller, ed., *Caste Today*, (New Delhi: Oxford

University Press, 1996), pp. 227–262; 'Family Biographies as Sources for an Historical Anthropology of Muslim Women's Lives in Nineteenth-Century South India', in J. Assayag, ed., *The Resources of History: Tradition, Narration and Nation in South Asia* (Paris and Pondicherry: Écôle Français d'Extrême Orient and Institut Français de Pondichéry, 1999), pp. 153–172; 'Older Women, Past and Present, in an Indian Muslim Family', in S. Patel, J. Bagchi and K. Raj, eds., *Thinking Social Science in India: Essays in Honour of Alice Thorner* (New Delhi: Sage Publications, 2002), pp. 247-263.

7 In the late nineteenth century much of this information was consolidated by a grandson of their common ancestor in an unpublished Persian manuscript (Maulvi Ahmad-ul Madani, *Tarikh-i Ahmadi* [Persian], unpublished ms., 1871–72). And in the mid-twentieth century, a woman living in Hyderabad began putting together a biographical register of both living and deceased members of the *khandan.* She added to it as relatives were born, married and died, keeping it up-to-date until shortly before her death in 1984 (Amatul Majid, *Biographical Register* [Urdu], unpublished ms., 1984).

8 A man's *mahram* are his corresponding female kin: mother, sister, daughter, etc. After marriage, a man and his wife become *mahram* to one another, as do their respective immediate family members.

9 For further details concerning the prohibited degrees and other requirements for a valid marriage in Islam, see M. Hidayatullah & Arshad Hidayatullah, *Mulla's Principles of Mahomedan Law,* 19th ed. (Bombay: N.M. Tripathi Private Ltd., 1990), pp. 223–234.

10 Pierre Bourdieu, *Outline of a Theory of Practice* (Cambridge: Cambridge University Press, 1977); Andre Gingrich, 'The Prophet's Smile and Other Puzzles: Studying Arab Tribes and Comparing Close Marriages', *Social Anthropology* 3(2) (1995): 147–70; and Ladislav Holy, *Kinship, Honour and Solidarity: Cousin Marriage in the Middle East* (Manchester: Manchester University Press, 1989).

11 See Cora Vreede-de Stuers, *Parda: A Study of Muslim Women's Life in Northern India* (Assen: Van Gorcum, 1968); Veena Das, 'The Structure of Marriage Preferences: An Account from Pakistani Fiction', *Man,* n.s. 8(1) (1973): 30–45; and Doranne Jacobson, 'The Veil of Virtue: Purdah and the Muslim Family in the Bhopal Region of Central India', in I. Ahmad, ed., *Family, Kinship and Marriage among Muslims in India* (New Delhi: South Asia Books, 1976), pp. 169–215. Mattison Mines, 'Urbanization, Family Structure and the Muslim Merchants of Tamilnadu', in I. Ahmad, ed., *Family, Kinship and Marriage among Muslims in India,* op. cit., pp. 297–317; Carroll McC. Pastner, 'Cousin Marriage among the Zikri Baluch of Coastal Pakistan', *Ethnology* 18(1) (1979): 31–47; and 'The Negotiation of Bilateral Endogamy in the Middle Eastern Context: The Zikri Baluch Example', *Journal of*

*Anthropological Research* 37(4) (1981): 305–318; Patricia Jeffery, *Frogs in a Well: Indian Women in Purdah* (New Delhi: Vikas Publishing House, 1979); Hastings Donnan, *Marriage among Muslims: Preference and Choice in Northern Pakistan* (New Delhi: Hindustan Publishing, 1988); Anjum Alvi, 'India and the Muslim Punjab: A Unified Approach to South Asian Kinship', *Journal of the Royal Anthropological Institute,* n.s.13(3) (2007): 657–78.

However, some fairly recent converts from Hinduism continue to follow their former caste customs in adhering to *gotra* (patrilineal clan) exogamy and prohibitions on marriage to those non-patrilineal kin who are classified as *sapinda* (for an example, see Raymond Jamous, *Kinship and Rituals among the Meo of Northern India* (New Delhi: Oxford University Press, 2003).

[12] R. Hussain & A.H. Bittles, 'Sociodemographic Correlates of Consanguineous Marriage in the Muslim Population of India', *Journal of Biosocial Science* 32 (2000): 433–442.

[13] R. Hussain & A.H. Bittles, 'The Prevalence and Demographic Characteristics of Consanguineous Marriages in Pakistan', *Journal of Biosocial Science* 30 (1998): 121–138.

[14] For an extended discussion of the issues see Holy, *Kinship.*

[15] There are few exceptions to the rule that the husband should be older than the wife. Out of 321 marriages contracted in the *khandan* between 1175 and 1949, in which the age of both partners is known, only seven wives were older than their husbands. In all but two of these marriages, the age difference was less than one year. Where the age difference was somewhat larger than this, the marriage was one of personal choice. See my 'Older Women', p. 251.

[16] Cf. Bourdieu, *Outline.*

[17] Even in those marriages that appear not to conform to the endogamic pattern, there is likely to have been some distant kin connection between the couple, though I am not always able to trace all the relevant links.

[18] The word *kufu* means 'likeness', 'similarity', or 'equality' in Arabic. The requirement that in making a match the 'similarity' of a couple must be considered, is an important principle of Islamic marriage law.

[19] Wala, *Tarikh*, pp. 58–59.

[20] C.J. Fuller & Haripriya Narasimhan, 'Companionate Marriage in India: The Changing Marriage System in a Middle-Class Brahman Subcaste', *Journal of the Royal Anthropological Institute* 14(4) (2008): 736–754.

[21] Of course, those whose ancestors include one or more 'outsiders' are more likely to be open to the possibility of their children marrying out of the *khandan* than are those descended 'on both sides' from a *khandan* ancestor.

[22] See Ch. 3 in this volume.

[23] Ibid.

[24] Yvonne Yazbeck Haddad, ed., *The Muslims of America* (Oxford: Oxford

University Press, 1991); Yvonne Yazbeck Haddad & John L. Esposito, eds., *Muslims on the Americanization Path?* (Oxford: Oxford University Press, 2001); Karen Leonard, *Muslims in the United States: The State of Research* (New York: Russell Sage Foundation, 2003); Garbi Schmidt, *Islam in Urban America: Sunni Muslims in Chicago* (Philadelphia: Temple University Press, 2004); Selcuk R. Sirin & Michelle Fine, eds., *Muslim American Youth: Understanding Hyphenated Identities through Multiple Methods* (New York: New York University Press, 2008); Moustafa Bayoumi, *This Muslim American Life: Dispatches from the War on Terror* (New York: New York University Press, 2015.

[25] Aminah Mohammad-Arif, *Salaam America: South Asian Muslims in New York* (London: Anthem Press, 2002); Ahmed Afzal, *Lone Star Muslims: Transnational Lives and the South Asian Experience in Texas* (New York: New York University Press, 2015).

[26] For example, Johanna Lessinger, *From the Ganges to the Hudson: Indian Immigrants in New York City* (Boston: Allyn and Bacon, 1995); Jean Bacon, *Life Lines: Community, Family, and Assimilation Among Asian Indian Immigrants* (New York: Oxford University Press, 1996); Karen Leonard, *The South Asian Americans* (Westport, CT: Greenwood Press, 1997); Aparna Rayaprol, *Negotiating Identities: Women in the Indian Diaspora* (New Delhi: Oxford University Press, 1997); Madhulika S. Khandelwal, *Becoming American, Being Indian: An Immigrant Community in New York City* (Ithaca: Cornell University Press, 2002); Sharmila Rudrappa, *Ethnic Routes to Becoming American: Indian Immigrants and the Cultures of Citizenship* (New Brunswick: Rutgers University Press, 2004); Bandana Purkayastha, *Negotiating Ethnicity: Second-Generation South Asian Americans Traverse a Transnational World* (New Brunswick: Rutgers University Press, 2005); Gita Rajan & Shailja Sharma, eds., *New Cosmopolitanisms: South Asians in the US* (Stanford: Stanford University Press, 2008).

[27] For example, Pnina Werbner, *The Migration Process: Capital, Gifts and Offerings among British Pakistanis* (Oxford: Berg, 1990); Alison Shaw, 'Kinship, Cultural Preferences and Immigration: Consanguineous Marriage among British Pakistanis', *Journal of the Royal Anthropological Institute* 7(2) (2001): 315–334; Katharine Charsley, '*Rishtas*: Transnational Pakistani Marriages'. Unpublished PhD Dissertation, University of Edinburgh, 2003.

[28] Charsley '*Rishtas*', pp. 315–16, 318–19.

# 7.

# What can Divorce Stories Reveal about Muslim Marriages?

## Introduction

Every Muslim woman and every man (with a few minor exceptions) is enjoined to marry, for—in the words of the most influential Indian clerical organisation—the perpetuation of the human race and the 'attainment of chastity, continence, mutual love, affection, and peace...in compliance with the injunctions of God's Book and His Prophet's *Sunnat*'.[1] The arrangement of a marriage is a difficult, often lengthy, and always expensive process, especially for the parents of the bride. However, after the negotiations have been successfully concluded and the wedding ceremonies completed, their fond hopes that the couple will 'live happily ever after' are too often doomed to failure.

Marriages break down for a variety of reasons: recent studies of separated and divorced women suggest that the most common areas of conflict between spouses revolve around a husband's failure to provide for the family, his involvement with other women, his addiction to alcohol or drugs, his dissatisfaction with the wife's housekeeping or cooking or the size of her dowry, and his suspicions that she is engaging in an extramarital relationship. Both women and men also complain very frequently of interference in the relationship by their respective parents-in-law. Domestic violence is practically ubiquitous in these cases, as is desertion by the husband, ejection of the wife from the marital home or her leaving it of her own accord.[2] One of the constants in these broken marital relationships arises out of the gap that frequently exists between the partners' religious and cultural expectations of what a marriage should be and the reality of life for Muslim men and women in India today. I argue here that a useful perspective on the cultural construction of the institution can be obtained by examining the narratives of marriages that have failed. Stories of separation and divorce can shed light on the nature and dynamics of contemporary marriage, the challenges that men and women face when trying to conform in their daily life to the prescriptions and norms of their religion, and the difficulties they experience when trying to perform to one another's satisfaction their assigned gendered roles, which in Islamic religious discourse are unproblematically complementary, but in practice are highly asymmetrical.

It is important to stress that the vast majority of Muslims remain married to their first spouse until death do them part. There is a widespread perception that Muslim marriages are exceptionally unstable and much more likely than Hindu or Christian marriages to end in divorce. Unfortunately, there are no hard statistics that one could use to either support or refute this notion.[3] Till 2013 India did not require marriages—let alone divorces—to be officially registered.[4] Most Hindus and Christians can obtain a legal divorce only by filing suit under their respective codes of personal law,[5] and it is thus possible to roughly estimate from court records the incidence of divorce among them. However most Muslim divorces take place extrajudicially. A man can dissolve his marriage by simply pronouncing the word *talaq* three times, without notifying any civil or religious authority.[6] A woman can also divorce extrajudicially—either by persuading her husband to release her in exchange for compensation (*khul*ᶜ) or by getting a *qazi* to annul the marriage for cause (*faskh-e-nikah*).[7] She may instead file suit under the 1939 Dissolution of Muslim Marriages Act[8] but most women prefer one of the cheaper, quicker, and more socially acceptable extrajudicial options, turning to a civil court only as a last resort. One advantage of a divorce under the DMMA is that a woman is entitled to ask for her *mehr*, whereas if she negotiates for a *khul*ᶜ she normally has to waive that right. However, in practice this advantage is not always realised. The divorce judgments I examined in the Chennai and Hyderabad family courts almost always included a settlement whereby the wife agreed not to press any monetary claims against her husband.

Another barrier to calculating the incidence of marital breakdown among Muslims is that many couples separate and live apart for years without either party taking the step of formally dissolving the marriage. Although this is true for Indians of all religions, it is probably more common among Muslims. Since Islamic law allows a man to have up to four wives at a time, he does not always have a pressing need to formally dispose of the first wife before marrying a second.[9]

## The data

I draw here upon data from fieldwork carried out intermittently over the past fifteen years in Chennai and Hyderabad. These include case files on Muslim suits for divorce, maintenance, and restitution of conjugal rights from the family courts of both cities and samples of marriage and divorce records kept by two Hyderabad *qazi*s. I have also used narratives of matrimonial disputes in the files of the Tamil Nadu State Legal Aid Authority and an all-woman police station in Chennai, as well as interviews with separated and divorced Muslim women, lawyers, legal aid staff, judges, court personnel, and Islamic clerics.[10]

The kinds of *qazi*s' records that I have are unfortunately not very useful for my purposes. *Qazi*s spend a significant portion of their time registering men's divorces and issuing 'divorce certificates' (*talaqnama*) that they can use to document their marital status. *Qazi*s also help broker *khul*ᶜ agreements between women and their estranged husbands. I was able to examine annual divorce registers in the offices of two Hyderabad *qazi*s. Each listed approximately 400 cases with names, dates, type of divorce (*talaq* or *khul*ᶜ),[11] amount of *mehr*, and whether and how it was paid. However the 'comments' column was usually left blank or contained only the formulaic phrase: 'For various reasons we have been unable to manage our married life and therefore I have pronounced *talaq* (or taken *khul*ᶜ) on such-and-such a date.' Even when a fuller explanation is given, it is invariably very brief and usually couched in euphemism. When I asked why there was so little information about the cause of the marital breakdown, I was told that it is not appropriate for an outsider to enquire into such matters. What goes on between a couple in the privacy of their own home is their business: it is not the *qazi*'s role to delve too deeply into it.

Legal petitions, counter-petitions, and criminal complaints are, of course, strategic documents, composed to meet the requirements of a particular law and to convince a judge that the petitioner should be given the relief asked for—or that she/he is lying and the plea should therefore be denied. Furthermore, they are written by advocates, not by the parties themselves, in a language (English) that few litigants command.[12] While containing some elements of a story that the client has narrated in the course of one or more interviews, that story has invariably undergone considerable editing in accordance with the lawyer's professional judgement about how much and what should be said, what needs to be highlighted, what suppressed, and what added, in order to win the case. The oral narratives that I have collected do not suffer from all the same defects but they represent only one party's version of the events that preceded the break-up and are, like court petitions, clearly self-interested.

Thus there is no way to assess the absolute 'truth value' of any of these materials. We can only learn from them what kinds of situations cause marital conflict in this society and how they are conceptualised and dealt with. We can also gain insight into people's understanding about how men and women *ought* to behave in a marital relationship, which behaviours are admirable, which are blameworthy and which constitute culturally acceptable justification—quite apart from *legal* justification—for parting from one's spouse.

## A divorce by *talaq* and a maintenance claim

In 1993 Batul Bi,[13] separated from her husband, Muhammad Basha, and living with her widowed mother, received a registered letter, written in English, from a (Muslim) advocate:

> Instead of living a happy life with my client ... you drifted away ... both temperamentally and emotionally. Over the years things did not improve ... [and now] you have deserted him. Finally ... he has come to the painful decision of pronouncing *talaq* on you ... in presence of Mr. M.A. and Mr. K.A. Client is sending demand draft for Rs. 585 (*mehr*) and Rs. 450 for *ʿiddat*. You gave false [sic] complaint on 30.12.91 and took away all *jahez* articles and acknowledged receipt of same.

This letter, together with one informing the chief *qazi* of Tamil Nadu of the divorce and a copy of a *talaqnama* notarised by another Muslim advocate, was included in Batul Bi's file at the Chennai family court, where she had recently filed a maintenance suit against her husband under Section 125 of the Criminal Procedure Code.

The couple had been married for four years and had one daughter. They began married life in her husband's family home. According to Batul Bi's petition, they were happy at first but soon her stepmother-in-law began interfering in their relationship and succeeded in turning her husband against her. The two hounded her for money, complaining that the dowry she had brought was inadequate.[14] Muhammad Basha began to abuse her physically, knocking out a tooth on one occasion. He spent money extravagantly and was generally irresponsible. Batul Bi tolerated the situation for some time, hoping that he would change; but he did not and finally, after one especially vicious beating, she left for her natal home and reported the family for dowry harassment, under Section 498A of the Indian Penal Code, at the local police station.

Her in-laws then called in a council (panchayat) of local elders to arbitrate. The council recommended that the couple separate from his parents, and Muhammad Basha found them alternative accommodation. But they lived there only briefly before he insisted that they move back to his parents' home. The abuse continued and she was eventually 'driven out of the house'. She went back to her mother and later filed the maintenance suit, asking the court to order her husband to pay Rs. 500 a month for herself and the same for the child—the maximum obtainable at the time.[15]

Muhammad Basha denied all these allegations. He described his wife as 'difficult to get along with' and related that she had ignored his 'repeated advice' to quit her job at a local hospital.[16] Nevertheless, he asserted, he had always tried to 'adjust' to her whims and had even moved to a separate house 'to appease her'. He also pointed out that the divorce had rendered her ineligible in any case to claim maintenance under the CrPC.[17] Batul Bi eventually ceased attending the required monthly court hearings and counselling sessions in the family court, and after two and a half years her suit was 'dismissed for default'.

These two contradictory versions of this couple's divorce story show what the parties felt they were entitled to expect from one another after marriage: submissiveness and obedience from the wife, material support, kindness, and consideration from the husband. Neither had lived up to the other's expectations. Muhammad Basha clearly anticipated that the woman he married would bend to his will, but the wife he got was, by his account, 'quarrelsome' and 'disobedient'. She did not stay at home as a respectable wife should, but insisted on keeping her job. They were living with his parents and he was loath to deviate from this arrangement, though he did so temporarily under pressure from community elders. He represented himself as a forbearing husband who, in the interests of preserving the marriage, had long accommodated his wife's ill behaviour and only took the drastic step of pronouncing divorce when she 'deserted' him.

Batul Bi claimed that her husband had neither met her material needs nor treated her with the kindness a wife deserves. Instead, he and his family subjected her to mental and physical abuse which she bore without complaint, as a good wife should, until they forcibly ejected her from the marital home.

### The Muslim marriage contract

The contractual nature of Muslim marriage is regularly cited, by Muslims and non-Muslims alike, as a key feature of the institution. While some regard it as materially distinguishing it from marriage in other religious communities, Islamic jurists are often at pains to stress that Muslim marriage is not *merely* a contract but also has great sacred and social significance. It makes sexual intercourse permissible, establishes the legal paternity of any children subsequently born to the woman, and gives each spouse certain rights against, as well as certain obligations towards, the other.[18] But, as historian Judith Tucker explains,

> [it] has a dual character…: it is the fulfilment of a moral imperative to marry as an essential part of leading a good Muslim life, and it is a binding legal contract that must meet certain conditions in form and content.[19]

A publication by one of India's most prominent clerical organisations, the AIMPLB, similarly states that '[i]n the eyes of the shari'at … marriage is not just a *civil* contract; it is also worship'.[20]

Juristically speaking, marriage is an agreement between a man and a woman and, as such, requires the consent of both, though, if the bride is a minor, her *wali* ('marriage guardian'—usually her father) may consent on her behalf. The agreement may be purely oral—all that is required is the presence of witnesses. Neither the imprimatur nor even the presence of a religious functionary of any kind is needed. In India, however, it is customary to ask a *qazi*, *imam*, *mullah*, or some other person with clerical qualifications to preside over the proceedings as *nikahkhwan* (reader of the *nikah*).

The couple does not sit together on this occasion. The groom, his male family members, and friends and those of the bride are in one room, along with the male witnesses to the marriage and the designated *nikahkhwan*, while the bride waits elsewhere with her female relatives and friends. In the men's quarters the pertinent details are taken from the male participants and recorded by the *nikahkhwan*, usually on a printed form, which the bride's *wali* then takes into the women's quarters to obtain her consent to the match. Given the context, the bride is most unlikely to feel free to express her true feelings about whether or not she wishes to get married to the person who has been chosen for her, someone whom she may never have seen and about whom she may know very little.[21] The two families' male elders have negotiated the terms of the contract. Even the groom is rarely involved in and may not even be informed about its details.[22]

It is, in any case, considered unseemly for a never-married girl to show any outward interest in the matter of her marriage. When asked for her consent, she is not expected to—and usually does not—utter a sound. She simply lowers her eyes and remains silent. These gestures are universally interpreted as signalling her agreement, an interpretation supported by the well-known *hadith* wherein the Prophet, responding to his wife Aisha's query, observed that a virgin is too shy to speak up at such a time and therefore 'her silence [means] her consent'.[23]

Printed marriage contract forms can be purchased at stationery stores in Muslim neighbourhoods but religious organisations and, in some states, government agencies also issue standard forms for the purpose. They ask for little information beyond the date, the particulars of the bride and groom and those of their parents and witnesses and the name of the officiating cleric. One might assume that, as marriage is, formally speaking, a contractual arrangement, the document would specify the *terms* or *conditions* under which the parties are agreeing to marry. However, in the vast majority of cases, the only condition stated in writing is the amount and payment schedule for the bride's *mehr* without which the marriage is not valid. The *mehr* is usually denominated in Indian currency but it can consist of any kind of valuable, such as gold jewellery or real estate.

In contract law, a distinction is often made between expressed and implied terms. An *expressed* term is one explicitly stated, usually in writing, in the contract itself. An *implied* term does not appear there in black and white, but is understood by the parties and all others concerned to be an intrinsic part of any contract dealing with the particular matter at hand and the signatories are therefore bound by it. One of the possible bases for such a shared understanding is that it is 'customary' within the trade or occupation, or the particular community or locality, to which the contracting parties belong.[24]

Except for the *mehr* agreement, the terms of a typical Indian Muslim marriage contract are similarly implied 'by custom', by shared religious and cultural understandings, and practices. Its key implied terms are that the husband must meet his wife's material needs and that she, in return, must obey his wishes. In Tucker's words:

> Once the contract has been signed and the marriage consummated, the rights and duties of a husband and wife ... are contained, in large part, in the twin doctrines of *nafaqa* (maintenance) and *nushuz* (disobedience).[25]

These terms recall the 'sexual contract' upon which, according to Carole Pateman, marriage has long rested in the Anglo-European historical tradition: the wife gives her husband exclusive access to her body, labours for him in the home, and submits to his will in return for sustenance, shelter and protection.[26] In earlier centuries in the west those terms were explicitly recognised and often legally enforced. Today, this is no longer the case and the social roles of women have greatly expanded, but the basic nature of the marital contract survives to a considerable extent.

The principles that Tucker cites as governing the spousal relationship in Islam are reflected in the *hidayat* or 'Instructions for the Couple', attached to a model marriage contract issued by the All India Muslim Personal Law Board in 2005. It instructs the husband to provide his wife with food, clothing, lodging, and medical treatment. He is also enjoined to safeguard her honour and respectability, that is, see to it that she dresses and behaves modestly and does not show her face to *namahram* (men who, were she not already married, could legally marry her).[27] He must treat her kindly, providing opportunities for her to visit her parents and non-marriageable male relatives (*mahram*). He must not take her to her parents' house and leave her there against her will nor should he divorce her, except under very compelling circumstances. However, if the couple's relationship has deteriorated to such an extent that living together is impossible, the husband must formally release her from the marriage by *talaq*, rather than leave her in the state of *mu'allaq*—living apart but still legally married to him and thus unable to marry anyone else.

For the wife's part, she is enjoined, first and foremost, to obey her husband (*farmanbardari karna*) in all religiously permissible matters (*jaᶜiz baton men*).[28] She must not leave the house without his permission, must care for his comfort and that of their children and must fully 'safeguard her own honour (*izzat*)', that is, behave 'modestly' and remain sexually faithful to her husband.[29]

All Muslims, even those without direct access to these published AIMPLB guidelines, are fully aware of their religion's prescriptions and proscriptions for the performance of gendered roles within marriage. Very similar lists are available in the myriad books and pamphlets with titles like *Miyan-Bibi ke Haquq* (the rights of husband and wife) that are readily available from any purveyor of Muslim-oriented literature. They are anyway part of every Muslim's repertoire of cultural knowledge, internalised while growing up in a Muslim family and in a predominantly Muslim social milieu.

## Stipulations to a Muslim marriage contract

Some schools of Islamic law allow either party to a marriage to make stipulations to the contract they are entering into.[30] Almost any kind of condition may be set down, as long as it does not require either party to perform a religiously forbidden act. Indian courts have upheld, for example, stipulations that the couple will live separately from the husband's parents, that the wife will be allowed to complete her education or work outside the home, or that the husband will refrain from taking a second wife during the lifetime of the first. The couple can even agree that, should the husband fail to fulfil any of the conditions they have written into the contract, she will have the power to dissolve the marriage herself, by a procedure called *talaq-i tafweez* (delegated divorce).[31]

At certain times and places in the Muslim world it was fairly common to insert stipulations into the marriage contract,[32] but in the Indian subcontinent they have never been widely used. Few lay Muslims in South Asia are even aware of the option. The standard printed *nikahnama* forms do not mention it as a possibility and, although the parties could dispense with the form and write up their own contract, this is seldom done. Indeed, even if the bride's elders are aware that stipulations could be made to the contract, few would risk scaring off the parents of a prospective groom by raising such a possibility during the marriage negotiations.

## Model *nikahnama*s

In the late 1930s a 'model *nikahnama*' that allowed for the insertion of conditions for the marriage, including for *talaq-i tafweez*, was drafted by the Muslim president of the non-sectarian All India Women's Conference, but the document was never widely distributed or utilised.[33] In recent years, a growing number of Muslim women activists have begun pressing for greater gender equity in the way that Muslim Personal Law (MPL) is administered.[34] Arguing that for centuries the patriarchal religious authorities have misinterpreted the Qur'an so as to deny women many of their 'God-given' rights, some have proposed that, if women added stipulations to the marriage contract, their status within marriage would be secured and even enhanced. This has led, beginning in the 1990s, to the drafting and public release of a number of 'reformed' *nikahnama*s.[35]

In 1994 one such document was presented to the AIMPLB for its consideration by a Mumbai group of women lawyers, academics, and NGO leaders. It encouraged the bride to enter stipulations into the contract and asked the groom to delegate to her the power of divorce, should he fail to honour them. It also required any groom who was contracting a polygamous marriage to affirm that he had informed his first wife of his intention and had made separate living arrangements for her.

The AIMPLB did not embrace this document but was apparently motivated by it to begin working on a model *nikahnama* of its own, which was finally released in 2005.[36] Some women's groups welcomed this effort as a step in the right direction but most were extremely critical, feeling that it failed to properly address women's concerns in a constructive way.[37] Women activists had strong objections to the guidelines for wifely behaviour contained in the *hidayat*, particularly those that enjoin strict obedience to the husband. They were disappointed that the AIMPLB document does not mention that the bride can insert conditions into the contract nor explain the procedures by which she can initiate dissolution of the marriage. And, with reference to polygyny, they found it highly unsatisfactory that the *nikahkhwan* is merely instructed to 'ascertain' that the groom will follow the Qur'anic injunction to treat both wives equally; how the cleric is to do this is not explained.

In 2006 a breakaway group of Shia clerics from the Sunni-dominated AIMPLB issued a *nikahnama* that was somewhat more 'woman-friendly' than the one produced by the latter organisation, in that it allows a woman to pronounce a 'delegated divorce' under certain circumstances and bans instantaneous divorce by 'triple *talaq*'.[38] Around the same time a *nikahnama* to 'better protect the rights of women in times of marriage, divorce, custody, and maintenance'[39] was issued by the Muslim Women's Rights Network, a Delhi-based group. It was later used in a few group weddings organised for poor Muslim young people.

The All India Muslim Women's Personal Law Board (AIMWPLB) was launched in Lucknow in 2005 by a group of upper-middle-class women, intended as a counter-balance to the mainly male[40]

AIMPLB. It immediately began to develop 'a set of marriage laws... [to] safeguard [women's] interests'[41], and three years later released a *nikahnama* in both Hindi and Urdu versions.[42] It contains seventeen guidelines for a proper Muslim marriage and ten for divorce, all based on teachings of the Qur'an and Hadith. It is structured in such a way that those who affix their signatures are knowingly entering into a contractual arrangement to which explicit terms and conditions are attached.

The most recent of these new marriage contracts was drafted by the Lucknow-based Bharatiya Muslim Mahila Andolan (BMMA) in November 2008.[43] Like earlier Muslim women's rights organisations, the BMMA claims to operate within an Islamic framework but it presents its *nikahnama* as 'a secular marriage contract',[44] whose provisions are designed to be in line with the codified portions of MPL as well as with Indian women's rights' laws. Despite all these efforts to introduce new versions of the marriage contract, none has been widely used in actual marriages. Some women's groups have used their own *nikahnama*s in highly publicised weddings[45] but none has achieved broad popularity.

## A court divorce

In 1991 Aqila filed for divorce in the Chennai family court, on grounds of cruelty and dowry harassment. She and Ahmad had married in 1987; her parents gave a dowry of cash and goods worth Rs. 30,000. When she moved to her husband's home, he soon began to physically abuse her, once even threatening to push her off the roof. Thereafter she lived in constant fear for her life. He was aided and abetted by his parents and unmarried sister, who complained that the dowry she had brought into the marriage was grossly inadequate.

In 1988 Aqila went to her parents' house to deliver her first child. When she returned to her in-laws the pattern of abuse resumed. Ahmad berated her for failing to bring expensive gifts for him from her parents' house. After some time he took up a new job in

Bangalore, leaving her and the baby with his parents, who allegedly beat her, forbade her to write letters to her family, 'treated her like a slave', and eventually threw her out of the house. She had to leave behind her silk saris and gold jewellery as well as her school certificates and other important papers. Back in her natal home, she filed a complaint of dowry harassment with the police, who made her husband return some of her personal property but not the bulk of her dowry goods.

Ahmad told a very different story. He claimed that their wedding was celebrated in a simple manner in an inexpensive government community hall and that neither he nor his family had received a dowry. He was indignant that Aqila's family had deceived him by not divulging that she was four years older than he and had an Intermediate diploma! He expressed concern for his son who, he claimed, needed surgery for undescended testicles, which his wife refused to allow. He alleged that she had never cared about the child's health, education or well-being and kept insisting that they live separately from his parents, a demand with which he, as an only son, could obviously not comply. His wife, he told the court-appointed counsellor,[46] was 'a very independent woman' and therefore was incapable of adjusting to his family. Nevertheless, he had always treated her 'with great love and affection'. He had never laid a hand on her and, in the interests of their child, wanted her to come back to his home and resume conjugal life.

When asked by the counsellor if he had remarried during his separation from Aqila, Ahmad denied it, though he admitted that his parents intended to find him another wife once the present case was settled. But Aqila reported having recently received a letter from one Aisha Bi, who identified herself as Ahmad's second wife! Aisha's parents had been told that Ahmad had divorced Aqila after learning that she was older than him, and because she was neglecting their child and having an illicit love affair. Aisha Bi soon discovered that there had been no divorce and that his allegations of child neglect and infidelity were false. Ahmad had also treated Aisha Bi with extreme cruelty and she had escaped after three months with the help of a nephew, leaving her jewellery and other belongings behind. In her letter she pledged to help in any way possible with Aqila's case, as she pursued her own against their common husband.

Both parties' testimonies indicate some of the expectations with which they went into the marriage. The husband was angry that his in-laws had deceived him, breaching the strict rule that a Muslim groom must be older (and preferably better educated) than his bride, thus ensuring his ability to exercise authority over her. In making this complaint, Ahmad assumed—probably rightly—that others would consider his strong reaction to the deceit completely justified. Other cultural expectations about gender roles are reflected in Ahmad's characterisation of his wife as 'too independent' and in his allegations of child neglect and adultery, all of which support his portrayal of Aqila as the very antithesis of a proper Muslim wife.

Aqila's primary complaint was that Ahmad failed to treat her with the kindness and consideration owed to a wife. Ironically, the fact that he shared her understanding of how a husband *should* behave is manifested in *his* assertion that he always treated her 'with love and affection'. Aqila also had complaints of a material nature: certain of her property rights had been abrogated both during the marriage and after she left him. In particular, she felt wronged by his and his family's retention of the many dowry gifts that her family had given when the two were married.

In her petition, Aqila also raises the issue of financial support, regarding it to be a husband's responsibility to support his wife as long as they remain married and to maintain their children even if they separate. She does not charge him with failing to provide adequately for her while she was living with him but complains that he stopped doing do so once she returned to her parents. His excuse is that she herself chose to live apart from him and unless she returns to him and resumes married life, he has no obligation to continue to maintain her. She insists that he be made to pay her *mehr* and thus fulfil the only explicit term of the marriage contract, but he counters by asserting that the *mehr* becomes due only upon divorce. They are still married, he has no intention of either divorcing her or allowing the court to dissolve the marriage, so the issue is moot.

The issue of sexual fidelity on the husband's part was also raised in this divorce case, though not in Aqila's petition, but her discovery that he had remarried made her determined not to return to him under any circumstances. Since Islam grants men such a right, polygamy is not a ground for divorce under the DMMA. Only if the husband has failed to treat both wives equally can the marriage of the one who is disfavoured be dissolved on grounds of 'cruelty'. In practice, as Aqila's example illustrates, when most Muslim women of today get married, they expect more than simply to be 'treated equally' with a co-wife: they anticipate having a sexually exclusive, monogamous relationship with their new husband. While they are well aware that polygamy is religiously permitted, they nevertheless feel that they have a legitimate grievance and even, perhaps, justification for exiting the marriage, should another woman enter the picture either as wife or paramour.

### Marriage to a deceitful stranger

The eldest daughter of her parents, Shahida was eighteen years of age, holder of an Intermediate diploma and employed as a schoolteacher, when her marriage was arranged to Salman, a young man recommended by a neighbour, who described him as the owner of a factory. Shahida's father visited the factory and spoke to the manager, who assured him that the match would ensure a comfortable future for his daughter. The prospective in-laws demanded furniture, household goods, and appliances as *jahez*, Rs. 45,000 for the groom as *jore ki raqm*, forty grams of gold jewellery for their daughter, plus a lavish wedding feast. In order to raise enough funds to meet these demands, they leased out their house and moved into a smaller, rental accommodation.

The groom's family then failed to give their new daughter-in-law the usual gold wedding ornaments, explaining that their son would soon be going to the Gulf to work and would purchase the gold there; but her husband never did travel abroad and the promised jewellery was not forthcoming. Indeed, soon after the wedding her husband asked her to give him the gold she had received from *her* parents, so that his family could pawn it to pay some pressing family debts. She never saw her gold again and learned only later that it was being saved for her sister-in-law's upcoming marriage.

After the wedding Shahida had moved in with Salman, his parents, three brothers, and an unmarried sister, all of whom soon began to mistreat her. They instigated her husband to beat her and, when she fell ill, they refused to take her to a doctor. They made her do all the housework, but didn't feed her properly. Her father-in-law and one brother-in-law were earning good salaries but her husband was unemployed and did not, in fact, own the factory that her father had inspected. Trying to pressure him to find a job, his mother decreed that Shahida would be fed regularly only after he began to earn a living.

Shahida told her parents what was happening but they felt helpless. They realised that they had not sufficiently investigated the groom but it was now too late. From neighbours in their new locality they learned that Shahida's husband had been married (and divorced) twice before and that his family had a reputation for exploiting brides in this way—taking large dowries, abusing, and ultimately divorcing the women and keeping whatever cash, jewellery, and household goods they had brought with them. Her husband's oldest brother had been compelled by his mother to divorce his first wife, but had refused to divorce the second and had moved out with her to live separately. A younger brother had also been forced to divorce his first wife, only two months after the birth of their first child.

Shahida considered going to the police to report the abuse she was suffering but feared that, once her husband and in-laws found out what she had done, her situation would become even worse. One day, while on a visit to her parents, she went with her father to consult a well-known woman lawyer/social worker with whom he was acquainted. She called in Shahida's husband and mother-in-law to discuss the situation and then recommended that the couple set up an independent household, but two days later a divorce letter arrived in the mail at Shahida's parents' home. Her father took her to the police station and asked them to help retrieve the money and goods they had given as *jahez.* However the police inspector—allegedly having been bribed by her in-laws—dissuaded them from pursuing the matter. Shahida did receive her *mehr,* but only because her husband had pronounced and registered the divorce at the office of one of Hyderabad's government-appointed *qazi*s, who refused to issue the desired 'official' *talaqnama* until Salman deposited the Rs. 10,000 that he owed his wife.

Since this story does not come from court records but was related to me in an interview with the wife, I do not have access to the husband's version of what went wrong in the marriage. According to Shahida's narrative, Salman had failed to live up to his primary husbandly duty, that is, to provide for her material needs, and, though they lived in his parents' home, the latter even withheld food from her. Furthermore, they had not given her the gift of gold jewellery that is customary when a new daughter-in-law enters one's home and, to add insult to injury, had tricked her into handing over the gold she had received from her own parents. Finally, after the marriage ended, they had managed to retain possession of all the cash and dowry goods that her parents had provided when the couple wed. This marriage was, from the outset, based upon a web of lies and deceit, and the relationship it created was characterised by extreme deprivation and domestic violence, inflicted by a husband who Shahida and her parents had been led to believe would support her in comfort and treat her with kindness and consideration.

### An incestuous affair

Khalida, a divorced woman in her fifties, currently lives in her natal home with her mother, younger sister, and mentally ill brother. Her former husband is her father's sister's son. She divorced him—by negotiating a *khulʿ*—several years ago, after discovering that he was having an on-going affair with his mother's brother's wife (who was also *her* father's brother's wife). When she told his parents about their incestuous relationship, they accused her of making it up. In retaliation, her husband began physically abusing her. She became pregnant but the beatings continued, and she suffered a miscarriage. She sought help from a local women's NGO whose staff advised her to get a divorce: 'Leave everything behind and get ahead in life!' But because she initiated the divorce, she had to forfeit her unpaid *mehr*—Rs. 25,000 and five tolas of gold—and none of her *jahez* was returned.

Here again, I have access to only one side of the story. Like other marriages, close kin unions do not always work out, whether because of unmet expectations peculiar to this kind of match or for unrelated reasons. Khalida's divorce was precipitated by her discovery that her husband was involved with another woman (and had been, even before the marriage). Predictably, he reacted with violence when she reported it to other family members. She was unwilling to share her husband with another woman and made the decision to seek a divorce. Khalida's case is unusual in that the woman with whom he was having the illicit affair was a close kinswoman. Otherwise, one can observe very similar divorce dramas being performed over and over again in this society, in which the only difference lies in the identity of the characters.

## Conclusion

I have endeavoured here, through the analysis of four different cases of separation and/or divorce, to suggest what one can learn about marriage as an institution in this culture from the parties' narratives about what led to its break-up. I have argued that men and women go into a marriage bearing expectations that are based upon religious prescriptions and proscriptions, as well as on a broader repertoire of ideas about the responsibilities and rights of husbands and wives that are derived from other sources in their social milieu. These include their personal experiences as members of a family and community, in which they have had ample opportunity to observe both successful and unsuccessful marriages among their relatives, neighbours, and friends. Some of these expectations, like those based on the dictates of Islam, are very clear and explicit—such as the requirement that a man support his wife and that a wife should be obedient. But others, like the idea that a man should be 'kind and considerate', are somewhat more vague and open to various interpretations. A wife is likely to feel that a husband who regularly beats her up is not adhering to this most important guideline for husbandly behaviour, while a husband will easily explain his resort to violence as something he was forced to do in order to 'keep her in line'. The fact that he has beaten his wife does not detract from his self-image as a long-suffering man who tried to 'adjust' to a woman who argued with him about his financial irresponsibility, his drunkenness, his illicit affairs, and the like—and furthermore, refused to obey his every command, as a good wife should.

As we have seen, some expectations actually contradict provisions of Islamic law of which everyone is well aware. Thus, for example, in two of these cases—and in others that I could cite—many Muslim women feel that a wife has a legitimate grievance if her husband has an extramarital affair or takes a second wife, even though the latter is something that their religious law clearly permits. A woman enters a marriage knowing that she must be sexually faithful to her husband but she also expects him to reciprocate, even though neither the clerical authorities nor the male-led community at large would strongly condemn him if he did not.

While these narratives, whether oral or documented in court or police files, cannot inform us directly about what goes on in intimate marital relationships, they do provide one kind of insight into what the parties to a broken marriage found missing in that relationship, based upon the prior understandings about proper gender roles in marriage that they brought with them when they were wed. By examining a large number of such narratives many common themes are revealed that, when put all together, present a vivid picture, not only of what marriages are supposed to be like in this society, but of why they sometimes fail. In this chapter, given the particular body of data that I have access to, I have shown how Indian Muslim divorce stories can be used as resources for understanding certain of the dynamics of the institution of marriage in that community. But, of course, such narratives can provide equally valuable insights into what couples in other societies, whether in India or anywhere else in the world, expect—or at least hope—to get out of marriage.

**Endnotes**

[1] All India Muslim Personal Law Board, *Compendium of Islamic Laws*, 2nd edition (New Delhi: AIMPLB, 2002), p. 12. *Sunnat* = 'exemplary practices, customs and traditions of the Prophet' (Ron Geaves, *Key Words in Islam* [London: Continuum, 2006]), p. 104.

[2] Kirti Singh, *Separated and Divorced Women in India: Economic Rights and Entitlements* (New Delhi: Sage, 2013), pp. 74–86. In her survey of 405 separated or divorced women, 83 per cent had suffered domestic violence and 13.5 per cent had been deserted by their husbands. For Muslims specifically see my 'Muslim Women in the Indian Family Courts: A Report from Chennai', in I. Ahmad, ed., *Divorce and Remarriage among Muslims in India* (New Delhi: Manohar, 2003), pp. 147–151.

[3] On the difficulty of calculating the Muslim divorce rate see ch. 2 in this volume.

[4] In August 2013, the Rajya Sabha passed the Registration of Births and Deaths (Amendment) Bill, the first step towards instituting a universal system of compulsory registration of marriages (http://timesofindia.indiatimes.com/India/marriage-registration-to-become-mandatory/articleshow/218145554.cms [last accessed 14 September 2013]). The principal rationales for this requirement are to discourage child marriage and to make it easier to prove that one is legally married, something that is often difficult for women seeking maintenance awards (see Gopika Solanki's discussion of this issue in *Adjudication in Religious Family Laws* [Cambridge: Cambridge University Press, 2011], pp. 105–108 and in 'Flawed Reforms: Debating Legislative and Judicial Efforts towards Compulsory Registration of Marriage', in S. Basu and L. Ramberg, eds., *Conjugality Unbound: Sexual Economies, State Regulation and the Marital Form in India* [New Delhi: Women Unlimited, 2014], pp. 217–250). The Supreme Court has twice directed all state governments

to frame such rules (http://timesofindia.indiatimes.com/articleshow/msid-1414370.cms [last accessed 13 November 2008]); http://www.thehindu.com/2007/10/26/stories/2007102656810100.htm [last accessed 13 November 2008]). However, to date few have complied. The Muslim clergy, by and large, are opposed to making marriage registration compulsory for members of their own religious community. For some recent reactions, including one from a representative of the AIMPLB, see Mohd Faisal Fareed, 'Cabinet No to Compulsory Registration of Marriages', 7 December 2014, http://indianexpress.com/article/cities/lucknow/cabinet-no-to-compulsory-registration-of-marriages (last accessed 1 February 2016).

[5] Under the Hindu Marriage Act 1955, exceptions are made for members of communities that have long-standing customary procedures for informally dissolving marriages.

[6] Although some high courts and more recently the Supreme Court of India have declared such instantaneous divorces by so-called 'triple *talaq*' to be invalid (see *Jiauddin vs. Anwara Begum*, 1981 [1] GLR 358; *Rukia Khatun vs. Abdul Khalique Laskar*, 1981 [1] GLR 375; *Shamim Ara vs. State of U.P.*, 2002 [7] SCC 518), these judgments have not reduced their prevalence.

[7] See Ch. 4 in this volume. See also Livia Holden, 'Divorce at the Woman's Initiative in South Asia and in the Diasporas', in R. Mehdi, W. Menski, & J.C. Nielsen, eds., *Interpreting Divorce Laws in Islam* (Copenhagen: DJØF, 2012); Sabiha Hussain, *Shari'at Courts and Women's Rights in India* (New Delhi: Centre for Women's Development Studies, 2007); Katherine Lemons, 'At the Margins of Law: Adjudicating Muslim Families in Contemporary Delhi', unpublished Ph.D. dissertation (Berkeley: University of California, 2010).

[8] This Act provides a number of grounds on which a Muslim woman can divorce an unwilling (or unavailable) husband. There is, of course, no need for a corresponding law for Muslim men who can divorce their wives extrajudicially and unilaterally, without providing any reasons or proving any grounds.

[9] The Hindu Marriage Act, 1955, Indian Marriage Act 1869, the Special Marriage Act, 1954, and the Parsi Marriage and Divorce Act, 1936, all prescribe monogamy. Nevertheless, non-Muslims often contract second marriages without legally dissolving the first. The crime of bigamy is seldom prosecuted, firstly because it is a 'non-cognisable' offence: i.e., the police do not take notice unless the first wife (or her parents) makes a complaint. Secondly, it must be proven that both women married the man in question in ceremonies meeting the definition of a legal marriage under the relevant law code. If the man can show that either woman is simply a 'paramour', there is no case.

[10] Over the years I was helped by a number of different research assistants, to

whom I am very grateful: R. Saraswathi in Chennai and Muhammad Ayyub, H. Raees Fatima, Rafia Anjum Masrath, Reena Ambikeshwar, Bhavana Avaneendra, and Mahfooz Nazki in Hyderabad.

11 Out of the almost 400 divorces recorded in one yearly register, 54 per cent were *khulʿ*. Hyderabad *qazi*s insisted that they lack the power to dissolve a marriage without the husband's consent, though elsewhere some *qazi*s will dissolve a woman's marriage without it, by *faskh*, provided that they consider her reasons compelling. For an example from Delhi, see Lemons, 'At the Margins'. Hussain (*Shari'at Courts*) found that the vast majority of the women approaching the Darul Qaza at Pahari Sharif, Bihar, are seeking dissolution of their marriages by *faskh*, but her data show that few succeed in persuading the *qazi* that such an annulment is warranted.

12 While court records are kept in English, hearings are conducted in Tamil (in Chennai) and Telugu (in Hyderabad). If the litigant is not conversant in the local language (or in English), he or she must be provided an interpreter.

13 All names in this and subsequent case studies are pseudonyms.

14 It is customary for a bride's parents to give the groom and his family cash and lavish gifts when they marry off a daughter. Islam neither requires nor condones this practice and clerical organisations, reformist groups, women's NGOs and the Muslim press have long sought to discourage what they consider an undesirable 'innovation', adopted from their Hindu neighbours. For example, the AIMPLB characterises demands for cash, dowry gifts, and lavish wedding feasts as 'strictly against the *shari'a* and a grave sin' (AIMPLB, *Nikahnama* [New Delhi, 2005]. Nevertheless, the practice has persisted and has even become more widespread and costly in recent years. See Ch. 3 in this volume.)

15 The Code of Criminal Procedure (Amendment) Act of 2001 removed this limit. The award amount is now subject to the court's discretion.

16 Though she does not mention this in her petition—probably because the amount she was earning would make her ineligible for relief under Section 125 of the CrPC—it is not unlikely that his lack of financial responsibility was one reason for her refusal to quit her job.

17 The 1986 Muslim Women (Protection of Rights on Divorce) Act rendered *divorced* Muslim women ineligible to claim maintenance from their husbands under Section 125, to which *married* Muslim women and all women of other religions can apply, if they have no other source of income.

18 AIMPLB, *Compendium*, p. 11. This work reflects the theological orientation of the Hanafi school of Sunni Islam, which most Indian Muslims follow. The specific rights and obligations of spouses differ slightly between Sunnis and Shias and between their respective schools of law. See Kecia Ali, 'Marriage in Classical Islamic Jurisprudence: A Survey of Doctrines', in A. Quraishi and F.

E. Vogel, eds., *The Islamic Marriage Contract: Case Studies in Islamic Family Law* (Cambridge, MA: Islamic Legal Studies Program, Harvard Law School, 2009), pp. 11–45.

[19] Judith Tucker, *Women, Family, and Gender in Islamic Law* (Cambridge: Cambridge University Press, 2008), p. 41.

[20] AIMPLB, *Compendium,* p. 12. See also, for example, M. Hidayatullah and A. Hidayatullah, *Mulla's Principles of Mahomedan Law,* 19th edition (Bombay: N.M. Tripathi, 1990).

[21] Marriages between cousins and other close relatives are quite common among Muslims (see Ch. 6 in this volume). In such cases the bride and groom may have known each other from childhood, though families try to keep marriageable relatives of the opposite sex apart once they reach adolescence.

[22] These remarks apply to a bride's first marriage. A previously married woman is in a different situation from both the legal and social points of view.

[23] This hadith is related by al-Bukhari (810–870). See Muhammad ibn Isma'il Bukhari, *Sahih al-Bukhari: The Translation of the Meanings of Sahih al-Bukhari/Arabic English,* Muhammad Muhsin Khan, trans. (Gujranwala: Taleem-ul-Quran Trust, 1971).

[24] Richard Austen-Baker, *Implied Terms in English Contract Law* (Cheltenham: Edward Elgar, 2011).

[25] Tucker, *Women,* p. 50. See also John L. Esposito, *Women in Muslim Family Law* (Syracuse: Syracuse University Press, 1982), pp. 22–28; and Frances S. Hasso, *Consuming Desires: Family Crisis and the State in the Middle East* (Stanford: Stanford University Press, 2011) on these concepts as incorporated into Egyptian marriage law.

[26] Carole Pateman, *The Sexual Contract* (Stanford: Stanford University Press, 1988).

[27] These include unrelated men, as well as first and more distant cousins in her own and ascending generations.

[28] That is, she must obey his commands only insofar as they are in accord with the precepts of Islam. He must not compel her to commit a religiously forbidden act.

[29] AIMPLB, *Nikahnama,* pp. 16–17.

[30] Ali, 'Marriage,' pp. 21–25; Tucker, *Women,* pp. 49–50.

[31] Lucy Carroll, '*Talaq-i-Tafwid* and Stipulations in a Muslim Marriage Contract: Important Means of Protecting the Position of the South Asian Muslim Wife', *Modern Asian Studies* 16(2) (1982): 277–309.

[32] Tucker, *Women,* pp. 61–63.

[33] Gail Minault, *Secluded Scholars: Women's Education and Muslim Social Reform in Colonial India* (New Delhi: Oxford University Press, 1998), p. 299.

[34] Nida Kirmani, 'Claiming their Space: Muslim Women-led Networks and the

Women's Movement in India', *Journal of International Women's Studies* 11(1) (2009): 72–85; Nadja-Christina Schneider, 'Islamic Feminism and Muslim Women's Rights Activism in India: From Transnational Discourse to Local Movement—or Vice Versa?', *Journal of International Women's Studies* 11(1) (2009): 56–70; Sylvia Vatuk, 'Islamic Feminism in India: Indian Muslim Women Activists and the Reform of Muslim Personal Law', in this volume.

[35] See Mengia Hong Tschalaer, 'Competing Model-*Nikahnamas*: Muslim Women's Spaces Within the Legal Landscape in Lucknow', *Journal of Law and Social Research* 3 (2012): 65–80; Nida Kirmani, 'Re-thinking the Promotion of Women's Rights through Islam in India', *IDS Bulletin* 42 (1) (2011): 56–66; Katherine Lemons, 'When Marriage Breaks Down, How do Contracts Matter? Marriage Contracts and Divorce in Contemporary North India', in R. Palriwala and Ravinder Kaur, eds., *Marriage and Globalization in India* (New Delhi: Orient BlackSwan, 2014), pp. 371–388.

[36] AIMPLB, *Nikahnama*. This document was originally posted in Urdu and English on the organisation's website (www.aimplboard.org) but has since been removed. A spokesman for the Board admitted in a 2011 interview that it had not been widely circulated and 'very few people were actually using' it. (IANS, 'Model Nikahnama Missing from Muslim Law Board Website', 20 February 2011, http://www.highbeam.com/doc/1P3-22271516801.html [last accessed 5 May 2013]).

[37] Geeta Seshu, 'Nikahnama: Time for a Gender-Just Model', June 2005, http://www.humanscape.org/Humanscape/2005/June/nikah/php (last accessed 26 April 2006).

[38] I have not been able to personally examine this document. For summaries of its contents see Tschalaer, 'Competing Model-*Nikahnamas*', pp. 69–70; Farzand Ahmed, 'Triple Failure: Approval of New Nikahnama by Shia Personal Law Board Hits Controversy', 11 December 2006, http://indiatoday.in/story/new-nikahnama-for-shia-muslims/1/180078/html (last accessed 30 August 2013).

[39] Seshu, 'Nikahnama'.

[40] The AIMPLB then had 201 members, of whom 25 were women. Currently it has 28 women out of a total membership of 251, but activists frequently complain that some are insufficiently committed to promoting women's interests within the organisation.

[41] Manjari Mishra, 'Muslim Women to Pen "Nikahnama"' *Times of India*, New Delhi, 31 January 2006.

[42] All India Muslim's Women Personal Law Board, *Shar'i Nikahnama* (Lucknow, 2008). See Lemons, 'When Marriage Breaks Down' and Tschalaer, 'Competing Model-*Nikahnamas*', for more details, analyses, assessments, and critiques of the document.

[43] Bharatiya Muslim Mahila Andolan, 'About BMMA', http://bmmaindia.com/about (last accessed 3 January 2016).

[44] Bharatiya Muslim Mahila Andolan, *Nikahnama and Iqraarnama* (Lucknow: BMMA, 2008). See also Tschalaer, 'Competing Model-*Nikahnamas*'.

[45] Nida Kirmani, 'Re-Thinking', p. 61.

[46] Under the Family Courts Act 1984, disputing couples must undergo one or more counselling sessions with an in-house social worker or psychologist before their case comes up before the judge.

# 8.

# Maintenance for Divorced Muslim Women after the Muslim Women (Protection of Rights on Divorce) Act, 1986

## a view from the lower courts

### Introduction

In recent decades there has been a good deal of controversy over one particular issue in MPL, that is, whether and for how long a Muslim man is responsible for the support of a wife whom he has divorced. Disputes over this question go back to the 1898 Criminal Procedure Code (CrPC), which is applicable to all Indian citizens, regardless of religion. Chapter 36 of that code (entitled 'Of the Maintenance of Wives and Children') was aimed at ensuring that destitute persons would not become a financial burden upon the colonial state. Section 488 (S488) of that chapter stated that any man who neglects or refuses to maintain his wife can be ordered by a magistrate to pay her a monthly allowance.[1] When the CrPC was revised in 1973, S488 was replaced by Section 125 (S125). The new section did not depart greatly from its predecessor, except that it added a provision for the maintenance of parents by their adult children[2] and, more controversially, redefined the word 'wife' to include 'a woman who has been divorced by, or has obtained a divorce from, her husband and has not remarried'.[3] This latter change met strong opposition from the Muslim clerical establishment, which insisted that Muslim men should be exempted from its provisions, since it contravened Islamic law. Their contention was that under Islamic law a Muslim man's financial responsibility for a divorced wife ends once she has completed the religiously prescribed post-divorce waiting period of approximately three months.[4] The clerics' demand was resisted by legislators but, in order to partially satisfy their objections, a clause was inserted into the subsequent section 127 that allowed a maintenance order to be cancelled if the woman had already received 'the sum which, under [the parties'] ... customary or personal law ... was payable on such divorce'.[5] While this passage does not specifically mention, it clearly references, the Islamic requirement that, upon divorcing his wife, a man must make good on the promise of a gift of cash or valuables to his wife (her *mehr*) that is part of every Muslim marriage contract. It also refers to the rule that he must maintain her until she completes her *ᶜiddat*. Notwithstanding the presence of this clause, divorced Muslim women continued for over a decade to file under S125 in order to obtain maintenance stipends from their husbands. The favourable judgments that they often received were regularly upheld by the various high courts when they went up on appeal.

Not surprisingly, the Muslim clergy continued to object to—and to participate in appeals against—such judgments, but it was not until 1986 that their demands for a change in the law met with success. The precipitating event was a maintenance suit filed in 1978 in a district court in central India by a married Muslim woman in her sixties named Shah Bano.[6] Her estranged husband was a successful lawyer who, she claimed, earned approximately Rs. 5,000 per month from his practice. The couple had been married for forty-six years and had five adult offspring; the husband also had another wife and children living in the same household. Shah Bano's husband had recently ejected her from the marital home. In the beginning he had regularly sent her a small monthly living allowance, but after a while he ceased doing so. She then had difficulty covering her living expenses and decided to file suit against him for maintenance under S125. Before the judge could render a decision, her husband informed the court that he had divorced her, had immediately paid her *mehr* and *ᶜiddat* expenses, and therefore had no further responsibility for her support. But the magistrate disagreed with his understanding of the law and ordered him to begin making maintenance payments of Rs. 25 per month. Shah Bano's lawyer soon applied to the high court of the state for an enhanced amount and in 1980 succeeded in having her stipend increased to Rs. 179.20. Her husband appealed that decision to the Supreme Court of India, but in April 1985 his appeal was dismissed and he was assessed an additional Rs. 10,000 towards his wife's legal costs.

That Supreme Court judgment was widely publicised and, not only because of its substance but also because of the way it was phrased, created a furore within the Muslim religious establishment. Mass demonstrations were organised all over the country, petitions were circulated, speeches were delivered on public platforms, and the issue was extensively publicised and debated in media. Pressure began to build for the passage of legislation that would clarify, once and for all, that Muslim men have no obligation to support their divorced wives after *ᶜiddat.*

The outcome of this prolonged agitation was the passage of the Muslim Women (Protection of Rights on Divorce) Act 1986 (MWA) by Parliament. It provided that, once a divorced Muslim woman's *ᶜiddat* expenses have been paid and she has received her *mehr* and any money or other property that at the time of their marriage had been gifted to her by her family, her husband or his relatives and friends, his financial responsibility for her is at an end. She can no longer turn to S125 for a maintenance order against him, as she could have in the past.[7] Should she have no other means of support at that time, she can ask a magistrate to order her adult children (if any) or one or more of her natal relatives to maintain her.[8] If she has no such kin, or if none are in a financial position to provide for her, the Wakf Board[9] of the state in which she resides can be ordered to pay her a monthly living allowance.

## The impact of the MWA: contrasting views

Not surprisingly, feminists and human rights activists were from the outset strongly critical of the MWA, characterising it as a discriminatory law that singles out Muslim women and deprives them of a fundamental right, in contravention of India's constitutional guarantee of equality for all citizens under the law. At that time, most scholars and legal activists took it for granted that the Act would have serious detrimental consequences for all divorced Muslim women. They predicted that men dissatisfied with their wives would now be motivated to formally divorce them—rather than simply abandon or eject them from the home—in order to avoid being subject to a maintenance order. They considered it unrealistic, in the existing Indian cultural context, to expect a divorced woman, no matter how needy, to take the extreme step of filing a suit for maintenance against an adult child, a parent or sibling: most women in such a situation would resign themselves to living in destitution, rather than alienate their closest kin by taking them to court. Untold numbers of Muslim divorcées would consequently be left penniless and starving, bereft of any avenue of relief. Indeed there is some evidence that the MWA does provide a convenient way out for Muslim men threatened by maintenance suits. Advocates routinely inform male clients that they can avoid a maintenance order by simply pronouncing a unilateral divorce (*talaq*). Judges in the civil and family courts that handle such cases often have a similar understanding of the Act's intent: upon learning that a Muslim petitioner has been divorced by her husband, they are frequently disposed to throw out her case immediately.

The original assumption underlying this negative prognosis for the MWA was that the courts would confirm the desire of those who had drafted the law to see that the Muslim husband's responsibility for his former wife would cease once he had paid her *mehr* and a modest amount for her *ᶜiddat* expenses, and had returned to her all of her wedding gifts. This perception of the Act is still the received wisdom for much of the non-Muslim public at large, for those politicians who favour enactment of a Uniform Civil Code of personal law[10] and for many, though not all, feminist legal activists and scholars. But before long, cases began to accumulate from different state high courts indicating that some judges were interpreting the law quite differently from the way its authors had intended. Most of these cases were appeals by men of lower court judgments awarding their wives or ex-wives maintenance stipends under S125. Citing the MWA in support of their stance, they claimed that since they had already divorced their wives and paid whatever was due to them, they were no longer legally bound to pay maintenance. But increasing numbers of high court plaintiffs found their appeals dismissed: instead they were ordered to make longer-term financial provisions for their former wives, in amounts that varied according to the particular judge's assessment of the man's income and assets and the wife's needs, usually taking into account the standard of living to which she had been accustomed before the divorce.[11]

The key concept in dispute here was the 'reasonable and fair provision', which the MWA directs the husband to make for his ex-wife during the *ᶜiddat* period: does this phrase simply refer in different words to the 'maintenance' that he is instructed to pay her during her *ᶜiddat*, or is it a reference to something that she is entitled to receive above and beyond that?[12] In at least 15 of the reported cases decided under the Act between 1987 and 2000, the woman's right to a 'reasonable and fair' amount *in addition to* her *ᶜiddat* expenses was upheld by the appeals courts.[13] In 2001 these judgments were confirmed by a Supreme Court judgment in a case challenging the constitutionality of the MWA for violating the fundamental rights of Muslim divorced women by excluding them from the protection of S125. There the apex court decreed, in the Danial Latifi case, that *during the ᶜiddat period* a Muslim man is liable to make a payment to his ex-wife that will secure her ability to sustain herself *in the future*.[14] Those who drafted the original legislation meant to ensure that a Muslim man would be obliged to provide for his divorced wife *only until she had completed* her *ᶜiddat*; but case law now required a different reading, and courts began in increasing numbers to order men to give their ex-wives substantial lump sum cash amounts (in addition to maintaining them during *ᶜiddat*) or to transfer to them some material asset, such as land, a house, gold jewellery or stocks.

Thereafter, opinions about the impact of the MWA underwent a change. Now some feminist legal scholars began to take a revisionist view of the 1986 law, suggesting that its passage had had an unintended *positive* effect on the ability of divorced Muslim women to obtain financial assistance from their ex-husbands. They began to feel that rather than being disadvantaged by the fact that they could no longer resort to S125, Muslim women were finding the 1986 Act 'a blessing in disguise, bringing ... newer alternatives for a more viable economic settlement', and 'scope for more innovative safeguards' for women's financial well-being after divorce.[15]

Those who cast this more positive light upon the MWA have, for the most part, relied upon their analyses of some of the high court and Supreme Court judgments I have mentioned to support their revisionist views. Indeed, almost all the literature on both sides of the issue is based on data from such sources.[16] While appellate cases are unquestionably of great importance, especially insofar as they produce judgments that set precedents for future litigation, they are clearly not fully representative of the totality of cases filed in the lower courts on a given subject. Thus, I argue, when attempting to determine the overall impact of the MWA, it is not sufficient to limit oneself to examining reported decisions from the high and Supreme Courts. The number of cases filed under the MWA even in the lower courts is very small; of these, only a tiny, highly selective sample goes on to appeal. Access to the appeals process is naturally limited by the high cost (in money and time) of pursuing a high court case. The cost of an appeal to the highest court of the land is, of course, far higher. Consequently, appellants tend to be considerably more well-to-do than the average respondent to an original suit under the Act. With few exceptions, the amounts at issue are correspondingly higher as well. Thus, in order to better gauge whether the Act has been detrimental or beneficial to the welfare of the generality of Muslim divorced women, it is important to also examine the case records of the lower courts, where litigants represent a broader and more diverse segment—economically and likely also in other respects—of the heterogeneous social category of 'divorced Muslim women'. Class is clearly a differentiating factor of particular salience in this regard.

The research upon which this paper is based was therefore designed to explore the question of how the MWA has affected divorced Muslim women in the years since its passage by looking at the experiences of those who have filed suits under the Act in the lower courts of two cities, Delhi and Hyderabad. I spent one month in Delhi and three months in Hyderabad in the autumn and winter of 2005–2006, interviewing local scholars, advocates, judges, Muslim clerics, Muslim women activists, and NGOs working with poor Muslim women. With the help of research assistants,[17] I also interviewed separated and divorced Muslim women on issues related to divorce and maintenance, focusing on their own perceptions of and experience with these matters. In both cities we observed court proceedings and examined court records of maintenance suits under MWA and CrPC S125.[18]

Most of our archival research took place in Hyderabad, in the criminal courts complex, where MWA cases are dealt with by a magistrate whose primary assignment is to adjudicate cases of crimes against women under various sections of the Indian Penal Code. This court, like similar ones in Delhi and other cities, is commonly referred to as the mahila (i.e., women's) court. The overwhelming bulk of its caseload pertains to charges of domestic abuse filed by wives and /or daughters-in-law under Section 498A of the IPC; it is only occasionally that the magistrate is called upon to deal with an MWA case.[19] S125 maintenance suits are heard in the additional family court, which is located within the same criminal premises; there we were able to examine case registers and some individual case files as well.[20]

## Factors that discourage resort to the courts

Only a small minority of financially distressed divorcées (of any religion) ever get to the point of filing a maintenance suit, either under S125 or the MWA. Few divorced women are well-informed about the law, and even the men of their families are unlikely to know very much about the legal remedies available to them. If they have any idea at all about avenues of legal resort, it is largely from hearsay. They are unlikely to know anyone else who has gone through the process of obtaining an award under the MWA. They may be somewhat more familiar with the options available to married women under S125, but are likely to believe that, since they are no longer married, no court will entertain their application for financial assistance.

## Uneven distribution of knowledge within the legal profession

As far as the MWA in particular is concerned, an advocate should be in a better position than the average woman to know what her legal options are. However, in practice, given the relatively small number of suits filed under the Act in most jurisdictions, few have had much, if any, experience arguing this kind of case. I found that both within the legal profession and between different jurisdictions, levels of awareness, knowledge about, and degrees of understanding of the provisions of the Act, and the possibilities it can offer a female client are highly unevenly distributed.

Since there is relatively little specialisation among lawyers, especially among those practicing in the lower courts, and since family law is in any case neither very prestigious nor very lucrative and does not necessarily attract the best talent, most suits under the Act are handled by advocates for whom such cases are merely a sideline. Even if an advocate is fairly accustomed to dealing with S125 pleadings, he or she is not necessarily also conversant with MWA and the relevant case law associated with it. This is especially so if he or she is not a Muslim. Muslim lawyers do tend to have a higher proportion of Muslim clients than lawyers of other religions and they are likely to be more knowledgeable about the options open to a divorced Muslim woman than the average Hindu or Christian lawyer. But Muslim lawyers are not very numerous, even in a heavily Muslim city like Hyderabad, and are not as likely as their Hindu and Christian colleagues to have been trained at one of the better law schools.[21] Like those colleagues, however, they tend to gravitate towards areas of the law other than MPL and only occasionally take on maintenance cases, whether under S125 or the MWA.

I have no data concerning the religion of the advocates who represented Muslim clients in the S125 cases we examined,[22] but for the 47 MWA cases filed after 1995 whose complete files we were able to examine and in which the advocate was identified, I found only five Hindu names. Each of them had argued only one case. Twenty-two Muslim lawyers were responsible for the rest of the cases; most of these had likewise argued only a single case,[23] as had the only woman among them, the young lawyer, Mumtaz Sultana.[24]

The uneven spread of knowledge about MWA within the legal profession and the stark differences between cities in terms of the extent to which—and the way in which—that Act is made use of was brought home to me in a very striking way when, in the first month of my research, I sought to discover how the MWA was being used in Delhi. I first interviewed several advocates, all Hindus, who had been recommended to me for their experience and expertise on personal law issues, women's rights, and crimes against women. None of them had ever handled an MWA case, nor indeed could recall ever having had more than one or two Muslim women clients in the course of their entire careers. All but one professed to be unaware of recent developments in the case law pertaining to MWA. Almost invariably, at some point in the interview, the predictable rhetoric about 'Muslim woman as victim of Islamic law, men, and the *mullahs*' was brought out, in the guise of informing me, the ignorant foreigner, of what I would be up against in undertaking the research project I had chosen.

I then sought out a well-known Muslim law professor, M.A. Wani. He was extremely helpful and was gratified to hear about my research plans, as he himself had published scholarly works on issues of maintenance for Muslim women.[25] Though he was naturally aware of the various high court decisions on the Act over the interpretation of the 'reasonable and fair provision' concept and was very familiar with the reasoning in the Danial Latifi decision[26] he had not personally heard of any cases filed under that Act in any of the lower courts in Delhi. He was not even sure where one would go to file such a case, he offered to assign a few of his better students to go to the criminal courts at Tis Hazari and Patiala House to look into the matter and, if possible, obtain some hard data on such questions as the number of cases filed, their outcomes, and the changes in these that may have occurred over time. The students pursued their task with diligence and enthusiasm but came up with a complete blank. None of the court officials, judges or registrars could provide any information about cases filed under MWA, either in any of the several mahila courts in their premises or in the special court at Tis Hazari to which all cases related to MPL are directed. The Hindu judge of this latter court explained that most of his caseload has to do with 'unauthorised construction' and only about ten per cent involve issues of MPL. He had never had a case filed under MWA in all the years that he had held his present post. The magistrates I interviewed who preside over the mahila courts at Tis Hazari expressed similar ignorance of the matter.[27]

Then I spoke to a number of Muslim advocates, one of whom practices exclusively in the high court, but has a particular interest in matters of Islamic law and has published articles on MWA, the Shah Bano case, the implications of the Latifi case, and other current issues related to Muslim law in India. Through him I was introduced to three more junior lawyers who had had considerable experience arguing MPL cases in the lower civil courts. They each indicated that their clientele is predominantly Muslim, and many are women. They were, of course, familiar in general terms with the MWA but none had ever filed a case under it. One told me that he had never heard of such a case being filed and that, as far as he was aware, the MWA is 'not the kind of Act under which one even *can* file a case!' There is no procedure for doing so, he asserted. The Act can only be used to defeat a suit for maintenance under S125.

When I asked how he would advise a divorced Muslim woman in need of monetary assistance to proceed, he said that his usual method was to file for maintenance under S125, just as if his client were still married. If the husband then claimed that he had already divorced her, the next step would be to contest the validity of the divorce. At that point the husband would doubtless pronounce *talaq* again. But in this way, at worst, the woman would be awarded maintenance from the time her husband had stopped supporting her, up to the effective date of the most recent divorce. He was, he said, currently defending a man in a case of just this kind. His client's evidence was a 'deed of divorce' with both his and his wife's signatures and thumbprints thereon. He also had two witnesses to the divorce having been pronounced several years before, but the wife was claiming that her signature had been taken on blank paper before the supposed 'deed' was executed. The case had not yet been decided at the time of our interview.

Thus any question about the practical impact of the MWA, whether it has been for good or for ill, must take this into account as one aspect of an overarching social context in which there are so many other factors discouraging women from ever considering an application to the court, when faced with the problem of how to survive after divorce. While the laws governing the maintenance of estranged wives and ex-wives could in theory provide a valuable 'legal resource' for women in such situations, it is one that relatively few divorced Muslim women and few practicing advocates either know about or actually make use of.

## The MWA in the Hyderabad courts

When I arrived in Hyderabad to explore issues of the MWA, I was gratified to find that the situation there was very different from the one that prevailed in Delhi. Advocates in Hyderabad had been filing cases under the Act ever since it came into effect, although, especially before 2001, it appears that most used it simply to get the husband to fulfil his obligation to pay *mehr*, maintain his ex-wife for the *ᶜiddat* period, return any dowry[28] items (or their value in cash) that had been left behind when she departed or was thrown out of the marital home, and perhaps also to recover cash gifts received by the groom as *ghora jora* or *jore ki raqm*.[29] Some advocates had become aware, even early on, that they could also ask for 'reasonable and fair provision' beyond the *ᶜiddat* period for their client. Nowadays, when a Hyderabad advocate takes on an MWA case, he almost always has the woman petition for as much as the Act allows and it is not unusual for them to obtain substantial monetary awards for their clients under this rubric.

The father-son partnership of Muhammad Hamid Ali and Muhammad Turab Ali,[30] whose practice is devoted mainly to criminal defence, especially for those accused of murder, represented more women in cases filed under MWA than any other advocate during the eleven year period for which I have information—14 in all. Mr. Hamid Ali told me that he had been filing such cases many years prior to 1995, usually acting on behalf of the wife, but occasionally representing husbands who had approached him because the court had ordered them to give 'too much' to their former wives. Another very senior criminal defence lawyer, Mahmood Hussain, deferred to Hamid Ali for his extensive record of experience in this kind of case. For his part, he claimed to have argued only 15 MWA cases in his entire career. He said he had filed the first of these in 1988. He has only represented women in cases filed under MWA and told me that he always asks for 'reasonable and fair provision' along with *mehr*, *ᶜiddat* expenses, the return of *jahez*, etc. By way of illustration he recalled a recent case that he had filed under Section 3 of MWA[31] for a woman who had married in 2000. She claimed that her parents had given her husband Rs. 25,000 cash in *jore ki raqm* plus a scooter worth Rs. 20,000. Her *jahez* had consisted of two *tolas*[32] of gold, plus furniture, utensils, and other household goods worth Rs. 60,000. The lawyer explained, 'He and his family were greedy. He was running a hotel, earning a lot, and also had some land business.'[33] A year after the wedding he sent his wife 'a divorce letter' through the *qazi*—she was apparently no longer living in the marital home—and deposited the Rs. 15,000 *mehr* in the *qazi*'s office. In court he denied all her claims, but the magistrate was persuaded that he hadn't fully discharged his liabilities at the time of the divorce. Rather than wait for the judge's decision, however, the couple agreed to an out-of-court settlement that gave her Rs. 55,000 out of her original claim of well over Rs. 1,00,000.[34]

In our examination of registers and case files in the additional family court of Hyderabad, we found that between 1999 and 2005 a total of 1,425 maintenance suits had been filed under S125.[35] The plaintiff was Muslim in 614 (43 per cent) of these, slightly above the proportion of Muslims in the city's population, which was 41 per cent in 2001.

Thus Muslim women, at least in Hyderabad,[36] appear to have been filing under S125 at a somewhat higher rate than women of other religions, even though only those who are *still married* are eligible to file for maintenance (on their own behalf), whereas Hindu and Christian women can do so even after divorce. The average number of Muslim cases filed per year during this entire period was 88, but it rose steadily from 2001 to 2005, from a low of 50 to a high of 122.[37] Still, these numbers are very small in relation to the city's one and a half million-strong Muslim population, within which there must be many thousands of estranged and abandoned women, and others ejected by their husbands from their marital homes, who have chosen or been forced to find ways other than resorting to the courts to sustain themselves.

**Table 1**
**Cases filed under S125 in the Hyderabad family court and additional family court, 1999–2005**

| | | *Muslim cases filed* | |
|---|---|---|---|
| *Year* | *Total cases filed* | *Number* | *Percentage* |
| 1999 | 168 | 70 | 41 |
| 2000 | 140 | 57 | 40 |
| 2001 | 119 | 50 | 42 |
| 2002 | 180 | 79 | 44 |
| 2003 | 268 | 116 | 43 |
| 2004 | 289 | 120 | 42 |
| 2005 | 261 | 122 | 47 |
| Total | 1,425 | 614 | 43 |

We were also able to examine court registers in the Hyderabad mahila court and thereby determined that 224 suits were filed under MWA in the years 1995–2005. Forty-six suits were filed in 1995: this was the largest number filed in a single year. Thereafter there was a significant drop: the number since then has fluctuated between nine and 31 per year. Most of the petitioners sought *mehr* and /or *ʿiddat* expenses, return of goods and cash given by the bride's family as *jahez* and *ghora jora*, and /or wedding gifts given by relatives and friends on the husband's side (*chadhava*). Many, though not all, had also submitted claims for 'reasonable and fair provision'. Some of these cases dragged on for years. Thus, by the end of 2005 65 (30 per cent) of the cases filed in the previous decade were still pending. Thirty-nine had been pending for more than a year and 15 for five years or more. Eighty-eight cases (40 per cent of the total number filed) had been dismissed, because the petitioner had either ceased making the required court appearances, had declared that she did not wish to pursue the case further, and /or had reached an out-of-court settlement with her former spouse. Thus in only one-quarter of the cases had a judgment been pronounced by the

**Table 2**
**Cases filed under MWA in the Hyderabad mahila court, 1995–2005**

| *Year* | *Total* | *Pending* | *Dismissed for default or not pressed* | *Settled out of court* | *Judgment passed* | *No information* |
|---|---|---|---|---|---|---|
| 1995 | 46 | 0 | 16 | 3 | 19 | 8 |
| 1996 | 31 | 0 | 15 | 0 | 11 | 5 |
| 1997 | 15 | 1 | 8 | 2 | 4 | 0 |
| 1998 | 9 | 0 | 4 | 1 | 3 | 1 |
| 1999 | 11 | 2 | 6 | 0 | 2 | 1 |
| 2000 | 22 | 6 | 4 | 7 | 5 | 0 |
| 2001 | 13 | 3 | 5 | 2 | 3 | 0 |
| 2002 | 12 | 5 | 2 | 0 | 5 | 0 |
| 2003 | 21 | 11 | 6 | 2 | 2 | 0 |
| 2004 | 17 | 11 | 4 | 1 | 1 | 0 |
| 2005 | 27 | 26 | 0 | 0 | 1 | 0 |
| Total | 224 | 65 | 70 | 18 | 56 (25%) | 15 |

time I left the field. In almost every one of these, the husband had been ordered to pay some amount to his former wife, though not always all that she had petitioned for.[38]

For example, in December 1999, by which time Afzal Bano's[39] MWA case had been running for four and a half years, her ex-husband, a private chauffeur, was ordered to pay her a combined amount of Rs. 3,100 for *mehr* and *ᶜiddat* maintenance, plus Rs. 36,820 as the value of her *jahez* and *chadhava* gifts. She had apparently not asked for 'reasonable and fair provision'. In this case the judge awarded her everything that she had asked for, though it took many years to achieve this outcome. Of those women who did ask for 'reasonable and fair provision', many were awarded fairly substantial amounts—in the range of Rs. 25,000 to 50,000—under that heading.

Thus in a case filed in August 1998 but not decided until June

2002, Rabia Begum was granted Rs. 4,100 as *mehr* and *ᶜiddat* expenses, plus Rs. 25,000 as 'reasonable and fair provision'. Another litigant, Amina Begum, apparently had a 'love marriage'[40] but lived with her husband for only five days, during which he allegedly tried to kill her by dousing her with kerosene. When she charged him with attempted murder, he divorced her and was later acquitted of the charge. Four years after the divorce, Amina filed a case under MWA. She asked for Rs. 3,400 *mehr*, Rs. 500 per month for maintenance during *ᶜiddat*, the return of her *jahez* articles or their value in cash, Rs. 25,000 as 'reasonable and fair provision', and Rs. 500 in court costs. Her ex-husband was ordered to pay her everything except for *ᶜiddat* expenses, since he was able to show that he had made a direct deposit to her bank account for that amount immediately after communicating to her that he had pronounced triple *talaq*. There is also no indication that he was ordered to return her *jahez* goods. One can only speculate upon the reason. Perhaps she was unable to provide written evidence of what she had been given;[41] or perhaps when she went to the police to report this attempt to set her afire, the police, as is their usual practice, had accompanied her to the home and compelled him to hand over all her belongings before taking him off to the police station.

## Judgments against a divorcée's relatives

I have mentioned the provision of the MWA contained in Section 4(1), wherein it is stated that if the woman has not remarried and cannot maintain herself after *ᶜiddat*, the magistrate may order her adult children, parents, or other natal kin to do so.[42] However, such orders are infrequently issued. Subramanian, after surveying some of the relevant MWA appellate case law from the 1980s and 1990s, observes that judges rarely 'direct the divorcée's heirs ... to support the woman'.[43] My own research in Hyderabad confirms that in the lower courts it is extremely rare for a woman to even invoke the MWA against a child or one of her natal relatives: I found not a single example in the magistrate's records that I examined.[44]

## Judgments against a Wakf Board

However, there is another option available to destitute Muslim divorcées, namely that contained in Section 4(2) of the MWA, which addresses situations in which the plaintiff either has no children or other potential heirs or has none who are financially able to contribute to her support. In such a case, the magistrate 'may, by order, direct the state Wakf Board ... to pay such maintenance as determined by him under sub-section(1)...'. Whereas Subramanian also asserts in the passage cited above that the courts rarely order a woman's state Wakf Board to provide for her, in fact it has become increasingly common in recent years for divorced women in need to successfully file under this sub-section of the law for a monthly stipend.[45] That they are entitled to ask for and receive such stipends, even if they have not first filed unsuccessfully against their potential heirs, was firmly established by a 1996 Supreme Court ruling.[46] Appeals by Wakf Boards, on a variety of grounds, against such maintenance orders did not entirely cease after that decision was issued, but they have rarely been successful.

States and their respective Wakf Boards have responded differently to the requirement that they provide financial assistance to poor divorcées when ordered to do so by the courts. Although, as I have noted, it was an appeal by the Tamil Nadu state Wakf Board that led to the definitive Supreme Court ruling on the subject, that Board, according to its own website, was maintaining only eleven women in 2012.[47] Eligible women in the state of Orissa also experienced difficulties in this regard. The state judiciary has been very proactive through 2007, issuing orders for as many as 546 divorcées to be assisted by the Orissa state Wakf Board with amounts ranging from Rs. 400 to Rs. 700 per month. However, that board was extremely dilatory in making the ordered payments. Once in 2007 and then again in 2011 hundreds of women took to the streets in the capital, Bhubaneswar, to protest the delays.[48] Whether after the second of these mass demonstrations the board began disbursing the funds is not known.

The situation in Andhra Pradesh appears to be much better. Until 2005 very few suits had been filed under the MWA against the Andhra Pradesh state Wakf Board. I discovered in the court records that, in the late 1990s, advocate Hamid Ali had argued one such case. The magistrate had allowed the petition but the Wakf Board had appealed. However, before the high court rendered a decision, a settlement was reached and the Board began paying the woman Rs. 500 per month.

On December 12, 2005, soon after my arrival in Hyderabad, I happened to see a news item in the local edition of the *Times of India* informing its readers that, although the Andhra Pradesh state Wakf Board had a fund of Rs. 30,00,000 set aside to support divorced Muslim women, only four women were drawing from it so far. The money had been accumulating at a rate of Rs. 10 lakhs per year for the past three years. Women 'could get anything between Rs. 500 and Rs. 3,000 per month ... depending upon the recommendation of courts'. However, the article explained, they cannot apply directly to the Board for this stipend but must file suit under MWA and obtain a court order. This had apparently discouraged women from trying to access the fund.[49] Within two weeks of the publication of that news report, seven new suits for maintenance had been filed against the Andhra Pradesh state Wakf Board in the mahila court of Hyderabad, six of them by advocate Hamid Ali! Evidently other advocates in the state soon began to follow his lead, because in March 2012 the Board was, by its own account, supporting 320 divorced Muslim women.[50] Funds for the purpose were reportedly being provided by the State Minorities Commission.[51]

## Conclusion

It is clearly not possible, either on the basis of my research or on that of previous scholars, to give a simple yes or no answer to the question of whether the MWA, in the quarter century of its existence, has been advantageous or detrimental to the generality of divorced Muslim women. Before one could even try to answer this question, it would need to be reframed, as the reality is much more complicated than it appears to be at first glance. There is no doubt that some women can and have benefitted from the MWA's clause—in Section 3(1)(a)—mandating 'reasonable and fair provision' for a divorced wife. In some cases the lump sum amounts awarded by the courts have been quite substantial, as Agnes[52] and others have documented on the basis of their studies of high court cases, and as my own data from the mahila court in Hyderabad confirm. But the women who receive these generous awards are not, by and large, the same women who would in the past have been able to obtain maintenance awards by filing under S125 of the CrPC. Well-to-do women are rarely in evidence among the litigants in the courts that deal with S125 cases. In order to obtain a maintenance order under that section one must first demonstrate that one has no other source of income, that one is essentially destitute.[53] A woman of a well-to-do or even a middle-class background cannot easily convince the court that she is in this position. Most of those who seek relief under this section of the CrPC, therefore, come from lower-income groups.[54]

Furthermore, until 2001 the maximum amount that could be awarded under S125 was Rs. 500, much too little to meet the needs of a woman accustomed to a comfortable lifestyle.[55] Solanki, who has analysed MWA cases from the Mumbai metropolitan magistrates' court, makes a similar point, observing that, prior to the enactment of the MWA, women of the middle and upper classes 'fell through the cracks, as there was no provision to address their financial vulnerability post-divorce [*sic*]. They could not seek recourse to Section 125 CrPC because the amounts granted ... were too low for them to go through the process of litigation. The [MWA] ... bridges this gap.'[56]

Under the MWA, as we have seen, the husband is required to make good on the unpaid balance of his wife's deferred *mehr*, return all her wedding gifts, including jewellery and cash, maintain her for three months after the divorce, and hand over an amount sufficient to enable her to get a new start in life. It therefore goes without saying that only those whose husbands have sufficient means to comply with such an order can hope to truly benefit from this clause in the Act. The MWA is much less well-suited to the needs of lower-class divorcées, those who used to be able to apply for maintenance under S125. A low-income man who has divorced his wife might be able to pay her a modest living allowance each month, should she go to court and succeed in winning an S125 maintenance award; but he is unlikely to be in a financial position to pay all of his religiously required obligations and also hand over a substantial lump sum in cash, which is what a judge normally requires that he do by way of 'reasonable and fair provision' under the MWA.

Thus, although in theory the revised interpretation of S3(1) (a) of the MWA can serve the needs of *any* Muslim divorcée, in practice a woman whose former husband has few or no assets, and earns a meagre and fluctuating income, is unlikely to be able to benefit from it, at least as long as the current practice of assessing a lump sum payment or the transfer of valuable assets continues to prevail. Even if a poor woman finds a way to pay for the costs of a court suit under the MWA and her advocate persuades the judge to decide the case in her favour, it is unlikely that her ex-husband will be able to come up with enough money to make the whole exercise worth her while. As Agnes has recently observed, one advantage of the 1986 law is that it entitles a divorced woman to receive a one-time payment, thus relieving her of the need to file, sometimes repeatedly, for execution of an order for a recurring monthly stipend, as would be required under S125. But the 'reasonable and fair' provision of the MWA has a negative side as well, in that 'a poor Muslim husband may not have the resources to pay an adequate amount as a lump sum'. This forces his ex-wife to resign herself to a meagre settlement that falls far short of ensuring her survival for the rest of her life.[57]

However, one fairly recent development in the case law on the MWA has begun to open up real possibilities for low-income women to be included in significant numbers among its beneficiaries. Somewhat surprisingly, this phenomenon has drawn very little, if any, attention from legal scholars. I refer here to the increasing willingness of magistrates to order state Wakf Boards to provide maintenance stipends to destitute Muslim divorcées. In that connection, increasing numbers of state governments have begun providing their Boards with funds specially designated for that purpose. There are, admittedly, persisting problems in some states with the implementation of these new judicial directives. It is understandable that Wakf Boards are often reluctant to take responsibility for divorced women: they were originally set up for very different purposes and have had no prior history of engagement in social service activities of this or any other analogous kind. Furthermore, there are many competing demands on state budgets and it is not a foregone conclusion that those in authority will always be prepared to prioritise the needs of minority institutions like the Wakf Boards or the poor minority women whom they are increasingly being required to serve. The actual numbers of women being helped in this way so far remain relatively small, but they are rising, particularly in some states of the Indian union, and there is every prospect of a continued upward trajectory in the years to come. This relatively recent trend in the creative use of a law that was originally thought to have no positive aspects for those whom it was allegedly designed to serve, has important implications for the ability of poor women to benefit from it, just as their better-off sisters have been able to do through a different, but equally novel, judicially inspired legal route.

**Endnotes**

1 Aziz-ud-Din Ahmad, *The Criminal Procedure Code, Being Act V of 1898* (Lucknow: London Printing Press, 1898), pp. 378–83.

2 Code of Criminal Procedure, Section 125(1)(d). This provision is only very seldom resorted to by destitute parents. The vast majority of suits under the section are filed by estranged and deserted wives against their husbands or by divorcées (Hindu or Christian) against their ex-husbands.

3 Code of Criminal Procedure, Section 125, Explanation (2).

[4] The *shari'at* prescribes that a divorcée remain at home, in seclusion, until she has completed three menstrual courses. Only after that is she free to remarry. If during this period it becomes evident that she is pregnant, her *ʿiddat* is extended until the child is born. Her former husband must continue to provide for her during the entire period.

[5] Code of Criminal Procedure, Section 127(3)(b).

[6] There is an extensive literature on this case, its background and aftermath, its significance and its legal, political, and policy implications. See, for example, Lucy Carroll, *Shah Bano and the Muslim Women Act a Decade On: The Right of the Divorced Muslim Woman to* Mataa (Bombay: Women's Research Action Group, 1998); Asghar Ali Engineer, *The Shah Bano Controversy* (Bombay: Sangam Books, 1987); Kavita R. Khory, 'The Shah Bano Case: Some Political Implications', in R.D. Baird, ed., *Religion and Law in Independent India*, 2nd ed., (New Delhi: Manohar Publishers, 2005), pp. 121–138; Gregory Kozlowski, 'Shah Banu's Case, Britain's Legal Legacy and Muslim Politics in Modern India', in Y.K. Malik & D.K. Vajpeyi, eds., *Boeings and Bullock Carts: Studies in Change and Continuity in Indian Civilization*, vol. 3, *Law, Politics and Society in India* (New Delhi: Chanakya Publications, 1990); Maitrayee Mukhopadhyay, *Legally Dispossessed: Gender, Identity and the Process of Law* (Calcutta: Stree, 1998); Archana Parashar, *Women and Family Law Reform in India: Uniform Civil Code and Gender Equality* (New Delhi: Sage Publications, 1992); Zakia Pathak and Rajeswari Sunder Rajan, 'Shahbano', *Signs* 14(3) (1989): 558–82; Sylvia Vatuk, 'A Rallying Cry for Muslim Personal Law: The Shah Bano Case and its Aftermath', in Barbara Metcalf, ed., *Islam in South Asia in Practice.* (Princeton: Princeton University Press, 2009).

[7] The MWA does not affect the eligibility of a *married* Muslim woman whose husband fails to provide for her to apply for a maintenance award under this section. Furthermore, whereas a Muslim divorcée cannot use S125 to obtain maintenance for *herself*, assuming that she has physical custody of the couple's minor offspring, she may file under it for child support.

[8] Specifically, any relatives who stand to inherit from her in the event of her death.

[9] The government office charged with the regulation and management of Muslim religious endowments (*waqf* or *wakf*, plural *auqaf*).

[10] That is, a code of family law applicable to Indians of all religions.

[11] As the news of these decisions began to spread, some within the Muslim clerical leadership became concerned that through such judicial activism the original intent of the law was being subverted. Flavia Agnes (*Law and Gender Inequality: The Politics of Women's Rights in India* [New Delhi: Oxford University Press, 1999, p. 105] notes, 'In response to the generous interpretations of the Act, Syed Shahabuddin ... moved a Private Members'

Bill (Bill No. 155 of 1992) ... to amend the Act and restrict its scope in clear terms to maintenance only for and during the *ʿiddat* period.'

[12] I do not have space here to go into detail concerning the reasoning behind such judgments and the points of Islamic law that were drawn upon in their support, but see Flavia Agnes, *Judgement Call: An Insight into Muslim Women's Right to Maintenance* (Mumbai: Majlis, 2001), for a detailed analysis of some of those decisions. See also Narendra Subramanian, 'Legal Change and Gender Inequality: Changes in Muslim Family Law in India', *Law and Social Inquiry* 33(3) (2008), pp. 645–649.

[13] Agnes, *Judgement*, pp. 32–33. Agnes statistically analysed 243 reported cases in which maintenance of a divorced Muslim woman was at issue and describes 67 of these in more detail. Almost all were appeals from lower court judgments, in which men had been ordered to pay maintenance to their wives or ex-wives under S125 of the CrPC. In only a few of these appeals had the original suit been filed under the MWA. In the vast majority of cases for which she has provided detailed information (52 out of 67, or 78 per cent), the petitioner was the husband (Agnes, *Judgement*, pp. 12–13, 104, 100–101).

[14] *Danial Latifi v. Union of India*, AIR 2001 [7] SCC 740.

[15] Agnes, *Judgement*, p. 72.

[16] But see Mukhopadhyay, *Legally Dispossessed*; Gopika Solanki, *Adjudication in Religious Family Laws: Cultural Accommodation, Legal Pluralism, and Gender Equality in India* (Cambridge, Cambridge University Press, 2011).

[17] I am grateful to Neeti Shikha in Delhi and to Mahfooz Nazki and Bhavana Avaneendra in Hyderabad for their valuable assistance and useful contributions to the project.

[18] The data are incomplete for a number of reasons. First, it was not possible to examine all the MWA and S125 files held in the record rooms or even to sample them systematically, because the officers in charge, while they were most accommodating and cooperative, retained the right to choose which files to show us. Whether they did this on the basis of convenience or with some other rationale in mind, it is impossible to say. Secondly, the files themselves are not always complete: vital information about the case is often missing.

[19] At the time of my research this court was presided over by the 13th Additional Chief Metropolitan Magistrate, Mrs. Ramani Krupavathi, for whose gracious help and willing cooperation with my investigations I am most appreciative.

[20] During the period of my fieldwork the judge of that court, Mrs. P. Shree Sudha, took much time out of her busy schedule to answer our questions and facilitate our access to the records we wished to examine. I am very grateful for her help. The court's official name is the Court of the Additional Metropolitan Sessions Judge for the Trial of Jubilee Hills Car Bomb Blast Case Cum Additional Family Court. It had originally been set up to try the

21 alleged perpetrators of a car bombing in November 1997 in an upper class area of the city. In January 2000, once verdicts had been reached in all those cases, a decision was made to transfer to this court the growing number of S125 cases then pending in the Hyderabad family court. Since then, the latter court has not dealt with maintenance issues but has jurisdiction only over cases filed under the various personal laws—Hindu, Muslim and Christian—which chiefly involve suits for divorce and for restitution of conjugal rights.

[21] According to the 2011 Census of India, 14.2 per cent of the population of India was Muslim. But, as a community, Muslims have lower average levels of education and are—not surprisingly—much more poorly represented in the professions generally than are Hindus (particularly those of the upper castes) and Christians (see the 'Sachar Report', Government of India, *Social, Economic and Educational Status of the Muslim Community of India*, 2006, http://www.minorityaffairs.gov.in/sites/upload_files/moma/files/pdfs/sachar_comm.pdf [last accessed 26 November 2012]). Although it is impossible to document this with official statistics, it is also the case that their representation in the legal profession is very much smaller than their representation in the population as a whole.

[22] In most large cities, as in Hyderabad, S125 cases are heard in specialised family courts whose procedure is laid out in the Family Courts Act, 1984. Under that Act, litigants do not have the right to be represented by legal counsel, except with special permission of the judge. This rule is intended to facilitate a more informal mode of interaction between the litigant and the judge, the parties being able to use ordinary language rather than the specialised legal jargon to explain their situations. However, in practice it is almost impossible for even a well-educated petitioner to navigate her (or his) way through the process of filing a suit in family court and pursuing it to completion, without the assistance of an experienced advocate. Most advocates do obtain such 'special permission' by applying for a *vakalatnama*. However, even in such cases, it is unusual for the advocate's name to be cited in the official case file.

[23] One father-son partnership had represented 14 women while two others had each argued three and five cases, respectively.

[24] There are very few female Muslim advocates, either in Hyderabad or elsewhere in the country. Several 'lady advocates' practice in the Hyderabad family court, the additional family court (for S125 cases) and the mahila court. Almost all these women lawyers are Hindu or, occasionally, Christian, and they are vastly outnumbered by their male colleagues. But in 2005–06, when I was conducting my research, women judges were presiding over both the additional family court and the mahila court. Whether that is still the case, I do not know.

[25] Mohammad Afzal Wani, *Maintenance Rights of Muslim Women: Principles,*

*Precedents and Trends* (New Delhi: Genuine Publications, 1987) and *The Islamic Law on Maintenance of Women, Children, Parents and Other Relatives: Classical Principles and Modern Legislations in India and Muslim Countries* (New Delhi: Qazi Publications, 1995).

[26] Danial Latifi v. Union of India.

[27] There was no family court in Delhi at the time of my research, and maintenance cases filed under S125 were heard by magistrates in specially designated mahila courts. The city set up its first separate family court in May of 2009, much later than most other large cities in India. A few more such courts have opened in different parts of the city since then. See 'New Family Court at Saket', *Times of India,* 1 June 2011, www.timesofindia.indiatimes.com/city/delhi/New-family-court-at-Saket/articleshow/8683528.cms (last accessed 8 August 2016); 'Second Family Court Opens in Rohini', *Indian Express,* 11 February 2010, http://www.indianexpress.com/news/second-family-court-opens-in-rohini/578348 (last accessed 10 January 2012).

[28] Gifts of clothes, jewellery, furniture, electronics, and household goods, including appliances, presented to the bride by her parents at the time of marriage.

[29] Literally 'horse and set [of clothes]' or 'clothes money'. Traditionally the bride's family provided the special outfit that the groom would wear for the *nikah* ceremony. However, the amounts given have now escalated to the point where in many weddings they bear little or no relation to their alleged purpose.

[30] I have used the real names of these and other advocates and of government officials whom I interviewed. For litigants, however, I have used pseudonyms throughout.

[31] This section, entitled '*Mehr* and other properties ... to be given to her at the time of divorce' lists the divorced woman's entitlements, including: '(1) (a) a reasonable and fair provision and maintenance to be made and paid to her within the *ʿiddat* period ..., (c) an amount equal to the sum of *mehr* ... and (d) all the properties given to her before or at the time of marriage' or thereafter by relatives or friends of either spouse.

[32] A *tola* is 11.66 grams, which was worth approximately Rs. 4,000 in 2000.

[33] The term 'land business', as used in Hyderabad, carries the implication of activities related to the acquisition of land through brute force, extortion, and the like.

[34] Whereas Mr. Hussain maintained that he always asked for 'reasonable and fair provision' above and beyond the woman's other Islamic entitlements, he could not recall how much he had asked for under that heading in this particular case.

[35] Figures for earlier years are not available, due to the practice in this court of destroying files once the deadline for appealing the case has passed.

[36] Unfortunately, statistics on the extent to which S125 (or the MWA) are made use of by Muslim women elsewhere in India are difficult to come by, so it is not possible to put these Hyderabad figures into a wider comparative context. Figures are not even available on the total number of divorced Muslim women in India. While data on marital status is indeed collected each decade by the Census of India, they are not cross-tabulated by religion in published tables. Official figures on the number of maintenance cases filed or pending in a certain jurisdiction or over a certain time period can sometimes be found, but not broken down by religion.

[37] The number of women of other religions filing for maintenance under this section was similarly on the rise during this period.

[38] Information concerning the disposal of the remaining five per cent of cases was not available.

[39] To protect litigant's privacy, this and the names of all others subsequently mentioned are pseudonyms.

[40] That is, a marriage of personal choice. In a society in which parents are expected to arrange the marriages of their children, usually with little input from the young people themselves, such unions represent a deviation from the norm that often causes serious rifts between the couple and their respective families.

[41] It is customary for the bride's family to make a list of the *jahez* items and the amounts given as *jore ki raqm*. Someone from each side signs the list and each retains a copy to serve as proof of the transaction. Typically, also, the *jahez* items are displayed for the wedding guests to admire and photographs or videos are often made at this time. But not all petitioners are able to either produce such a list or provide photographic evidence of what they brought into the marriage. In such cases the judge may regard the wife's claim as unsubstantiated or greatly exaggerated and refuse to comply with her request.

[42] The relevant passage reads 'where a Magistrate is satisfied that a divorced woman has not re-married and is not able to maintain herself after the *ʿiddat* period, he may … direct … *such of her relatives as would be entitled to inherit her property on her death according to Muslim law* to pay … maintenance to her [my italics]'. It is not necessary that in her petition the woman herself cite any specific relatives as potential providers, though she may do so.

[43] 'Legal Change', p. 647.

[44] It is likewise very rare for a parent to invoke S125 for a maintenance order against an adult child. I found no such examples among the Muslim cases that I examined in the records of the Hyderabad additional family court that deals with S125 suits. Likewise, when investigating maintenance cases in the family court of Chennai in 1998–99, I found only one such suit among the total of 55 filed by Muslims between 1991 and 1998. In that case, an elderly father

was asking that his son be ordered to provide for him. A search of an online database (www.indiankanoon.org) of high and Supreme Court judgments does, however, bring up a very small number of appeals by Muslim men against maintenance orders awarded under S125 by lower courts in different parts of India to one or both of their parents (e.g. *Rafiuddin s/o Quazi Zainul Abeden v Smt. Saleha Khatoon d/o Yaqub Ali*, 2007 [109] Bom. L. R. 2059; *Makiur Rahaman Khan and Anr. v Mahila Bibi*, [2003] CALLT 422 HC, 2002 C Cr LR [Cal] 39).

45 See, for example, *Tripura Board of Wakf and Anr. v Tahera Khatoon*, II (2001) DMC 401. Though in her original petition the divorced woman had asked that her mother *and* the Wakf Board be issued orders to maintain her, the lower court absolved the former of any responsibility and placed the entire burden on the Wakf Board. The latter then proceeded to appeal. The Gauhati High Court rejected this appeal, as it did a later appeal by the same Wakf Board in a similar case (*Tripura Board of Wakf v Ayasha Bibi*, AIR 2008 Gau 10).

46 *The Secretary, Tamil Nadu Wakf Board and Anr. v Syed Fatima Nachi*, AIR 1996 SC2423.

47 'Maintenance Allowances Paid to the Divorced Muslim Women', www.tnwakfboard.org/forwomen/htm# (last accessed 1 July 2012).

48 'Muslim Women Agitate for Stipend', *The Hindu*, 6 June 2007, http://www.hindu.com/2007/06/06/stories/2007060609680300.htm (last accessed 8 July 2012); 'Delay in Maintenance Money: Women Stage Dharna', 14 October 2011, www.ibnlive.in.com/news/delay-in-maintenance-money-women-stage-dharna/193031-60-114.html (last accessed 5 August 2012).

49 'Not Many Divorcées Avail Wakf Board Scheme', *Times of India*, Hyderabad, 12 December 2005.

50 'Divorced Women Get Financial Aid from Wakf Board', *The Siasat Daily, 20* March, 2012, www.siasat.com/english/news/divorced-women-get-financial-aid-wakf-board (last accessed 26 November 2012).

51 Interview with Shaik Saleem Basha, law officer of the Andhra Pradesh state Wakf Board, 9 January, 2006.

52 Flavia Agnes, *Give Us This Day Our Daily Bread: Procedures and Case Law on Maintenance.* Gender Justice Series, Book II (Mumbai: Majlis, 1992), pp. 76–106.

53 This condition is laid out in CrPC, S125(1)(a).

54 They do not necessarily come from the very poorest strata of society. The great expense of filing and pursuing such a suit is one factor: such women can indeed sometimes obtain court-ordered maintenance awards with the help of free legal aid, women's NGOs, and the occasional (usually female) advocate willing to work on a pro bono basis. However, they often encounter insurmountable problems getting their orders executed, in part because their

husbands typically have such extremely low and irregular incomes that they would be unable, even if willing, to comply, no matter how many maintenance orders are issued against them.

[55] In practice, most awards were for amounts much lower than the Rs. 500 maximum. The Code of Criminal Procedure (Amendment) Act, enacted in 2001, removed all limits and made the award amount subject to the court's discretion: much higher awards are now possible.

[56] Solanki, *Adjudication*, pp. 146–7.

[57] Flavia Agnes, *Family Law, Volume II: Marriage, Divorce, and Matrimonial Litigation* (New Delhi: Oxford University Press, 2011), p. 124.